Growing Roses

Growing Roses

Michael Gibson

Illustrated with colour photographs
by the author

CROOM HELM
London & Canberra
TIMBER PRESS
Portland, Oregon

© 1984 Michael Gibson
Croom Helm Ltd, Provident House, Burrell Row,
Beckenham, Kent BR3 1AT
Croom Helm Australia Pty Ltd,
28 Kembla St, Fyshwick, ACT 2609, Australia

British Library Cataloguing in Publication Data

Gibson, Michael
 Growing roses.
 1. Rose culture
 I. Title
 635.9'33372   SB411

 ISBN 0-7099-1147-5

First published in the USA 1984 by
Timber Press,
PO Box 1632,
Beaverton, OR 97075
USA

Line drawings by the
author and David Henderson

Typeset by Columns of Reading
Printed and bound in Great Britain

Contents

List of Figures and Tables vii

Foreword *R.C. Balfour, President of the World Federation of Rose Societies* ix

Why Roses? An Introduction 1

1 The Rose in the Garden 5

2 The Rose Families 24

3 The Species or Wild Roses 28

4 The Gallicas 34

5 The Damasks 39

6 The Albas 43

7 The Centifolias and Moss Roses 47

8 China Roses 52

9 The Bourbons and Portland Roses 56

10 The Hybrid Perpetuals 62

11 Tea Roses 68

12 Large-flowered Bush Roses (Hybrid Teas) 73

13 The Polyanthas 97

14 Cluster-flowered or Floribunda Roses 101

15 Modern Shrub Roses 120

16 Climbing Roses 134

17 The Ramblers 144

18 Miniature Roses 150

19 Choosing and Buying Roses 156

Contents

20	Cultivation	163
21	Routine Maintenance	176
22	Growing Roses from Cuttings	196
23	Hybridising and Budding	201
24	Exhibiting	207

Appendix: USDA Hardiness Ratings by Zone for Groups of Roses Discussed in the Text — 216

List of Suppliers — 217

Bibliography — 219

Glossary — 223

Index of Roses — 228

General Index — 233

Figures and Tables

Figures

1.1	Achieving a balanced effect in the rose bed	8
1.2	The use of standards to give height to a rose bed	10
1.3	Hedge of cluster-flowered roses	11
1.4	Hedge of big, rugosa-type shrub roses	12
1.5	Hedge of climbers on horizontal wires	13
1.6	Weeping standard growing as a specimen	14
1.7	Tripod with rose trained on it	15
1.8	Pegging down	16
1.9	Roses on a patio in troughs and tubs	17
1.10	Miniatures growing in terraced beds	18
1.11	Ramblers on a catenary	19
1.12	Ramblers on a pergola	20
1.13	Roses tied on to a larch pillar	21
1.14	Rose hips	22
20.1	Planting a bedding rose	167
20.2	Planting a climbing rose	168
20.3	Planting a standard rose	169
20.4	Training a climbing rose on a wall or fence	170
20.5	Training a climber or rambler on a pillar	171
20.6	Growing a climber up a tree	172
21.1	Pruning a large-flowered (hybrid tea) rose	182
21.2	Pruning a cluster-flowered (floribunda) rose	183
21.3	Pruning a climbing rose	184
21.4	The effects of four of the commonest insect pests	186
21.5	The two commonest rose fungus diseases	191
21.6	Dead-heading	192
21.7	Disbudding	193
21.8	Finding suckers	194
22.1	The preparation of a rose cutting and four cuttings in a planting trench	198

Figures and Tables

23.1   Cross-section of a rose flower   202
23.2   The three main stages of budding   205

Tables

21.1   Insect Pests and Diseases   187

Foreword

R.C. BALFOUR, MBE, DHM
*President of the World Federation of Rose Societies and Past
President of the Royal National Rose Society*

I am pleased to write the Foreword to Michael Gibson's latest
book, not only because he is a friend, but also because he shares
my love of roses and appreciates their value in the garden,
particularly in association with other plants.

The message of this book is 'Enjoy roses and make the best
use of them. Choose carefully, buy the best and treat them well
and they will reward you over many many years from early
summer even to Christmas.'

Thanks to the dedication and perseverance of rose breeders
over the last two hundred years, aided by a fair degree of luck
or divine intervention, there are now roses suitable for nearly
any site in most gardens, except deep shade. There are ramblers
which will grow up tall trees and miniatures ideal for troughs
and window boxes, shrub roses to brighten any shrubbery or as
specimens on lawns, ground-cover roses for banks and short
roses to edge paths and drives and roses for colourful hedges.
There are bush roses to produce show blooms and strongly
scented flowers for the house or a mass of colour in the garden
and climbers which will beautify pergolas and pillars, fences and
walls throughout the summer and into autumn with relatively
little attention.

All these uses are covered in the book, with examples of the
best roses to choose for each purpose, coupled with valuable
advice and tips based on his own experience and experiments
about planting, pruning and the general maintenance of roses.
He explains the modern classification of roses and even deals
with such specialist aspects as showing, propagating, hybridising and growing under glass. The accompanying line drawings
should be helpful to anyone new to rose growing.

He describes in detail his selection of the various types of
rose, with coloured illustrations of some from his own photographs. Although he fully covers modern roses, his own love
and knowledge of the old roses will be obvious to the reader.
Since the habit of growth of the old roses varies so much even

within particular groups, the choice of the right variety for a chosen site is even more important than with modern bush roses, for which colour will often be the predominant factor, so anyone thinking of planting any of the older roses should benefit greatly from studying his advice carefully. For many it may come as a surprise that quite a lot of these are suitable for smaller gardens, to which they will add a special interest for visitors as well as the owners. As a result of the recent revival of interest in the older roses, a much wider selection of them is now available from general rose nurseries and from a few which specialise in them. The time to see them at their best is from mid June to mid July and a number of gardens open to the public have collections of them, but I would strongly recommend a visit to the Royal National Rose Society's Gardens of the Rose near St Albans, which are open throughout the summer and where there are also large displays of modern roses and the newest roses in the Trial grounds, besides examples of small gardens. Anyone thinking of planting more roses, as I hope this book will encourage them to do, would find a visit most helpful, because they would be able to check that the varieties they may have chosen at a show or from a catalogue or from this book really are suitable in habit and colour for the selected position in their garden.

I hope that this book will make many more gardeners appreciate how rewarding and versatile roses are and so widen the world of roses.

Why Roses?
An Introduction

Sixty per cent of public or private gardens in anything that could be said to resemble, however marginally, a temperate climate have one or more rose bushes in them. This is said with a confidence not entirely generated by the fact that nobody is likely to have the time or the inclination, or indeed be dotty enough, to try to disprove it; one has only to pass any group of houses that have gardens or the gardens of public parks and the truth of it becomes pretty well self-evident. Except perhaps in the Far East, in the lands of the chrysanthemum and paeony, the rose has always been man's favourite flower.

It is difficult to say just why this should be so. Why the rose, beautiful as it is, rather than another flower that is equally old? The rose in the wild is not even distributed all over the world, for none occur naturally south of the equator, and it might be difficult for early man to recognise what he knew of as a rose in our sophisticated hybrids today. Over the centuries the rose has either changed itself or been changed by man so dramatically that it might almost be a different flower altogether. There is little resemblance between the original five-petalled wild roses which gripped the imaginations of the early Persian manuscript illuminators and the modern large-flowered bush roses (hybrid teas), and yet not one fraction of the rose's popularity has been sacrificed.

Of course, the change came about very gradually, and was in the main a natural progression. A cross between two five-petalled species or wild roses is likely to produce a new rose with more petals than either of the parents. As John Parkinson, writing in 1642, put it: ' . . . assuredly all such flowers did first grow wilde . . . but for how long before they were found they became double no man can tell'. In other words, the progress from single to double blooms was first achieved without the help of man, and these early double roses had short centre petals so that they opened cupped or flat. Man's influence only really began to be felt with the coming of the much longer

1

petalled tea roses from China early in the nineteenth century – little more than 150 years ago – which more or less coincided with the realisation that humans could actually carry out deliberately the transfer of the pollen of one rose to another to produce a hybrid. This was something that insects, and of course the wind, had been doing since the beginning of time and man had been slow to catch on, but once he did the shape of the rose's flowers was utterly changed. Careful selection from crosses made with the long-petalled teas resulted eventually in the high-centred blooms which are so much admired today.

So where have we got to? How near are we to discovering a constant factor which links the old roses with the new and which can account for man's unbroken loyalty? Colour might certainly have been expected to play a part, for the flowers of the rose come in a range of colours matched by few if any other plant families. Yet the bright yellows, the orange and flame colours, and the more subtle blends of these so often found have only been present in our garden roses since the beginning of this century. Before that they were all, as far back as memory goes and beyond, either white, various shades of pink, red, crimson, maroon, purple or lilac and sometimes a beguiling combination of several of these. Colours, therefore, have changed, too.

All in all, and discounting characteristics only to be perceived by a botanist, the only easily recognisable and unchanging link between the old roses and the new – apart from their thorns, which only a *fakir* would consider an endearing attribute – is fragrance. There have certainly always been scented roses, but even here it is difficult to produce what Humpty Dumpty would have called a 'nice, knock-down argument' which cannot be contradicted, or at least disputed, for there have always been scentless roses, too.

Ancient Greek writers such as Theophrastus and later on Pliny the Elder in Rome in about 50AD both compared the roses of their time from the point of view of fragrance. They came up with the rose of Cyrene (in North Africa) as having the sweetest scent of all, and condemned others for having none, so the complaint that modern roses have no scent is not a new one as we shall realise even more fully when we come to discuss the damask roses in Chapter 5. But long before the times when either Theophrastus or Pliny the Elder were writing, both Greek and Roman myths contained accounts of how the rose first got its fragrance. One version tells of how Cupid: 'In the midst of a light and lively dance, overthrew, with a stroke of his wing, a cup of nectar; with which precious liquor, falling on a rose, embalmed it with the delightful fragrance which it still retains.'

And retain it it does, despite both ancient and modern doubters.

So much for the arguments, but of course the only way really to satisfy oneself as to why the rose in all its multitudinous forms has been so beloved by man is to grow at least a few examples of each rose family so that their own particular magic is revealed, and more people would, I think, have done this if it were not for the unfortunate attitude of a few. Some gardeners who, solely because they grow and in some cases write about the old roses, have taken to themselves what Swift called (with in his case reference to having seen Athens and a thinking more closely linked to the Grand Tour than the package tour) an 'Invisible Precedence' over mere ordinary mortals. This is much more than the rivalry that exists, sometimes as a strong undercurrent, but at other times erupting in green-eyed spleen among the garden owners of a district. It is more subtle than that, but that does not absolve it from the charge of being balderdash, and damaging balderdash at that. It has made the more timid gardeners who might otherwise have been prepared to venture away from what could perhaps be called the run of the mill hesitate on the brink. They feel that old roses are in some way difficult and that they will not fit in with a small, modern garden.

Wrong on both counts as will, I hope, become clear as you read this book, for one of my aims in writing it is to show what is being missed by those who grow nothing other than the large and cluster-flowered varieties. There is nothing wrong, of course, in growing tried and trusted favourites such as 'Peace' or 'Wendy Cussons'. Equally there is nothing wrong in being a rose lover who takes off each year with the acceleration of a minnow after the latest rose novelties red-hot from the hybridists, and there are quite a lot of suggestions in the pages that follow as to how these and all the other kinds of roses can be used. Also, there are ideas as to the other flowers and shrubs that roses can be grown in association with. I have endeavoured to show up the myth that roses must always be kept on their own for what it is, a myth. If the right roses are chosen, they will blend beautifully into mixed plantings.

I have not, however, included any garden plans as I cannot see that these can be drawn in a vacuum. Unless one can see the surroundings of a garden plot, and by that I mean what is outside the boundaries of a garden, how is it possible to produce a design that will even be adequate? If there is a pickle factory next door, nothing but a screen of trees (or another pickle factory) will hide it. Only if you know that it is there can

3

you make sensible suggestions as to what needs doing. So no plans.

Above all, rose growing should be something to enjoy. I hope that I have managed to convey something of the enjoyment it has given me.

CHAPTER 1

The Rose
in the Garden

The rose in the garden does not mean quite the same thing as the rose garden. The latter implies that what is grown should be predominantly roses with maybe a few other plants here and there to set them off; the former means something which I much prefer, the blending of roses in all their incredibly wide variety with the multitude of other flowers from which one can choose.

There is, however, a firmly entrenched belief that roses do not mix with other plants, that one should have a kind of rose monastery, a closed order, but since so many gardens nowadays clearly demonstrate how false this is, it is interesting to speculate how the idea came about in the first place.

It can be taken as a reasonable certainty, I think, that the Empress Josephine, wife of Napoleon, had quite a lot to do with it, even if inadvertently. She loved flowers with a great passion and created, at her Villa Malmaison not far from Paris, the first rose garden that can be said to have been truly documented. Her idea, which she fully achieved, was to form a collection of all the varieties and species of roses then known to be in existence, and such was her influence in the higher diplomatic circles that she could arrange the shipping of roses from England at the height of the Napoleonic Wars. The documentation of her garden is both written and, very fortunately for us, visual, for it was at Malmaison that the Belgian artist, Pierre Joseph Redouté painted most of the plates for his *Les Roses*, handing down to us a record that it unique.

Although the Empress's idea was to gather together as many different roses as possible rather than to form a rose garden as such, the result must have been very pleasing. Certainly friends admired what she had done and the idea caught on. The fashion spread, first to the gardens of the French chateaux, and later it was taken up by the owners of country estates elsewhere on the Continent and in the United Kingdom. Possibly for the first time, roses were being used on a large scale purely as decorative plants, for although there had been gardens with roses in them in earlier times, a very large number of these would have been attached to religious institutions and the roses grown for their value as herbs rather than because they were beautiful to look at.

So it would seem that the idea that roses should be grown on their own was sown in France, and it must be admitted that the rose families then popular rather lent strength to this line of thought. It was well before the time of the upright and compact bedding roses we know today, and the old garden varieties with their long, lax shoots and comparatively untidy habit did not fit into the rather formal garden schemes that were then popular. Roses were best kept to themselves, often in walled gardens or so it was thought until Gertrude Jekyll and William Robinson came along. In a sense, these could be paralleled with the kitchen garden, and in them the ladies of the house would stroll to gather blooms for their bowls and vases, much as their gardeners would collect the vegetables for the kitchen. On the big estates nobody actually wanted to be without roses. They would have them and enjoy them – as long as they knew their place and kept to it.

This kind of thinking was perpetuated and maybe reinforced late in the nineteenth century by the publication of books on roses and how to grow them – practically all, strangely enough, written by clergymen. Reynolds Hole (later Dean of Rochester) came first in 1874 with *A Book About Roses*, then came A. Foster-Melliar with *The Book of the Rose* and H.H. D'Ombrain with *Roses for Amateurs*, both in 1894, and finally Joseph Pemberton, just into the twentieth century in 1908 with *Roses, Their History, Development and Cultivation*. Dean Hole, who was co-founder of what was to become The Royal National Rose Society, said in the preface to the first edition of his book:

And now I write about roses, because, having grown them for twenty years, having won more than thirty cups 'open to all England', having originated the first Rose-show – that is, the first show of roses only – having attended most of the subsequent meetings, either as judge or exhibitor, I ought to have something to say worth hearing to those who love the rose.

About one-third of Hole's book is devoted to rose shows and this typifies the intensely competitive outlook of all four writers. All were dedicated to exhibiting roses at national rose shows, and if there is one kind of rose that really must, because of the special cosseting it needs, be isolated from the rest, it is the kind that in due course will compete for challenge cups. Almost inevitably, the advice that they give in their books reflects this principle of segregation.

And it was, of course, at just about the time when these writers were making their mark that the large-flowered (hybrid tea) rose was also coming to the fore. The first had appeared in 1867 and the group can be said to have launched the rose as a bedding plant. Cluster-flowered (floribunda) roses came a good deal later, but they, too, have the rather stiff, upright carriage that does not lend itself too well to mixing and blending in with other plants. It is difficult to put your finger on just why this should be, but it may have something to do with the fact that bedding roses are not particularly beautiful or graceful plants in themselves. They are, as I said just now, rather stiff, and while the flowers may be the most lovely in the world, the same cannot be said of the bushes that bear them. An additional factor is that spraying against both mildew and black spot becomes a real problem if you are not sure of the reaction of the surrounding plants to the chemicals that make up the spray.

To do him justice, Dean Hole did recognise and describe uses for roses that were not exclusively destined for exhibition. If I may quote him just once more, he said:

There should be beds of Roses, bowers of Roses, hedges of Roses, edgings of Roses, pillars of Roses, arches of Roses, fountains of Roses, baskets of Roses, vistas and alleys of the Rose. Now overhead and now at our feet, there they should creep and climb. New tints, new forms, new perfumes should meet us at every turn.

Beds of Roses

All these uses mentioned by Hole and uses for roses unthought of in the Dean's time will be discussed in due course, but perhaps it is most logical to start with bedding roses as this is the way that most people grow roses. On the face of it, this is a pretty straightforward kind of planting, using roses of a more or less uniform size to fill a level piece of ground, but there are nevertheless a number of points worth making.

I have mentioned size, and this and the habit of growth effects bedding with roses in two different ways. First of all, if several different varieties are planted haphazardly in a single bed and their heights differ even by as little as 1 ft (30 cm), the result will be far from pleasing. If, however, the tall roses are planted in the centre of a circular or square bed, or at the rear of a bed running along a wall or fence with the shorter ones in front of them, a balance will have been achieved. This to some people may seem to be stating the obvious, but when buying

Figure 1.1
Tall roses at the
back of a border,
short ones in front.

roses the height to which a variety will grow is not always considered. Colour, flower form and scent are the factors that govern the choice as often as not, and this can lead to trouble for the uninitiated when being beguiled by some of the special collections – at a bargain rate – offered in the nursery catalogues. I have seen the 6 ft (1.8 m)-plus cluster-flowered rose 'Queen Elizabeth' in the same collection as 'Zambra', which will reach all of 2 ft (60 cm), and while this may have been exceptional, the heights of roses in collections should always be checked, with the supplier if his catalogue does not give information about heights under the entries for the individual varieties. Otherwise, you may end up with a very odd-looking rose bed indeed.

The height of a rose variety is also important in relation to the size of the bed to be planted. A big bed will look perfectly proportioned whether the roses in it are short or tall, but a small one with very tall roses, particularly if they are of the kind that carries all its flowers at the top, may look top-heavy. The smaller the bed, the smaller the roses is a good rule to follow.

Considerations of height apart, it is generally held to be wrong to mix different varieties in one bed, and while not going all the way with this I would agree that large-flowered and cluster-flowered types are best planted separately. The whole point of the cluster-flowered types is that they should provide a solid mass of colour, formed from a multitude of small flowers over the whole bed, which will not be achieved if they are broken up by large-flowered roses. With the large-flowered roses, the aim is for refinement of the individual blooms, giving a good overall show of colour, though neither so comprehensive nor so continuous as cluster-flowered varieties would provide. Whether different varieties of large-flowered and different varieties of cluster-flowered bedding roses should be mixed is another matter.

The argument against mixing varieties is that: a) the colours may clash and b) that some varieties come into bloom much later than others so that the overall effect of the planting, except maybe for a very limited period not long after mid-summer, is likely to be 'spotty'– a dot of colour here, a dot of colour there, which could hardly be said to make up a coherent whole.

Both these points, and particularly the last one, have some substance, but with a little thought both can be circumvented, if you want to, that is, for there is, of course, nothing wrong with keeping your scheme to one variety a bed. This can be most effective, but so, too, can a bed in which a number of varieties are used, not dotted about at random but planted in blocks of not less than four or five of one rose. 'Blocks' is a clumsy word although I cannot think of a better one, but whatever you call them they could, to take one instance, form radiating segments of a circular bed, or concentric rings of different heights which diminish towards the perimeter, and there could be a standard rose in the centre round which the whole pivots. Standards can often be used to advantage in a large bedding scheme to give the height variation the human eye appreciates in a garden. Bed after bed of roses, or of any other plant, all at more or less the same level can become monotonous if not broken up by a standard, a pillar or a pergola which the eye can follow upwards.

A standard in a bedding scheme can be of the same variety as the rest of the roses (supposing they are all of one kind), but it is often more effective if its colour is a complete contrast. The colours of comparatively few roses clash, and it is not difficult to keep apart those that do. One would not, for instance, plant the brilliant cerise-pink of the large-flowered 'Wendy Cussons' next to the scarlet of 'Alec's Red', but if you do want to grow them both, even at a pinch in the same bed, put a white, cream, buff or a pale-yellow rose in between them. These pastel colours, which nurserymen say are the hardest to sell, are quite invaluable in the garden for colour blending and for separating

Figure 1.2
The use of standards
to give height to a
rose bed.

the more strident juke-box tones. Even the so-called 'blue' roses such as 'Blue Moon', which everyone says they dislike but which continue to appear in catalogues and so must sell in reasonable quantities, look much more at home in the company of quieter flowers. Too many people do, I think, expect them to compete with the general range of rose colours, which simply overwhelm them.

Paths and Drives

For lining paths and drives there is a wide choice of roses from the taller miniatures such as 'Angela Rippon', 'Darling Flame', 'Easter Morning' or 'Fire Princess', through the complete range of more or less conventional cluster-flowered roses ranging between 1 ft (60 cm) and 3 ft 6 in (105 cm), to the less conventional such as 'Chinatown', 'Queen Elizabeth' and 'Fred Loads', taking you in stages from 4 ft (1.2 m) to 7–8 ft (2.1–2.4 m) and all reasonably economical of space. Where space is not a consideration, shrub roses such as the low-growing, spreading 'Ballerina' or 'Marjorie Fair', or one of the taller hybrid musks would be suitable. The only kind of rose to avoid beside a path is one, like, for instance, the cluster-

10

flowered variety 'Europeana', which has lax shoots and very double blooms. These, weighed down with water after rain, will be only too willing to share their wetness with your trouser legs as you walk past.

In trying to decide at what height something ceased to be a row of plants and became a hedge, I looked 'hedge' up in the dictionary. It was rather baffling to be met by: 'Fence of bushes or low trees, living (quickset~) or dead (dead~)' (*The Concise Oxford Dictionary*). That lets out miniature roses I think, but taller dead roses round the garden? Surely not. But living roses, yes and yes again, for they will make the most colourful hedges of all and give you everything else you want in a hedge except an evergreen screen in winter.

In talking about roses to line paths and drives, we have already been discussing rose hedges for a particular function. Mention has been made of the space they may occupy, and this may well be one of the main considerations in a small or medium-sized garden. Not many people would disagree that the ideal hedging roses from the point of view of dense leaf coverage right to the ground, complete immunity from the usual rose diseases, continuity of flowering and with the single-flowered varieties autumn hips to follow, are members of the rugosa group, in particular 'Roseraie de l'Hay', 'Scabrosa' and *R. rugosa alba*. But they do take up a lot of room and are 5–6 ft (1.5–1.8 m) tall by 4–5 ft (1.2–1.5 m) across. This makes a very substantial hedge and one which, armed with the usual

Figure 1.3
Hedge of cluster-flowered roses, showing staggered planting.

11

Figure 1.4
Hedge of big,
rugosa-type shrub
roses.

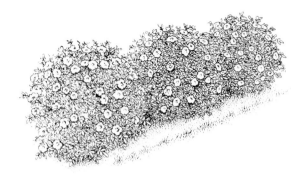

rugosa thorns and prickles, would repel anything that tried to get through it that was much larger than a centipede. 'Frau Dagmar Hartopp', to use the stage name of 'Fru Dagmar Hastrup', with the most lovely soft-pink single flowers set off by cream stamens is a more unassuming rugosa at about 4 ft (1.2 m) by 3 ft (90 cm).

Excessive width can also be a problem with those otherwise fine hedging roses the hybrid musks, which include the ever-popular 'Penelope', 'Cornelia', 'Prosperity' and 'Moonlight' among others. These roses, in addition to making rather large bushes, are apt to be unpredictable in habit, often sending out, particularly in late summer and autumn, very long and substantial flowering shoots at the most unexpected and sometimes highly inconvenient angles. However, the width of hybrid musks can be very well curbed and reduced to about 3 ft (90 cm) by training them like climbers on horizontal wires strung between upright rustic poles of about 5–6 ft (1.5–1.8 m) in height. The hybrid musks have a reputation of putting on as fine a display of bloom late in the year as they do just after midsummer, but in my experience this is not entirely true. I have found that a certain amount of dead-heading is necessary if the second flowering is to go any way towards matching the first, and dead-heading a large shrub is not always easy. Nevertheless, unpredictable as they may be in a number of ways, hybrid musks for hedges take a lot of beating.

The same approach with wires and posts may be adopted if one wishes to make a hedge of climbing or rambling roses, though with the more vigorous ones it would be possible to take the screen higher than 6 ft (1.8 m). Of course, it must depend on the vigour of the varieties you choose, but one could say on average that the climbers should be planted about 5–6 ft (1.5–1.8 m) apart and the shoots then fanned out along the

Figure 1.5
Hedge of climbers
on horizontal wires.

wires so that each rose will in time intertwine with its neighbours. The result can be one of the loveliest rose hedges of all, though you are unlikely to have created an impenetrable screen. With such a large area to cover, it is most unlikely that the roses will grow shoots exactly where you want them to fill every gap.

Specimen Planting

There are certain roses, particularly among the taller shrub roses, that make fine specimens if planted on their own, perhaps isolated on a lawn or perhaps serving as a focal point at the end of a path or at the junction of two paths, or else to light up a dull corner where two hedges meet. One which immediately springs to mind is the spring-flowering 'Frühlingsgold' (its name means Spring Gold) which makes a 7-ft (2.1-m), arching shrub and is a Pimpinellifolia hybrid with the most enchanting semi-double, scented yellow blooms, or if you want something rather smaller with very similar though in this case single blooms, there is 'Golden Wings', which is scarcely ever out of bloom throughout the summer. With 'Frühlingsgold's' cousin, 'Frühlingsmorgen', the very large single flowers of which shade enchantingly from pink at the petal edges to primrose at the centre, there is often some repeat as well. Creamy-white 'Nevada' and its pink sport, 'Marguerite Hilling', are two others that put on a really breathtaking display early on and a rather less spectacular one later, but with these two one must certainly allow for a spread of 5–6 ft (1.5–1.8 m) and a wide path is needed to accommodate them.

If one is planning for a garden of the size where a map is needed to find your way around, it will not matter particularly if you choose once-flowering varieties for at least some of your specimen plantings, possibly a wild rose like *R. moyesii* or 'Canary Bird', for they will not necessarily dominate the scene. If on the other hand you are one of those people whose garden

Figure 1.6
Weeping standard
growing as a
specimen in a lawn.

reflects the fact that you have to live with the gas turned down, a recurrent rose makes much more sense. This would eliminate the true weeping standards formed from ramblers, which can otherwise be added to the list of roses that make good specimens. Mostly members of the wichuraiana group, they put on a really spectacular display over many weeks, beginning a few weeks after midsummer, but there is nothing later. However, there is a substitute which makes use of one or other of the not too vigorous modern climbing roses that are fully recurrent. This is to grow them on a pillar or a tripod of rustic poles, and suitable varieties would be 'Golden Showers', 'Aloha', 'Compassion' or 'Dortmund'. Some of the older recurrent Bourbon roses like 'Mme Isaac Pereire' would be equally good.

Roses for Ground-cover

It is only comparatively recently that roses have seriously been considered as ground-cover plants, though for a number of years about four varieties have been suggested for the role, in a good many cases, I suspect, by people who have never grown

14

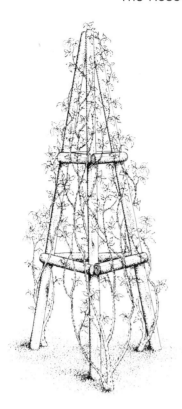

Figure 1.7
Tripod with rose
trained on it.

them. These have been the rugosa hybrids *R. × paulii* (white), its slightly less vigorous pink form, *R. × paulii rosea*, 'Max Graf' which is also a rugosa hybrid, this time crossed with the rambler *R. wichuraiana*, and a 'Macrantha' hybrid called 'Raubritter'. The first two, both singularly beautiful in leaf and flower, will eventually mound up to 4–5 ft (1.2–1.5 m) tall, which to my mind is not an altitude to which a ground-cover plant should aspire. True, they will eventually cover an area of earth perhaps 12 ft (3.7 m) in diameter, and smother every weed beneath their thorny stems and dense canopy of leaves, but it will take quite a few years before this really becomes effective and there are other shrubs which nobody considers in terms of ground-cover which will do the same. The two versions of *R. × paulii* should, I think, be grown simply for their beauty, forgetting any other function, and the same thing really applies to the other two, if perhaps to a lesser degree. 'Raubritter' is a lax sprawler with cupped, pink, semi-double blooms in tremendous profusion at midsummer and lots of mildew later, and 'Max Graf' spreads along the ground by rooting where its long, spreading canes touch the earth. Neither grows densely enough

Figure 1.8
Pegging down.

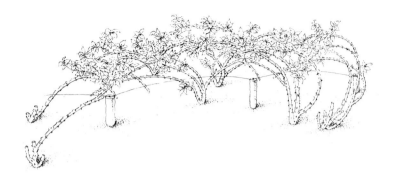

for true ground-cover according to my book, but they can be of great value if in their wanderings the shoots are allowed to trail at random down an awkward bank or to tumble like a waterfall from a terraced bed or over a low wall.

Having done something of a hatchet job on the traditional if somewhat misattributed qualities of these four, let us now look at the more positive side of roses for ground-cover, for labour-saving plants have become all the rage in recent years. Rose breeders have not been slow to follow up this trend, and although I would not say that they have come very near to achieving what they are aiming at as yet, they are trying hard. Varieties such as 'Rosy Cushion', 'Fairyland', 'Fairy Prince' and others of this Harkness series, 'Swany', and what is actually a miniature climber from Japan called 'Nozomi' are appearing in these breeders' lists. Apart from the last, which sends its shoots far and wide across the ground like the spokes of a wheel (and not a great deal closer together), the name 'Rosy Cushion' does, I think, indicate the trend. They form cushions of growth maybe 18 in (45 cm) tall, widespreading but not really as dense as they ought to be to be effective. Couch grass would curl its lip at their attempts to smother it.

However, with the work that is going on at the moment to improve them, it cannot be too long before these roses really carry out the function now claimed for them. By far the nearest approach so far to the ideal is a recurrent miniature with pure white double flowers called 'Snow Carpet'. It was only introduced in 1980 and so has yet to prove its true worth and durability, but the promise is certainly there. It really does form a mat, hugging the ground, but, of course, as it is a miniature it is limited in size. So far, I have seen it spread out to about 3 ft (90 cm).

'Snow Carpet' is a rather special miniature, but to what use can the others be put in the garden? With a few exceptions such as 'Toy Clown', 'Fashion Flame', 'Beauty Secret', and 'Baby Darling', they are, despite their size and in some cases rather fragile appearance, just as tough as the majority of other roses and will grow quite happily out of doors in a climate akin to that of the United Kingdom. The fact that they are so often sold in pots has led to the belief that they are house plants, but neither the light nor the humidity in the average house – there being too little of either – will be right for them. With a certain amount of trouble one can create the right conditions indoors by using gravel trays and fluorescent tubes, but the roses will really be much happier in the garden.

Nowadays one is finding increasing difficulty in defining the limits of the uses to which miniature roses can be put. Over the years they have been hybridised with many other roses – in the main the cluster-flowered types – largely in order to extend the colour range. Other attributes of the larger roses have, however, also been transmitted, notably their size, so that we now have a race of roses more or less halfway between the two, some of which are listed in catalogues as miniatures and some as dwarf cluster-flowering roses.

This is something that is waiting to be sorted out and illustrates well the point that any classification scheme must be flexible and easily adapted to change as the roses change.

Miniature Roses

Figure 1.9
Roses on a patio in troughs and tubs.

The true miniatures, growing no more than 9–10 in (23–25 cm) tall, are in themselves excellent for small-scale patio planting in tubs, troughs and sinks. In this type of container, which is as a rule raised some way above ground level, it is easier, especially if you have a creaking back, to appreciate the full beauty of the tiny blooms and to smell those of them that are scented.

Another effective way of growing miniatures is in terraced beds, with climbing miniatures, of which there is a reasonable if not very large selection available from nurseries, draping down over the vertical brickwork or stonework used to face the steps of the terracing. Miniature standards can be added to give variety.

Colour blending and choosing roses of the right size is just as important for these terrace beds as it is for bedding schemes of large roses, for there is every bit as much variation on both counts. For instance, a bush variety that might well grow taller than the standards that are intended to set it off would not make much sense.

Miniatures used for lining paths have already been dealt with, and they can also be useful for edging beds of larger roses provided the latter do not shade them too much from the sun. And any of them, of whatever size, will look very well on a rockery, the smaller ones perhaps in clumps of three or four.

Figure 1.10
Miniatures growing
in terraced beds.

The tallest climbing roses will reach something in the neighbourhood of 40 ft (12 m), which would be rather overdoing it in most gardens. The only way these giants can really be accommodated as a rule is by sending them up trees, but the sheer weight of their incredibly vigorous growth and the additional wind resistance their leaves give to the tree through which they are meandering, means that the tree must be not only large but strong. Something like an ornamental cherry or even an apple tree would be liable to be smothered in time, but this does not mean that some of the less rampant climbers or ramblers cannot be used, for there is no lovelier way of growing them. Varieties like 'Climbing Cécile Brunner', 'Seagull', 'Wedding Day', 'Sanders's White' or 'Albéric Barbier' would be quite suitable for a medium-sized tree in a medium-sized or even a small garden. All of these varieties have reasonably flexible shoots, which means that they are also easy to train over arches and pergolas or along a catenary which, in case you are in doubt, means the curve formed by a chain hanging between two points but in the gardening sense is a substantial rope suspended so that it hangs in a graceful curve between two or more uprights 8 ft (2.4 m) or so high. The number of uprights and the distance between them will obviously depend on how much space you have, but 8 ft (2.4 m) pillars ought really to be about 12–14 ft (3.7–4.2 m) apart. The roses are trained up

Climbers and Ramblers

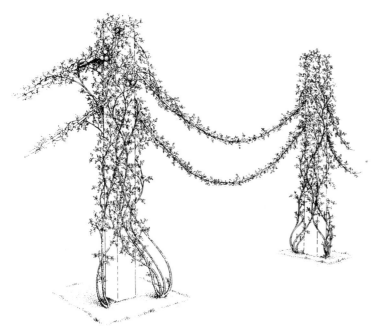

Figure 1.11
Ramblers on a catenary — Regent's Park.

19

Figure 1.12
Ramblers on a
pergola.

these and then along the ropes and the effect is enchanting. It
can be seen on a grand scale all the way up Weather Hill in the
RHS gardens at Wisley and also in Queen Mary's Rose
Gardens in Regent's Park in London. One can make a pergola
from rustic poles but for permanence brick pillars are certainly
better. However, a brick-pillared pergola and for that matter a
catenary form fairly large and substantial structures which are
perhaps best avoided unless you are quite sure that they will not
look out of scale with their surroundings. On the other hand, a
gateway of whatever size would take a rose arch.

Not too many people grow ramblers nowadays (always
excepting 'Albertine', which is immortal and hence, for those
who know their Greek mythology, has ichor rather than sap in
its veins) as they are not recurrent and many of them are
particularly prone to mildew. However, many people still have
an affection for them, as the fact that most rose-growers'
catalogues still contain a limited selection would seem to prove.
If you buy any, keep them away from walls, where air
circulation is likely to be poor, as this will encourage disease.
Train them on open-work fences, trellis, on pillars if they are

Figure 1.13
Larch pillar with
sections of the
branches left to
which roses can be
tied in.

not too rampant, or as outlined above, on arches, pergolas and
so on.

There is a fine range of recurrent climbing roses in the middle
range of vigour from which one can choose nowadays. They
come in every colour and are ideal for the walls of most modern
houses, or for growing as pillar roses unless, to revert briefly to
the ancient past once more, you happen to live in a Greek or
Roman temple. They include the varieties listed above under
the heading 'Specimen Planting' together with 'Autumn Sunlight', 'Galway Bay', 'Handel', 'Leverkusen' and 'Maigold', the
latter being such a marvellous coppery-yellow rose that it

Figure 1.14
Rose hips.

cannot be left out even though it only flowers once. None of these will go much over 10 ft (3 m) and if they are properly trained they will carry their blooms at all levels, even quite near to the ground. Some of the older and more rampant climbing roses such as 'Paul's Lemon Pillar', lovely as they are, do tend to get very bare at the base after a number of years, leaving the lower half of your house wall looking as if it had been subjected to the worst excesses of a mad Victorian plumber. Cutting back hard does not always help.

The majority of modern climbers do, in addition to the purpose for which they are intended, also make very effective if rather lax free-standing shrubs, or else they can be allowed to ramble up through surrounding shrubs of other kinds, giving an extra dimension to something like a lilac, which can be a pretty dull individual from midsummer onwards.

I have not touched on old garden or shrub roses here except briefly under hedging. They vary so much that it seems better to cover some of their uses in the garden in the chapters devoted to each, but there are some general pointers that can be given that apply to them all, with particular reference to the other plants that go well with them.

Contrast in plant form is always interesting in a garden, and in mine I have inadvertently acquired it. Wild foxgloves seed themselves each year among a large group of shrub roses which has been underplanted with heather – though not too closely as the heather needs the sun, too, and must not be shaded too much. The tall spires of the foxgloves give the kind of contrast I might have planned for if I had thought of it, although I have used Canterbury bells in the same way. However, perhaps the most beautiful of all – if you have the soil that suits them so that they do not quietly steal away in the night – are lilies. Both the guardsman-like stance and the trumpet flower form are so different from that of the rose that they are just what is needed. The cool whites and pinks of such lilies as *L. regale*, *L. rubellum* and *L. speciosum* which carries the flowering period through to early autumn, are best for blending with the old rose colours.

So too are both shrubs and plants with grey or silvery-grey leaves like the shrubby potentillas *P. mandschurica* and *P.* 'Vilmoriana' which have white and creamy-white flowers respectively and are better than the silver-leafed but yellow-flowered *P.* 'Beesii', anaphalis, *Stachys byzantina* (*S. lanata*), artemisias such as 'Lambrook Silver', sage (*Salvia officinalis*), which will get the fairly regular snipping over it needs to prevent it straggling if you combine this decorative use for it with its culinary one, and *Senecio* 'Sunshine' (*S. greyii*). The latter is really best if the yellow flowers are removed before opening each year, for they seem to me neither to blend with the rose colourings nor their own leaves. They are on a par with the purple foliage and pink flowers of the flowering cherry *Prunus* 'Kanzan'. Someone up above nodded at the planning stage.

Lavender in its many forms and sizes will always go well with roses, especially as an edging to a rose bed. In addition to the attractive blue-grey of its foliage, it will provide, assuming you are not growing something like 'Loddon Pink', the only colour missing from the rose spectrum: blue. Clumps of nepeta will do the same, though it may be rather too spreading to make a good edging plant, and finally there is rosemary (*Rosmarinus officinalis*), making in time quite a sizeable shrub and another one with a double use, for it, like sage, can be picked over for the kitchen.

CHAPTER 2

The Rose Families

The earliest roses were the species or wild types which, coming true from seed when crossed with one of their own kind, remained unchanged down the centuries. We see them today just as they were before man inhabited the earth, and there are probably something like 150 of them. I say 'probably' because there is disagreement among botanists. Some hold, and they are known as the 'splitters', that all the different forms of rose such as *R. canina*, the dog rose, which have perhaps been caused not by interbreeding with other wild roses but by differing environmental conditions over the centuries, should be classified as separate species. This applies to a number of roses and, if the splitters had their way, it is anybody's guess as to how many there would be, though certainly the number would run into four figures. I tend to go along with the second group of botanists, the 'lumpers', if only because it makes things simpler all round. Rose history is confused and uncertain enough already without people, however well intentioned, thinking up ways of making it worse.

One of the wild roses was *R. gallica*, low growing with single light-red flowers and native to the regions bordering the Mediterranean. This, probably making a natural cross with *R. moschata* (the musk rose) and/or *R. phoenicia*, brought us the first damasks, which included not only the summer-flowering but also that odd-man-out among the Western roses of the time, the 'Autumn Damask', which did produce some late flowers and was one of the most important varieties in the whole rose family tree. For, crossed with recurrent roses newly arrived from China, the 'Autumn Damask' produced two closely related groups, the Portland roses and the much more numerous and important bourbons. Although both groups were strong-growing (inherited from the damask side and not from the rather tender and far from vigorous early Chinas), the bourbons were much easier to breed new varieties from and so they prospered while the Portlands languished.

Further introduction of China rose blood into the bourbons and to a lesser extent to the Portlands gradually brought a more dependable remontancy, resulting in a new class, the hybrid perpetuals. This was a misleading name as they were not even as perpetually in flower as many of the China roses from which they were descended. However, a lot of them did put on a show in the autumn after a longish gap to get their breath back after their midsummer display. It was not until a fresh introduction of China rose blood, this time from the newly arrived tea roses, that anything like the flowering performance we now expect of our bedding roses was achieved.

The tea roses, with very few exceptions, were too tender to survive out of doors in Western Europe – or perhaps one should say the northern part of it – but crossed with the hybrid perpetuals they produced the hybrid teas. These, as we know, are, with only a few exceptions, a tough and hardy race, and the tea roses also passed on to them something of the much more refined and delicate beauty of form of the tea rose flower.

That, in broad outline, is the family tree of the hybrid tea. I have given no dates for the formation of a new class or group as in most cases they are unknown or at least far from certain. New types of rose do not suddenly happen. Development takes place gradually over many years and what happened with the hybrid teas can be taken as typical of the whole. The rose 'La France', nowadays generally accepted to be the first hybrid tea, dates from 1867, but for some years after that date it was still being sold under its original classification as a hybrid perpetual. After a while, it was realised that 'La France' (and a number of other varieties) were sufficiently different from what had gone before to make up a new class, and then it was a question of looking back to try to decide which of them had been the first. 'La France' was chosen, although it must be said that there were other claimants and that a pretty strong case could be put forward for a number of them.

More will be said about the development of each of the groups of roses in the separate chapters devoted to them, but there are still a few branches of the family tree that have not been touched on. Of equal importance to the line that resulted in the hybrid teas is the one that produced our other most popular type of modern rose, the floribundas. Once again hybrid China roses feature, crossed in this instance with the dense-growing, thicket-making *R. multiflora* (*R. polyantha*) whose influence provided the clusters of comparatively small flowers typical of the polyantha pompon roses which were the first result. The China rose influence gave recurrence and later

25

on tea roses and hybrid teas introduced into the polyantha pompon strain brought bigger flowers in a wider colour range and better health. The floribundas (known initially as hybrid polyanthas) thus arrived, having taken a rather shorter route than the hybrid teas.

Two other lines of development ought to be mentioned briefly, in the first of which the 'Autumn Damask' once more played a part. A cross with *R. corymbifera* (or some say the closely related *R. canina*) resulted in the alba roses. From these – though as far as I can see there is very scanty evidence – it is generally considered that the first centifolia came, but there is no doubt at all that the moss rose race originated in a sport from a centifolia. Then there were the rugosas which, originating in the Far East, have not figured in any of the main lines of development of the rose except that of the Kordesii climbers. The varieties we know are almost without exception hybrids produced at about the turn of the century and very little influenced by or having very little influence on any other rose family.

From what I have said so far it may have been gathered that all roses fit snugly into one class or another, but this is far from being the case. There is too much uncertainty in the early history and too little proper recording of pedigrees later on for anyone to be dogmatic about anything. In addition, the rose is still in a state of change. Not too long ago one could tell if a rose was a floribunda without having to look at it twice. But crossing floribundas with HTs has resulted in floribundas with flowers of such a size (coupled with fewer in a truss) that one is unsure about which group they belong to. Then to cap the confusion, names were adopted for new classes which were imprecise or botanically incorrect. One such was 'Grandiflora', used for tall-growing and large-flowered floribundas, and so at length the Royal National Rose Society, after many previous attempts to devise an acceptable new classification, produced one which was adopted, after slight amendment, by the newly-formed World Federation of Rose Societies in 1971. Things were on the move.

They were concerned to sort things out for the befogged gardener rather than for the botanist and, having taken all considerations into account and rejecting faith and hope, decided that the greatest of all considerations was clarity. Their deliberations succeeded to a degree although, as has already been said, it was always intended that the new classification should be a developing thing, for the rose as we have seen is always moving on, ever changing. The new classification is being introduced gradually by member countries of the World Federation, which means the majority of the rose-growing nations. As most gardeners will come across at least some aspects of it, here is a summary of the new categories. There are subdivisions of most of these, such as Wild Rose (as the species are now called) and Wild Rose, Climbing, or recurrent and non-recurrent, but these need not concern us here. Basically the picture is as follows:

1. Species and varieties that bear a strong resemblance to them have become Wild Roses.

2. All hybrid roses dating from before the coming of the HT are to be known collectively as Old Garden Roses. Within this general title the ancient names such as Gallica, Damask, Alba, Centifolia, Moss Rose, Bourbon, Portland, China, Hybrid Perpetual and Tea are retained, since they are unlikely to be changed or developed further by hybridisers.

3. The term 'Modern Shrub Rose' (meaning a rose that is unsuitable through size or habit of growth for bedding) is now confined to roses fitting this description introduced since very roughly the turn of the century. This works well enough for the roses produced fairly and squarely in this century, but does put something like the rugosas and the vast *R. pimpinellifolia* (*R. spinosissima*) group on the spot. Most of the hybrids we grow of both groups are clearly modern shrubs, even though many more closely resemble their wild ancestors in looks and habit of growth. And it has been argued that the name 'Hybrid Musk' should vanish and the varieties simply be called Modern Shrub Roses, lumped in with all the rest, but I see no reason why the old name, which after all commemorates the work of the great Joseph Pemberton who created this individual group of roses, should vanish. I doubt if it will and I certainly do not intend to be the first to try to do away with it.

As for the rest of the new terms:

4. Climbers are unchanged.

5. Ramblers are unchanged.

6. Polyanthas are unchanged.

7. Miniatures are unchanged.

but:

8. Hybrid Teas have become Large-flowered Bush Roses.

9. Floribundas are Cluster-flowered Bush Roses.

For most gardeners these last two are the most significant changes as they are the only ones that will really affect them. They are not difficult to remember anyway, and do mean what they say, which the old terms no longer did.

CHAPTER 3

The Species or Wild Roses

These are the roses which grew in the wild, many thousands of years before man was even aware of their existence. In fact most of them would have been able to regard the first men as intruders into a world in which they themselves had long felt at home, which means that their early history cannot be charted with any accuracy. It can really only start with the date on which each new wild rose was first discovered by the early plant hunters, or was introduced to the West, so the dates which are given after the names of the various wild roses in this book – and in other books and catalogues – do not really mean the same as those given for hybrid roses. In the latter case, the date is either that of the actual creation of the new hybrid or, more likely, of its introduction to the gardening world. The wild rose, *R. bracteata*, flowering right through the summer months and one of the parents of the lovely climber 'Mermaid', carries the date of 1793 in reference books, but that is when it came to us from China. Nobody knows how old it actually is, but the date of 1918 after its hybrid 'Mermaid' is the date of that rose's creation.

In the introduction to this book I have already said a little about the difficulty in deciding which is and which is not a true species owing to the natural increase in the number of petals which may have taken place through crosses between different roses which happened quite by chance to be growing near to each other. But two sets of people have confused the situation still further.

First came early botanists, who on occasion gave Latin names that should properly have belonged to species to hybrid roses. All the alba roses are now considered hybrids, probably descended from a damask rose and the species *R. corymbifera*, as are the centifolias and moss roses, even though here the lineage is less certain. Thus the Great Double White Alba *R. × alba* 'Maxima', the cabbage rose *R. × centifolia* and the moss rose *R. × centifolia muscosa* should properly have the '×'

inserted before their names to indicate hybrid origin.

Modern or comparatively modern hybridists have added to the confusion by producing hybrids such as Wilhelm Kordes's 'Frühlingsgold' and 'Frühlingsmorgen' and the Spanish rose 'Nevada' which in habit of growth and flowers closely resemble species and are only once or twice removed from species in their pedigrees. So when trying to group roses in some sort of order, does one count these as wild rose hybrids in the same category as those that have happened through the agency of insects or wind-blown pollen, or does one class them as modern shrub roses? This is the sort of problem one all too often encounters when dealing with the different groups of roses. In this book I have followed the latter alternative.

A word, too, should be said about the sizes given for the roses in this chapter and in later ones. These should be regarded as indications only, for the ultimate size to which any shrub will grow can depend on many factors – the soil, the climate, the situation in which it is planted in relation to sun or shade, and on whether or not it is neglected or cherished. Some shrubs may thrive on neglect, but by no means all, and roses are always that much better for some loving care.

There are possibly 150 different species roses altogether, although, as we have seen, botanists are by no means unanimous about the total. Of these only a small proportion make really worthwhile garden shrubs and in what follows I have picked out for description some of the best. And it must be said that with few exceptions such as *R. ecae* and *R. pimpinellifolia* (which sends out suckers all over the place at the speed of light) they are on the big side for modern gardens. *R. soulieana*, for instance, will reach 10 ft by 10 ft (3 m by 3 m). If cut back to fit a limited space, they lose much of their grace and charm, so all in all they are for biggish gardens, for solo planting as specimens or for mixed shrubberies provided they can have plenty of sun. In mixed shrubberies the lack of late flowers is less noticeable, though a number of species do make up for this by a fine display of red or orange hips.

Most species can be increased quite easily from cuttings, but this is not always an advantage. There is a tendency when they are on their own roots for them to put most of their energy into producing an impenetrable tangle of spindly shoots rather than into flower production on a limited number of fine strong ones.

Here is a selection of some of the loveliest species roses:

'Canary Bird' is usually listed under this, its popular name although it can sometimes be found under *R. xanthina* *spontanea*, a rose which is very similar. The latter may, in fact, be one of the parents of 'Canary Bird', and if so, 'Canary Bird' is not a true species. In other words, nobody is quite sure of the origin of this lovely rose except that it came originally from Northern China and Korea. When it came is again in doubt, but as *R. xanthina spontanea* arrived from the same area in 1907 we can presume, I think, that 'Canary Bird' must date from rather later.

Late spring in a good year brings out the brilliant yellow 2-in (5-cm) single flowers all along the gracefully arching canes. The display is spectacular, a real herald of the rose season, and will last for several weeks. There may be the odd flower or two later in the summer but even without these the shrub remains singularly attractive, both because of its habit of growth and because it has healthy, fern-like foliage. It will make a big bush if left to its own devices, probably about 7 ft × 7 ft (2.1 × 2.1 m), but several nurseries offer it grown as a standard. In this form it will make a big head certainly but one that it unlikely to exceed 4–5 ft (1.2–1.5 m), more easily accommodated in a small garden.

I have seen die-back mentioned as a possibility with this rose but have never had any problems with it myself, perhaps because the soil in my garden is light and sandy, which appears to make die-back less likely.

R. × dupontii. A rose I would never willingly be without for it has an elegant beauty probably unmatched by any other. The blooms come in small clusters of four to five but are quite large in themselves, with wide overlapping petals so that they give the impression of being semi-double. They are creamy white with an occasional blush of pink on some of the petals, set off by the central ring of golden stamens and by the background of soft-green leaves. Fragrance is marked, which is not surprising as it is thought that a musk rose figures in *R. dupontii*'s breeding line. It was raised some time before 1817, possibly in the Empress Josephine's garden at Malmaison, and named after the Director of the Luxembourg Gardens in Paris, André Dupont. Not a terribly rampant grower, in time it will make a fairly open bush with few thorns about 6–7ft (around 2 m) high and the same across, blooming at midsummer. Not by any means spectacular but with a quiet beauty very much its own. With a spray of its flowers in your hand you can understand why it is said that the Romans, in order to cool the anger of an antagonist, would give him a rose to smell.

R. fedtshenkoana is the first true, unadulterated species on our list and very nearly unique as it is pretty well perpetually in flower all through the summer, the later flowers being produced on short side shoots from the main canes. The single blooms, about 2 in (5 cm) in diameter, are white with yellow stamens and the soft, grey-green leaves are an added attraction which make this a good candidate for a mixed shrub planting. Orange-red hips covered in fine bristles come in the latter part of the summer, but they are not particularly showy. Introduced from Turkestan in 1890, this will make a tall (8-ft or 2.4-m) rather twiggy shrub which will sucker readily – a point to remember when planting it among other shrubs.

R. × *harisonii* (**'Harison's Yellow'**) probably came from a cross between a Scotch rose (*R. pimpinellifolia*) and *R. foetida*, the latter the only rose known at the time of 'Harison's Yellow's' introduction in 1830 to have such brilliant yellow colouring to pass on to its offspring. For this one is a real dazzler for several weeks from just before midsummer onwards. The flowers are semi-double and open rather informally on a bush with the brightest of green leaves but rather an unpredictable habit of growth. By this I do not mean that it lacks vigour, which certainly does not. It will reach 6 ft (1.8 m) or so but becomes rather unbalanced unless some corrective pruning is carried out. Raised in New York, 'Harison's Yellow' is said to have spread westward across the continent with the pioneers, so that it can be found nuturalised along the old covered wagon trails. I have seen it, too, described as being The Yellow Rose of Texas, but this is denied by American rose-growing friends. It should not be confused with 'Williams Double Yellow', which was raised about the same time in England from the same parents. The latter has green carpels in place of the yellow stamens of *R.* × *harisonii* in its otherwise very similar flowers.

R. moyesii **'Geranium'**. Almost every description of this variant of *R. moyesii* includes the words 'the most suitable form for the small garden'. Well, maybe, but the statement must be understood to be relative, for 'Geranium' will make a fairly open bush fully 9 ft (2.75 m) high and almost as much across. Bright-scarlet single blooms decorate the long arching almost thornless shoots in early summer and are followed by a perhaps even more startling – and certainly longer lasting – display of clusters of the most remarkable, flagon-shaped, bright-red hips, each one fully 2 in (5 cm) long. This is an outstanding characteristic of pretty well all the moyesii hybrids, some of which, including *R. moyesii rosea* (*R. holodonta*), 'Fred Streeter' and 'Sealing Wax' have pink flowers of varying intensity. *R. moyesii* itself was introduced from Western China in 1908, and 'Geranium' raised at the RHS Garden, Wisley, in 1935.

R. × paulii rosea is the light-pink and, I feel, more attractive sport from the white but otherwise similar *R. × paulii* and both have for long been recommended as ground-cover roses as was mentioned earlier. Well, they will cover the ground and they will smother weeds, but after a time they form a dense hummock some 12–15 ft (3.7–4.5 m) across, under which nothing that would not be equally happy living under a stone would thrive. But as they will also mound up to something like 4 ft (1.25 m) they are simply, to my mind, low-growing bushes for foreground planting or for sprawling down awkward banks. For such purposes *R. × paulii rosea* has a rare beauty, at midsummer being almost submerged under its large single, scented flowers with their creamy-yellow stamens. The fact that this is a rugosa hybrid is reflected in its fine, wrinkled leaves. It has multitudinous and horrendous thorns. William Paul, about 1903.

R. pimpinellifolia altaica is another of the very large Scotch or burnet rose family, completely differnt from *R. × harisonii* in that the flowers, coming in late spring in great profusion all along the gently arching canes, are single and creamy-white with golden stamens. They are followed by round hips of so dark a purplish-red as to appear black. A more upright grower than many species to about 7 ft (2.1 m). The leaves are greyish green and the rose's name is derived from the Altai mountains in Siberia where it was first unearthed sometime around 1820.

R. rubrifolia (R. glauca). Clusters of tiny pink and rather fleeting flowers decorate this rose at midsummer, to be followed by a fine display of round red hips in the autumn, but the reason that this open growing, arching 7-ft (2.1-m) shrub is so often grown is for the plum-red colour of its usually thornless young shoots and the purplish red leaves with their coppery sheen. Flower arrangers are at its beck, let alone its call. A native of Europe, self-sown seedlings germinate readily.

R. virginiana is later flowering than those so far described, producing its single, cerise-pink flowers when we are well into the summer. It makes an informal, fairly lax, 6-ft (1.8-m) shrub which will spread if allowed to by suckering, and in autumn its leaves take on in turn every colour of the gaudiest sunset. The double form 'St Mark's Rose' or 'Rose d'Amour' is preferred by many people and is perhaps a little more compact.

CHAPTER 4

The Gallicas

This is the most important group in the history of the rose in that it almost certainly contains the first roses cultivated by man and because practically every rose we grow in our gardens today is descended from it. All the old groups, the damasks, centifolias (and through them the moss roses), the albas and so on, came down to us from hybrids of the original species *gallica*. Gallicas were certainly known to the Greeks and the Romans as they are native to most of the Mediterranean and western Asia.

One of the gallicas especially has made its mark, *R. gallica* 'Officinalis', also known as The French Rose and The Apothecary's Rose. The former name comes from the long association the gallicas in general have had with France, but they are also more specifically known as Provins roses after the town of Provins not far from Paris. It was in this area, from the Middle Ages onwards, that 'Officinalis' was grown commercially in large quantities for the manufacture of preserves from its petals and also for the effusions and potions that could be prepared from it to cure pretty well every disease known to man. Hence the link with the apothecaries.

'Officinalis' also links France and England together for Edmund Crouchback, the first Earl of Lancaster, had estates in France through his French wife, and it seems likely that it was in her country that he first saw the semi-double crimson-scarlet blooms of 'Officinalis' and decided to make it his badge. After the Wars of the Roses, when the houses of Lancaster and York came together under the Tudors, they combined 'Officinalis', the Red Rose of Lancaster, with *R. × alba semi-plena*, the White Rose of York, to form the Tudor rose, which became the badge of England. If you examine it you will see that it is not one rose but two, one inside the other, and you can still buy and grow both of them. For a detailed description of 'Officinalis' look in this chapter under 'Rosa Mundi'. The latter is a striped sport from the former and identical in every way except for the flowers.

Both 'Officinalis' and 'Rosa Mundi' could be said to be typical gallicas in size and habit, and this family is perhaps the most suitable one among the old roses for small gardens. Few of the varieties grow much above 4 ft (1.2 m) and many of them are compact and upright, so that they do not take up too much room. If, however, they are on their own roots (as they would be, for instance, if they had been raised from cuttings), they will spread very freely by suckers. This can be useful if one wishes to thicken up a gallica hedge, but can be much less welcome in most other situations.

In summer gallicas carry some of the most beautiful flowers among the old garden roses. They come in the full range of the old rose colours except for pure white, and include a number of striped varieties other than 'Rosa Mundi', among them 'Tricolore de Flandre' and 'Perle de Panachées'. Their leaves, however, are less attractive, rather rough and coarse, and they certainly can look very much the worse for wear by the end of the summer, particularly if mildew has struck, as it very well may.

Gallicas which are more lax in habit and therefore need rather more room than most include 'Tuscany' and 'Empress Josephine' and then there are two hybrids with single flowers, 'Complicata' and the aptly named 'Scarlet Fire', which will ramble up through other shrubs or make handsome fence or pillar roses. But these two are far from typical and in cultivation would need pruning (if at all) only to confine them within bounds. The more typical upright, rather twiggy growth of the others of the family benefits from some thinning out and the bushes can even be gently clipped over in winter to keep them neat. Some of the best gallicas are:

'Belle de Crécy' is one of the lax-growing gallicas really needing a surrounding of low shrubs or something else to rest its elbows on if the canes are not to be bowed right to the ground by the weight of the profusion of flowers at midsummer. The shoots are typically gallica in their lack of thorns, though also typically they have plenty of short bristles instead. The sweetly-scented, fully double flowers are a rich mauvish-pink on opening and change through tints which are blends of lilac, slate-grey and paler pink to purple. At all stages the combinations of colours are both striking and beautiful and many people consider this the most lovely gallica of all, even though the leaves are something of a let-down, being matt and a rather dull green. Raised or at least introduced by Roeser some time before 1848, this is, of course, quite a modern hybrid in comparison with a rose like 'Officinalis'. The majority of the gallicas one can buy nowadays date from the nineteenth century.

'Cardinal de Richelieu' is a rose that really needs good soil and a certain amount of cosseting to give of its best, which is not a usual gallica trait. Generally they are tough and very hardy roses, which will grow almost anywhere, but though 'Cardinal de Richelieu' may need that little bit more attention, most people will think it worthwhile after seeing the rich and sumptuous beauty of the dark, maroon-purple blooms, the many petals of which reflex almost to a ball. As with other gallicas, they come in small clusters at midsummer only on shoots which in this case are well covered with dark-green leaves and on a bush that will reach 4–5 ft (1.2–1.5 m) if given a little support.

'Charles de Mills' makes a compact, upright bush to 4 ft (1.2 m) or so with a multitude of slender shoots which will almost certainly need the support of a stake once the flowers come out. Unpromising-looking in bud, they open to large blooms fully 4 in (10 cm) across, cupped to flat, the massed petals often quartered, and the whole in the richest crimson-maroon which holds undimmed until the petals fall. The scent is only moderate.

'Complicata' is a most unlikely gallica in every possible way. Nobody seems at all sure of its parentage and as it is thought that *R.* × *macrantha* hort. (which 'Complicata' much more closely resembles) may come into the lineage too, it would have seemed more sensible to have given this side of the family precedence. A botanist may have reasons for not doing so, but they are not obvious, any more so than the reason for this rose's strange name is obvious. It is a strange name because this rose has some of the simplest and least complicated of single blooms of great beauty, like saucers of the most delicate, transluscent porcelain. Fully 4 in (10 cm) across, brilliant pink paling to a white eye, and with golden stems, they are carried at midsummer all along the enormously vigorous canes. These love to ramble up and through surrounding shrubs and small trees or, if isolated, 'Complicata' will make an enormous, mounding bush fully 8 ft by 8 ft (2.4 m by 2.4 m). There are healty, matt, rather pointed leaves, which are nothing like the rather rounded gallica type.

'Du Maitre d'Ecole' is an upright plant about 3 ft 6 in (105 cm) high and reasonably compact when out of flower, but with its fairly slender shoots arching in midsummer under the weight of the large, double, quartered flowers, it can reach a spread of 4 ft (1.2 m). Buds of the typical rounded gallica type, but with long feathered calyces, open to large and very double carmine blooms, the petals veined purplish-pink, the whole fading attractively after a time to lighter tones. It is a pity that nobody knows who the schoolmaster may have been or the date of this lovely variety's introduction.

'Empress Josephine' (**'Francofurtana'** or **R.** × **_francofurtana_**). As already mentioned, this makes a loose, spreading bush, ideal for the foreground of a shrub planting provided it is in full sun. It will reach about 4 ft by 4 ft (1.2 by 1.2 m) with loosely-formed double flowers in bright-pink with deeper veining on the waved petals. This was one of the roses in the Empress Josephine's collection that was painted by Redouté in the garden at Malmaison, but it was then known as 'Francofurtana' or 'The Frankfurt Rose'. It was renamed in memory of the Empress at a considerably later date. Not very much scent, I am afraid, but a very well-worthwhile rose in every other way.

'Gloire de France' dates from 1819, and is the smallest gallica in stature that I am going to describe, reaching no more than 3 ft (90 cm) tall and spreading out to about the same measurement. The flowers, which are carried with great freedom, are particularly striking with the mauve-pink fading to the palest tints at the petal edges. On the whole, it is less likely to be attacked by mildew than many of this family.

'Président de Sèze' has blooms with the same colour contrasts as those of 'Gloire de France' only, as one might say, more so. The flowers are larger, fully 4 in (10 cm) across and just as full and quartered and scented, but with the centre petals a vivid crimson-purple shading dramatically outwards to a soft lilac-pink as the outer ring is reached. In full bloom and at its peak a few weeks after midsummer, a bush of this rose is a memorable sight. It is a sturdy grower, reaching 4 ft by 3 ft (1.2 m by 90 cm) and with leaves larger than is usual for a gallica. Introduced by a discerning (and certainly lucky, as this was long before deliberate hybridising was carried out) Madame Hebert, some time prior to 1836.

'Rosa Mundi' (**R. _gallica_** **'Versicolour'**). A brief mention of this rose was made at the beginning of this chapter when discussing R. _gallica_ 'Officinalis', of which this was a sport and to which the odd shoot or two will occasionally revert. Quite when it came into existence nobody knows for certain, although there is a mention of a rose which fits the description of 'Rosa Mundi' in 1581. It is said to have been named after Fair Rosamund, who was the mistress of Henry II, but there is no trace of any contemporary record to link the two. On the face of it they are separated by some 400 years, but it is by no means unlikely that this gallica could date back to a much earlier time than we are aware of. At any rate, whether this connection is a myth or not, it is one of the small but intriguing snippets one keeps chancing on in rose history and which I am reluctant to disbelieve unless some real proof is forthcoming that they are pure fable.

Certainly, when once one has grown it, one can see why 'Rosa Mundi' should have survived for so long. It will fit in anywhere as it will not go over 4 ft by 3 ft (1.2 m by 90 cm) and it stays upright and compact even when in full bloom. This is at least partially because the clustered blooms are only semi-double and so much lighter than those of most gallicas that they arch over only a little, if at all. They are, in fact, held well above the rather coarse, light-green leaves and are really eye-catching. The palest of blush-pink backgrounds (which fades white after a few days) is splashed and striped with crimson and deep pink in gay abandon and the flowering period stretches over several weeks. Sometimes one sees 'Rosa Mundi' put forward as a hedging rose and there is in fact a notable and often mentioned hedge of it at Kiftsgate Court in Gloucestershire. I would not, however, advocate such a mass planting of this rose in a garden which was a great deal smaller, as once the flowering period is over mildew can be a problem. In a garden the size of Kiftsgate Court, what could become an unsightly line of bushes can quite easily be lost in late summer among a wealth of other features. In a small garden it might dominate the scene. As I mentioned earlier, *R. gallica* 'Officinalis' is similar in every way to its sport 'Rosa Mundi' except for the colour.

'Tuscany' has superb dark-crimson double flowers which open to reveal a mass of golden stamens. Its date of introduction is unknown, but in 1848 the great nurseryman William Paul put on the market an improved version, 'Tuscany Superb', which has larger leaves and bigger, more double blooms in which the stamens are largely hidden. Not too much scent, which is unusual in a dark-red rose, but it makes a strong-growing, reasonably upright bush of about 4 ft by 3 ft (1.2 m by 90 cm).

CHAPTER 5

The Damasks

All the old roses and perhaps particularly the damasks have always been thought of as among the most strongly-scented of flowers. Conversely, modern roses are thought to lack scent. However, neither statement is really correct. At the most they are only partially correct as instanced by Pliny the Elder remarking in his *Natural History* on the lack of scent in many roses. He actually makes a comparison between roses from various areas in relation to their scent, placing those of Cyrene in North Africa top of the list. Probably the truth of the matter is that we have treasured particularly and so kept growing those of the old roses that had a scent (as well as other good qualities) and so it is these that have survived. The others have been forgotten, but more recently it has been the coming of the cluster-flowered (floribunda) roses, mostly lacking in scent because they come from a scentless line, that has appeared to distort the picture even more. Their rise in popularity since the last war has been phenomenal, but if people really want them there are just as many fragrant large-flowered (HT) roses and roses from other groups as there ever were, notable among them the damasks.

This is one of the oldest of the groups of roses, second only to the gallicas, from which they are descended. It is said that they originated in the Damascus area and that they were brought west by the returning Crusaders, but there seems to be no evidence to support this. However, they probably did come from somewhere in the Middle East and from descriptions by Pliny and others it is fairly certain they were known by the Romans, who grew sweetly-scented roses in vast quantities, particularly in the area round Paestum in the Gulf of Salerno in south-western Italy. These were for use in all sorts of ways, for the preparation of rose water and various scented oils and balms, to decorate their festivals and triumphant processions, and not least to give the ultimate touch of decadence to their orgies by being strewn on the beds on which they lay, to say nothing of being ankle-deep on the floor all around.

It has been mainly damask roses which have been used over many hundreds of years for the distillation of attar of roses. The mountain valleys of the Balkans and parts of Turkey were found to have the ideal growing conditions and it was here particularly that the industry flourished and is still carried on today.

Apart from their notable fragrance, which, as we have seen, may well have kept the rose in general in the topmost place in man's esteem, the damasks have a further and perhaps even more noteworthy claim on our attention. Right up to the beginning of the nineteenth century there was only one western variety of rose that produced any flowers after the single, midsummer flush. This was a damask, *R. × damascena semperflorens* (*R. × damascena bifera*), also known as the 'Autumn Damask' or the 'Quatre Saisons'. The autumn flowering was certainly not profuse and the rose could not really be recommended as a must for the garden nowadays, except for its historical interest. The blooms are of poor form, but it so happened that the 'Autumn Damask' was planted in a hedge together with some fully recurrent China roses (probably 'Old Blush') on the Ile du Bourbon, a French possession right in the middle of the Indian Ocean. Cross-pollination resulted in seedlings in which a botanist called Bréon saw possibilites. Brought back to France, these became the first of the bourbon roses and direct ancestors of all the roses that grace our gardens from midsummer until the first frosts of autumn.

The 'York and Lancaster' rose is *R. × damascena versicolour* and is thought to be the one growing in the Temple Gardens in Shakespeare's Henry IV Part I from which the opposing Yorkists and Lancastrians picked their emblems, because the blooms may be anything from the palest blush-pink to a deep-pink or parti-coloured with petals or sections of them in either shade. They are, however, never pure white, so my own preference for the Yorkists' rose is the truly white *R. × alba semi-plena* described in the next chapter.

The damasks are naturally more lax and wide-spreading in habit than the gallicas and have an informality that blends in well with plants other than shrubs. They vary quite widely in size from 3–4 ft (90 cm–1.2 m) up to the 7-ft (2.1-m) 'Trigintipetala' which is one of the oldest and is used extensively in the production of attar. Rather slender pedicels or flower stalks mean that the blooms of damasks tend to nod. Downy foliage is typical of the group.

Here is a selection of recommended damasks:

'**Blush Damask**' is included in this group because, although its ancestry is very uncertain, it would appear to have a lot of damask about it. And it has one particular advantage over the others. Most of them really should have good soil to give of their best, but 'Blush Damask' does seem to thrive almost anywhere, making a large and exceptionally twiggy shrub about 6 ft by 6 ft (1.8 m by 1.8 m). Graham Thomas has suggested that there may be a Scotch rose somewhere in the background and certainly that is a family that will grow on anything short of solid concrete.

The flowering period at midsummer is maybe a little shorter than with some of the others but the blooms do appear against the deep-green leaves in the greatest profusion, double and neatly quartered, reflexing gradually and of a deep lilac-pink, fading away a little towards the petal edges.

'**Celsiana**' was introduced some time before 1750 and has lost none of its vigour with the years, making a substantial, well-branched bush some 5 ft (1.5 m) tall and about 4 ft (1.2 m) across, well covered with grey-green leaves. The flowers, semi-double, may reach 4 in (10 cm) across and come in clusters at midsummer only. They open a deep rose-pink but gradually the crinkled petals, of an almost transparent texture, fade to lighter tones. The fragrance is strong and after the flowers have finished small, narrow hips are produced, although these cannot be counted as showy.

'**Ispahan**' is the damask rose I would choose if I were restricted to one only, and not solely because it is longer in flower than any other members of the family, for five to six weeks at least. First noted in 1832, it is almost certainly very much older and makes a strong-growing, reasonably upright bush with a plentiful covering of leaves which are smoother and less downy than is usual with the damasks. The flowers are carried in large clusters and are of medium size and loosely double. The colour is a clear, soft, unshaded pink, and there is a rich fragrance. Growing to 5 or 6 ft (1.5 or 1.8 m) in height, 'Ispahan's' compactness will prevent it taking up too much room. It can be quite at home in a small garden.

'**Madame Hardy**' Many people, when asked which is the most beautiful of the old roses, will give the name of this one. I am often asked that question myself and though I have to say that such is the variety to choose from that I could not possibly give an answer, 'Madame Hardy' would certainly be on my short list. The buds before opening have great charm for they are decorated by long feathery calyces. Then they open to snow-white, flat, double, quartered blooms with a green carpel in the middle, giving the final touch. In my experience, however, they are far from fond of rain, and from what I have seen of its vigour elsewhere, the light soil of my garden does not really suit this rose. My flowers are smaller than they should be and the growth of the bush, which ought to reach 5 to 6 ft (1.5 to 1.8 m), is inclined to be spindly where it should be strong and freely branching. It is generally said that the scent is good, but here again mine disappoints, and to be truthful I have never found it particularly noticeable elsewhere. The matt, light-green leaves may need watching for mildew. It is a rose that clearly has some faults, but you do not love your best friend any the less because he or she has some too.

'St. Nicholas' is a very showy and attractive rose, both at midsummer when the semi-double rich pink blooms with their golden stems literally cover the bush, and later when hips appear in their place. The flowers do fade a little after a time but are still pleasing against the dark-green leaves. It is a compact and sturdy grower to about 4 ft (1.2 m).

This rose is something of a mystery, as it appeared out of the blue in a garden in Richmond in Yorkshire in 1950. It is suggested that it was a self-sown seedling of a damask/gallica cross, but nobody knows for certain.

CHAPTER 6

The Albas

From the name they bear one would imagine that all these should be white. They are not. Most of them are pink, but the two oldest varieties by a very long way are white and it must have been from them that the group took its name. They are probably descended from damask parentage, crossed it was thought until very recently with *R. canina*, the dog rose. The latest botanical edict is that *R. corymbifera* should be substituted for *R. canina*, but the two are so closely allied that the news is unlikely to cause alba lovers to lose any sleep. At any rate the albas, like the three other groups which we have already dealt with, are so ancient that nobody can be certain even of their country of origin.

The Romans certainly knew them and seem likely to have introduced them into Western Europe. Needless to say, however, following the almost inevitable pattern when dealing with rose history, there is also a theory that the Romans called England Albion, not because of the White Cliffs of Dover, but because of the white alba roses they found growing there when they first arrived. It is quite true that the white albas did at some stage become naturalised, especially in the north of England, but never, I think, on such a scale as would have led to them being considered a national flower by a conqueror. It is really much more likely that the first roses were planted after the Roman invasion than before, and if it was indeed a white rose that gave the country its Latin name, it was more likely to have been the native field rose, *R. arvensis*, then, it would appear, much commoner than it is now.

The albas have for long played a supporting role to the damasks in the production of attar, and roses of typically alba type with many reflexed petals can be recognised in the pictures the Dutch masters of the seventeenth century and those of the very much later French artist called Ignace Henri Jean Théodore Fantin-Latour. He lived until 1904, but following the snipe-like flight of rose history we will now dart back again in time.

The Albas

There has always been and most surely will continue to be an argument as to whether *R.* × *alba semi-plena* or the field rose already mentioned is the White Rose of York. The former gets the vote by a considerable majority, possibly because its comparatively large semi-double creamy-white blooms are vastly more impressive than the small and very fleeting single ones of *R. arvensis*. On the other hand it seems to be fairly generally agreed that the double form of the alba rose, *R.* × *alba maxima* or the Great Double White, is the Jacobite Rose or Bonnie Prince Charlie's Rose. His followers either wore it openly when it was not too dangerous to do so, or else planted bushes of it round their crofts or manses, silent witnesses to their loyalty to him, but not evidence that could be produced and proved against them.

Having said all of which, it is only fair to point out that a few authorities do state quite categorically that *R.* × *alba semi-plena* is the Jacobite Rose and that *R.* × *alba maxima* is the White Rose of York. In rose history it does not take long for one to be, if I may so put it, up to one's hips in a swamp of contradiction.

Although there are one or two smaller ones such as 'Félicité Parmentier' and 'Königin von Danemarck', the albas as a family tend to be large and very robust shrubs, their strong, rigid canes with only a scattering of thorns keeping them fairly upright. As some of them will comfortably exceed the height of a tall man and be almost as much across they certainly do need a fair amount of room, but, if you can possibly manage it, do have at least one of them, for they are among the finest garden shrubs of any kind. Their blooms are, as has been said, either white or the softest pink which fades little as the flowers age, and they are scented, too. The foliage is outstanding for the leaves are a grey-green which maintains its beauty long after the flowers have gone and enables the albas to add distinction to any mixed shrub planting. *R.* × *alba semi-plena* has worthwhile hips, too.

For garden purposes the two big white albas are more or less interchangeable, depending only on whether you prefer double or semi-double flowers. Both will reach 7–8 ft (2.1–2.4 m) and can be used as back-of-the-border roses, in a mixed shrub or shrub rose planting, or they can be trained quite effectively against a wall as short climbers. Flowering will be good, even against a north-facing wall, which may be linked with the fact that they are roses that seem to thrive especially in the northern counties of the United Kingdom.

Here is a selection:

'Celestial' ('Celeste') is a more lax and spreading grower than the average alba, which means that it will probably finish up wider than it is tall. As the ultimate height is likely to be 6 ft (1.8 m) or more, this is another one that needs room. The blooms are singularly lovely, quite large and loosely semi-double, the delicate soft pink petals seeming almost to be transparent. Clusters of them appear among the typically blue-grey leaves at midsummer.

'Félicité Parmentier' is unlikely to exceed 4 ft by 4 ft (1.2 m × 1.2 m) and so can be accommodated almost anywhere. It would do for foreground planting in a big garden, or could be given a solo spot in a small one. The flower buds are, I believe, unique, as with all other roses these show early tints of pink or red, regardless of what the eventual colour of the flower may turn out to be, whereas here the early colouring is a most attractive primrose yellow, but yellow flowers do not follow. Quite small and very double and reflexed – sometimes with a button eye – they are of the palest blush-pink, which in hot sun is likely to fade almost to white. It is a pity that the petals do not always drop cleanly as the earlier blooms fade and die, and a brisk shaking of the bush may be needed to get rid of them. The 'Félicité Parmentier' in my garden was grown from a rooted offset so that it is flourishing on its own roots. Further suckers appear yearly, as will happen with all the albas if they are not budded on to stocks, so it is not entirely true to say that you need not worry about suckers if a rose is on its own roots. You will not have a different rose to worry about, it is true, just the same one, and with the albas the spread is easily controllable and nothing like as exuberant as that of the gallicas or the Scotch roses which send sucker growth through the soil at the speed of an underground train. Introduced in 1834.

'Great Maiden's Blush' and 'Maiden's Blush' are, as one might expect, of different sizes, but would appear to be 6 ft (1.8 m) and 5 ft (1.5 m) forms of what is virtually the same rose except that 'Maiden's Blush' has rather fewer petals. 'Great Maiden's Blush', sometimes appearing under the alternative name of R. × alba incarnata, would seem to date back at least to the fifteenth century. The blooms are not unlike those of 'Celestial' in colour, but they are more double and come rather later, as this is the last of the albas into flower. They have a delicacy and refinement matched by a sweet fragrance that is certainly not exceeded by any other rose.

'Königin von Danemarck' has its name spelled in a number of different ways and it is probably impossible to find out, since it was introduced as long ago as 1826, which is correct. It also sometimes appears in catalogues under the English translation of its name: 'Queen of Denmark'. In habit it much resembles 'Félicité Parmentier', although it will grow upwards and outwards perhaps an additional 1 ft or 18 in (30 cm or 45 cm). The flowers are larger, too, but similar in form and have just as many petals. They open an intense carmine-pink, deeper in the centre, which gradually changes to a soft rose-pink. The flowering period, starting a few weeks before midsummer, lasts for an exceptionally long period – six weeks or more. Weather resistance is good, surprising in so double a flower.

CHAPTER 7

The Centifolias and Moss Roses

We do know that the original moss rose (*R.* × *centifolia muscosa*) was a sport from a centifolia, occurring some time prior to 1750. But where the much older centifolias originated nobody can say for certain. Pointers indicate Eastern Europe or the Near East, but their undoubted merits seem to have been first recognised in Holland – so much so that they were at one time called Holland Roses. This name has long since ceased to be used and a French one, Provence Roses, substituted, for, following the example of the Dutch, growers in France, particularly in the south, took centifolias up with great enthusiasm and introduced many new varieties.

It is not surprising that a rose with the name 'Centifolia' should have something approaching 100 petals. Strictly speaking, the name means 100 leaves, but early botanists often spoke of leaves when they obviously meant petals. And 100 petals means that the stamens are rarely exposed to pollen-carrying insects so that hybrids are rare. However, centifolias do sport readily and in one case produced a rose in all ways true to type except that its calyces and flower stalks were covered with a 'mossy' growth of small glands. This was the first of the moss roses so beloved of the Victorians and Edwardians.

Whether or not the centifolias were also the roses that early Greek and Roman writers called by the same name is more doubtful as what rather scanty descriptions there are do not really fit. 'Centifolia' in Roman times may well have been used simply to indicate that a rose had a lot of petals (as opposed, once again, to leaves), which could have applied, for instance, to a number of the damasks then certainly in existence. The centifolias were, however, without any shadow of doubt, the original cabbage roses, even though the blooms of some of the much later bourbons and hybrid perpetuals more closely resemble cabbages as we know them today. The typical centifolia blooms, with their short centre petals, open to a goblet shape, but in many of them the petals gradually reflex, almost in some cases to a ball or pom-pom – something I have never seen a cabbage do. One can see them in many old paintings, but perhaps even more often they were worked into floral designs on porcelain, especially that of the nineteenth century.

In describing the general characteristics of the centifolias and moss roses and their uses in the garden, one can regard the two groups as one, for, as we have seen, apart from the moss on the moss roses, they are pretty well identical. All have flowers, mostly many petalled, of great beauty, but unless the plants are given the support of a stake or a pillar they may not show them off to the best advantage. For they are carried on long and usually rather lax canes which can be weighed down right to the ground. The nodding blooms on their rather slender foot stalks (or pedicels if you prefer) could then be adequately viewed by a flamingo with its head in the feeding position but not by much else, which means they require careful placing in the garden so that they can drape themselves happily and with a careless elegance over something else. The leaves of the group are very large, and droop, too. In one case, that of a variety called 'Bullata', they are wrinkled like, and much resemble those of, a lettuce. Mildew can be a problem on all of them.

Some of the best centifolia and moss roses are, taking the former first:

'**The Bishop**' is the one our alphabetical list starts off with, but it is not a typical centifolia in its habit of growth, in that it will stay reasonably erect without outside help, making a bush perhaps 5 ft by 3 ft (1.5 m × 90 cm). As a matter of fact, it is not really a very typical example of its group in other ways, for the leaves are glossy – not a common attribute on any of the old garden roses – and the flowers open into rosettes rather than goblets. The flowers are an attractive cerise-purple with a lilac-mauve reverse to the petals, the latter colour taking over completely as the flowers fade. Nobody knows where this rose came from or when, and only a botanist (which it has probably become obvious by now that I am not) could tell you just why it is considered one of the centifolia group.

'**Centifolia**'. Although once again there can only be guesses about its early history, this rose is held to be the original Rose of a Hundred Leaves or *Rose des Peintres* of the Dutch masters of the seventeenth century. It is certainly of a great age, but whether or not it was actually the first centifolia or simply the earliest one to have survived to the present day, I doubt if anyone could say. Not really surprisingly, as it is (or may be) the founding father of the family, it conforms in every way to my description of a typical member of the group. In other words, it makes a lax, rangy shrub, which will reach about 5 ft (1.5 m) if not left to sprawl, which would be its natural inclination, and which has large, dull, drooping leaves. The flowers, as always with the centifolias, more than make up for other deficiencies, being large, globular, very fragrant and of a soft pink, deeper in the heart.

'Chapeau de Napoleon' (*R.* × *centifolia cristata*, 'Crested Moss'). Vibert, 1827. Why Napoleon's Hat? Well, the very strange-looking buds, the edges of the calyces of which are covered with very pronounced 'moss', on beginning to open do look rather like the hat one normally thinks of when visualising Napoleon. Rather – but not to my mind very – like, but it is a suitably imaginative name anyway for an intriguing rose. It is on occasion also known as the 'Crested Moss' but the glandular protuberances in this case are confined only to the calyces, so it is not a true moss. Forming a graceful bush with quite slender canes, it will occupy a space 5 ft by 4 ft (1.5 m × 1.2 m), carrying quite large rose-pink blooms which are globular in their early stages and then open flat and often quartered. A rose of considerable character which will make a talking point as you take non-gardening visitors on their duty tour of your garden.

'De Meaux', introduced by Sweet in 1789, once again stays reasonably upright on its own and is one that will fit into the smallest garden, not growing much over 3 ft 6 in (105 cm). The flowers are suitably in scale, only about 1 in (2.5 cm) across, and are carried on slender but well branched canes that arch gently over. They are soft-pink and sweetly scented, globular at first but opening flat and on occasion quartered. The leaves are on the small side even for a rose of this comparatively dwarf stature, and to the mortification of those who confidently assert that all shrub roses are too big for the average garden, here is one which, together with the slightly larger 'Petite de Hollande', would add distinction to a rockery and look quite in place.

'Fantin Latour'. So far I have given an upright habit a lot of weight in choosing which centifolias to recommend. Not that those I have mentioned so far are inferior in other ways; they are as good as any, but if one does not have to deal with staking or otherwise supporting a rose, things are easier all round for everybody. Such a one is 'Fantin Latour' which would, however, pick itself in any company for the sheer beauty of its blush-pink, many-petalled flowers, which reflex and sometimes show a button eye. Coming in small clusters with tremendous profusion over a long period, they really do cover what in this case will be a big, sturdy and once again upright bush. It will go up to 7 ft (2.1 m) and spread out almost as far eventually. The dark-green leaves are smooth and handsome, but not, and this must be said for all the centifolias, proof against mildew, so that they really should be sprayed.

And now for the moss roses:

'Common Moss' ('Old Pink Moss', 'Communis', *R.* × *centifolia muscosa*). A number of alternative names generally indicates a very old rose indeed and the last of the four names above would seem to indicate this is the original moss rose. It would appear, however, that this is not so as 'Common Moss' arrived on the scene in France in about 1696 and, as far as is known, the moss roses, like the centifolias, originated in Holland. However, this is yet another of the multitudinous hazy areas that one peers through in rose history trying to catch a glimmer of the truth, so it is best not to be dogmatic one way or the other. 'Common Moss' is probably in the ancestry of most if not all of the many later moss roses. It is a reasonably bushy grower to 5 ft (1.5 m) or so, spreading fairly wide. The moss on the buds in this case has a reddish tinge and the lovely pink, fragrant, double blooms follow the usual pattern of being globular early on and then reflexing. The first in the field or not, many people feel this one has never been surpassed.

'Général Kléber' was one of a really vintage crop of moss roses produced in France in the 1850s, in this case by Robert. Others include 'Capitaine John Ingram', 'Duchess de Verneuil', 'Gloire de Mousseux' 'Henri Martin', 'Jeanne de Montfort', 'Madame Delaroche-Lambert', 'Mousseline' and 'William Lobb'. Many of them were put on the market by Monsieur H. Laffay, the man who later played such a prominent part in the early story of the hybrid perpetuals, and although there is not space here to describe all those listed above, they are without exception well worth growing. 'Général Kléber' itself makes a fairly lax 5-ft (1.5-m) bush which does need some form of support and which carries a profusion of fragrant pink flowers with a silky sheen to the petals and up to 5 in (13 cm) across, which is quite a size. They open flat and some are quartered.

'Henri Martin' is one of Laffay's best, though it is not as well mossed as some. The bush, with fine bright-green leaves, grows to about 5 ft by 4 ft (1.5 m by 1.2 m) and carries clusters of double blooms in a striking light-crimson, the only moss as far as I know in this particular colour. The flowers appear a little later than most others and so help to prolong the season in a mixed planting.

'Mousseline' (also known as **'Alfred de Dalmas'**). Without wishing to raise hopes too high it can be fairly said, I think, that here is a recurrent moss rose. There is the usual fine early summer flush that they all have and then there is usually sporadic blooming right through until the autumn. Nothing, mind you, to take your breath away, but a very satisfactory bonus just the same. The flowers are of medium size (3 in or 7.5 cm) as a rule, although sometimes there will be much larger ones amongst them. They are scented, of a soft flesh-pink, and although fully double tend to remain cup-shaped and without the usual reflexing of the petals. The moss on the buds is a brownish-green and on average the bush will be 1 ft (30 cm) or so smaller than the last two described. Introduced by Portemer in 1855.

'William Lobb' (**'Duchesse d'Istrie'**) has flowers of singular beauty, double and of dark, soft magenta-purple at first, with a lighter reverse, which fades after a day or two to a pale lilac-grey that is equally attractive. The mossing on the flower stalks and sepals is exceptionally heavy. So far a fairly normal moss rose one would think, but as a grower 'William Lobb' is exceptional. It has such vigour that it is probably best used as a pillar rose or as a short climber on a wall, and it will go up to 6 ft (1.8 m) without exerting itself unduly. Do not plant it in a border and hope for the best or it will sprawl all over the place and trail its blooms in the mud. But wear gloves if you are training it on a pillar or wall as it is quite inexcusably thorny.

CHAPTER 8

China Roses

Many of the earliest roses to come to the West from China – and I am talking now about the middle of the eighteenth century – were clearly cultivated varieties. However, because China under the rule of the mandarins was a society more closed to foreigners even than it was under Chairman Mao, we know very little about their earlier history or to what extent they were grown in what is after all the land of the paeony and the chrysanthemum. They were, however, to Western eyes, extremely desirable because they were recurrent or in some cases very nearly perpetually in flower from midsummer until well into the autumn. There was also a deep crimson colour in some of them so far unseen in Western roses, which was eventually to be brought into European breeding strains through 'Slater's Crimson China'.

Although later on China roses came to us from the Far Tee nurseries in Canton, at first it was through the agency of diplomatic missions, missionaries of various religions who were plant enthusiasts, and other travellers who were prepared to take something of a chance, that a few China roses did begin the journey west across the Indian ocean. And it was a long journey in those days, so that the plants were often rested for a while at the Botanical Gardens in Calcutta. The fact that this was only a stop-over on the way from their true land of origin seemed somehow to be forgotten when they finally completed their journey and they were for many years known as Bengal Roses, or by botanists as hybrids of *Rosa indica*. You can see a number of them under one or other of these names in the plates of Redouté's *Les Roses*.

Although the China roses did, as we have seen, come to Europe nearly 250 years ago, they did not at first make the impact that their introducers had expected. True, they kept on flowering, but many of them were far from hardy and they made on the whole rather small, spindly shrubs. They were in the main used as pot plants in conservatories and out of doors only by gardeners who liked to grow the difficult and the unusual. It was not until much later that they began to be more generally planted and it might have been thought that, somewhere along the line after they came to the West, their potential as breeding material might have been exploited in order to bring recurrent flowering to Western rose varieties. However, it was not until early in the nineteenth century that it was realised that a deliberate crossing of two different plants by the transfer of pollen from one to the other in order to produce a new variety – a hybrid – could be carried out. This had been happening purely by chance since time began, of course, through the agency of insects and the wind, and it was, as I mentioned in Chapter 5, one of these chance crosses with a China rose something like 100 years after they came on the scene in the West that was to revolutionise our garden roses by making them recurrent.

Most of the China roses are suitable shrubs for a small garden and those that have survived in the (perhaps more specialist) nursery lists are pretty hardy. They make light, airy shrubs with noticeably pointed and usually very healthy leaves and the clusters of small flowers are carried probably more continuously and over a longer season than those of any other rose group. They mix well with other plants and some of them can even be used for bedding, though not if you want a big forceful splash of colour as their tones are discreet.

Here is a small selection:

'Cécile Brunner' and **'Bloomfield Abundance'** must be logically bracketted together because current thinking is that the latter is a sport of the former. I say current thinking because a different parentage has been cited for each of them in the past. 'Cécile Brunner' was supposed to be a tea rose crossed with polyantha and 'Bloomfield Abundance' a hybrid tea crossed with a rambler, but there has always been a question mark added and it does seem unlikely that with two roses so unlike all others and so incredibly similar to each other, one should not be a sport of the other. 'Bloomfield Abundance' grows much taller than 'Cécile Brunner' – it may reach 5–6 ft (1.5–1.8 m) – and the buds have long, feathery calyces which those of 'Cécile Brunner' lack, but the rather long pointed leaves and the clustered blooms, each one an enchanting, lightly scented blush-pink miniature hybrid tea in form, which each of these roses have, are virtually identical. They have appropriately bestowed on 'Cécile Brunner' the additional name of 'The Sweetheart Rose'.

As a matter of fact, there is a further area of controversy about these two roses, in that there are those who have held, and I have been one of them in the past, that these are polyanthas and not China roses at all. However, the RNRS (Royal National Rose Society) has come down firmly on the side of the Chinas and I am content to abide by that – until somebody produces a stronger argument for the other side. Certainly in its light, airy, twiggy growth and with the leaves on which I have already commented, 'Cécile Brunner' does fit well into the Chinas and so in fact do the flowers once they have passed the tight, scrolled bud stage, for they then become loose and informal. The bush will not often exceed 3–4 ft (90 cm–1.2 m) but will be spreading and well branched. 'Bloomfield Abundance' has a habit in the latter part of the summer of sending up one or two incredibly long and strong shoots, each one covered by what one can only describe as a candelabra of up to a hundred or so flowers.

'Comtesse du Cayla' has some of the most attractive flowers of all the Chinas. Semi-double and in the clusters usual in this group, they open a coppery-flame colour which gradually shades to salmon-pink with yellow tints on the petal reverse. It will make a fair-sized and spreading bush of 5 ft (1.5 m) with healthy dark-green leaves. Introduced by Guillot in 1902.

'Mutabilis' ('Tipo Ideale') is nothing if not an original, for its quite large single flowers, as do those of 'Comtesse du Cayle', open a coppery flame, but then they turn first to a coppery buff-yellow, then fade to pink and finally deepen once again to a coppery crimson, all the colours contrasting with each other on the bush at the same time and giving a very gay effect. It is of course fully recurrent and the usual dark leaves of a China rose set the blooms off well on a bush that will probably reach 3 ft (1 m) in an open border but, if used as a short climber against a wall, it will show its appreciation of the protection provided by going up to 8 ft (2.4 m) or so. Nobody knows the origin of this most distinctive, not to say distinguished rose, but it would appear to date back several hundred years at the very least.

'Old Blush' ('Parson's Pink China', 'Common Monthly Rose') was the China that passed on to Western varieties its repeat-flowering habit, and it is, even among the prolific Chinas, one of the most continuously in bloom. It is an upright grower to about 3 ft (90 cm), freely branching and spreading out well, and carrying clusters of pale-pink double flowers, which are cupped when fully open, the colour deepening with age. Its long flowering period, often up to Christmas, makes it likely that this is 'The Last Rose of Summer' of the famous Victorian song.

***R. chinensis viridiflor* ('The Green Rose')** is not a variety which the average person would grow for the beauty of its blooms. It is a novelty, fairly obviously a mutation or sport from an earlier China rose, in which the 'flowers' open from perfectly normal-looking blue-green buds to reveal what appear to be imperfectly and irregularly formed leaves instead of petals, green at first and quickly becoming streaked with purple and brown. Beloved of flower arrangers because of its novelty, it makes quite a substantial bush up to maybe 5 ft (1.5 m) high. Nobody is quite certain when it first arrived on the scene but it has certainly been in cultivation since the early part of the nineteenth century.

CHAPTER 9

The Bourbons and Portland Roses

These groups can be conveniently (and logically, which is not always the same thing) placed together because they much resemble each other and because the first of each group resulted from a very similar cross. This was between the 'Autumn Damask' and 'Parsons' Pink China' ('Old Blush') in the case of the bourbons and probably the 'Autumn Damask' and 'Slater's Crimson China' in the case of the Portlands. Both crosses happened by chance very early in the nineteenth century, though at places many hundreds of miles apart, and both resulted in hybrids that were the first really vigorous and what one might call home-grown recurrent Western roses.

With *R.* × *borboniana*, as the first bourbon was called, the best of both worlds was combined. It was East meeting West, resulting in a true Eurasian beauty, and once back in France the botanist Bréon, whose part in the story is outlined in the damask rose chapter, together with French nurserymen, rapidly developed the new group and it went from strength to strength.

There is less documentation on the Portland side, and while one school of thought holds that the parentage given above is correct (resulting in the Portlands being known at one time as perpetual damasks), others maintain that the cross was between an unspecified China rose and a gallica. Certainly there is a good deal of the typical gallica in the compact, upright carriage and in the way that the flowers are held erect above the foliage in the 'Duchess of Portland', which was the first of the race, so this may be true. It is known for certain, however, that 'The Portland Rose', as it is also called, came into existence in Italy, which naturally leads one to wonder why it ended up with these two very English names. It would seem that, although it originated in Italy, it was English nurserymen who took it up and developed it, and though it was common practice at that time to name roses after members of the nobility regardless of whether they were interested in plants or not, the Duchess of Portland of those days was actually a figure in the world of

56

horticulture. When the Empress Josephine was forming her collection of roses at Malmaison and needed varieties from England to complete it, it is said to have been the Duchess who, despite the fact that England and France were at war, organised the trip made by a certain Mr Kennedy across the Channel, carrying with him the roses the Empress had asked for. It is a story that could just be true, given the attitudes to and of the privileged classes in those times, but despite such illustrious beginnings, the Portland roses were not destined to make their mark in the way that the bourbons did. They were not very fertile breeders and the range of new varieties produced remained limited as a result. This was a pity as there were some very good roses, such 'Comte de Chambord', among them, very sturdy growers, much resembling the bourbons though probably not quite so vigorous, and very reliably recurrent, which not all the bourbons were.

Although the flowers of R. × *borboniana* were not really fully double, those of most of the later hybrids were (and still are) large, cupped or globular, and sometimes with the outer petals reflexing. The colour range is that of the old roses in general – white, pinks of varying intensities, maroon and some purple, and a few, such as 'Variegata di Bologna' and 'Commandant Beaurepaire', striped. The leaves are large and smooth and the canes thick and strong. Growth is vigorous and some varieties need considerable restraining in anything other than a big garden. This can be achieved by treating them as short climbers and growing them up pillars or on tripods of rustic poles – or even against a wall – or else by pegging down the longest shoots. They will respond well, too, to quite hard cutting back of the laterals in winter which, in addition to keeping the size of the shrubs under some sort of control, will also in many cases give you more and better flowers. 'Zéphirine Drouhin', often called 'The Thornless Rose' (because it is, practically), is a bourbon and a true climber which will reach perhaps 15 ft (4.5 m), so that it is suitable for a substantial arch or a pergola.

Some of the best bourbons to grow are:

'Blairii No. 2'. Its rather strange name beginning with a 'B' forces me, if I am to follow the alphabet, to start off with a bourbon that is not even partially recurrent, which, as I have hailed bourbons as the first Western hybrids to be recurrent, is unfortunate. The name comes from Mr Blair, the raiser, who produced his No. 1 and No. 2 seedlings in 1845. The first one was not a patch on the second and, although I understand that it does still survive, I have not found it listed by any nursery. Even No. 2, fine rose that it is, is not as well known as it should be.

'Blairii No. 2' is a really rampant grower and I have seen its chestnut-brown 15-ft (4.5-m) shoots trained into an old apple tree with great effect. It would be equally suitable for a wall or pillar or it can make a very large, rambling shrub, either standing on its own, in which case you must allow for a 6–7 ft (1.8–2.1 m) minimum spread, or weaving its way like a floral python up through the branches of neighbours. Flowering only at midsummer, it carries all along its arching canes a truly breathtaking display of large, sweetly fragrant, fully double blooms, deep pink in the centre and paling towards the petal edges. The minimum of pruning should be done, any cutting back necessary being carried out immediately after flowering as one would with a rambler. Unlike most bourbons, flowers come only on shoots that have grown the previous summer and not on growth of the current season.

'Boule de Neige' (1867) is in almost every way a contrast to 'Blairii No. 2'. Short of stature, it will not go much above 4 ft (1.2 m) and only spread out sideways to any noticeable degree when the weight of the small clusters of very double, globular blooms arches over some of the more slender canes. The flowers are fragrant and creamy-white, with an occasional pink blush. Dark-green leaves make a good background for them, and this rose, while perhaps not the most notable of a family whose most endearing characteristic is sheer exuberance, is a very pleasing one and quite easily accommodated in a limited space. It is fully recurrent, too.

'Commandant Beaurepaire', on the other hand, cannot be relied on to produce more than the odd bloom or two in the autumn, showing that although there was a strong influence of China rose in the bourbons there was also a fine Irish stew of genes from the past whose influence was not always overcome completely by those from the East. However, here is a rose which puts on such a magnificent display at midsummer that it can really be forgiven for shortcomings later. Every shoot bears both large and small clusters of medium-sized flowers that open cupped, the scented, deep-pink petals of which are decorated in the gayest way with splashes and stripes of purple, maroon and a paler pink. Allow plenty of room for a bush which will reach 6 ft by 5 ft (1.8 m × 1.5 m). It has light-green leaves.

'Ferdinand Pichard', introduced in Germany by Tanne in 1921, is out of its time for a bourbon, the heyday of which was really coming to an end in the last quarter of the nineteenth century. It is even out of time as one of the hybrid perpetuals which followed the bourbons and in which family some people claim that it belongs. The light yellowish-green leaves and also the flowers suggest a possible link with 'Commandant Beaure-paire'. The blooms are cupped and could not be called fully double, deep-pink (which fades a little) and striped with the most intense crimson-red, but the real glory of them is that they keep coming all summer and well into the autumn. This is without doubt the most recurrent of all the striped roses and one that is relatively restrained in its growth. It will make a fairly wide-spreading, arching shrub of about 4 ft by 4 ft (1.2 m by 1.2 m), which may need watching for mildew in the late summer, its only weakness.

'La Reine Victoria', introduced by Schwartz in 1872, is one of a small group of three bourbons – the others being 'Mme Pierre Oger' (which see below) and 'Louise Odier' from some twenty years earlier – which have relatively slender main shoots which make the support of a pillar or tripod a necessity. They also have quite small but exquisitely delicate, goblet-shaped blooms in medium-sized clusters and, a less desirable attribute, a tendency towards some mildew and black spot. One can, however, almost (if not quite) disregard this for the common diseases seem to be much more easily shrugged off by the old roses than by their more highly bred successors. Concentrate instead on the flowers, which are produced continuously and, in the case of 'La Reine Victoria', are of a pink which, following the pattern of the China roses, will deepen in hot sunshine. The petals are singularly delicate and shell-like and there is a good scent. Autumn flowers tend to be smaller than those of the early summer. This is a rose that will produce 6 ft (1.8 m) canes, but if these are, as they will have to be, tied in to a pillar, the lateral spread need only be about 3 ft (90 cm). New growth produced during the summer will need to be tied in regularly or the weight of the late flowers will bear it right to the ground.

'Mme Issac Pereire' dates from 1881, when it was introduced by Garçon. If ever the term 'sumptuous' could be applied to a rose, it would be to the blooms of this one. They are huge and fully double, opening sometimes cupped and sometimes globular, with the outer petals reflexing. The colour is a deep, unshaded cerise-pink, and they are probably more strongly scented than those of any other rose, old or new. They are carried with considerable freedom and seem to take on an added lustre and intensity of colour in the autumn crop. Some, though by no means all, of the early blooms may be distorted, although nobody knows why this should happen and they can easily be removed. Or at any rate, those within reach can, for this is an enormously robust grower, its great thick canes clothed in dark-green leaves taking it at its best to 6–7 ft (1.8–2.1 m) and to almost as much across. This is pretty big to accommodate, but the two plants I have were grown from cuttings and have, after quite a number of years, reached only about two-thirds of this size. 'Mme Ernst Calvat' is a sport from 'Mme Isaac Pereire' and was introduced in 1888 by Schwartz. It is in all ways similar, except that the blooms are a softer and much lighter pink.

'Mme Pierre Oger' has, as a sport of 'La Reine Victoria' introduced by Oger in 1878, been pretty fully described already. The only real difference lies in the colour of the flowers, in this case a blend of very pale pink and cream, the pink tones deepening even more markedly after a few hours of sunshine than those of the older rose.

'Variegata di Bologna' was, like 'Ferdinand Pichard', a late-comer on the scene in 1909, introduced then by Bonfiglioli as a striking novelty. It is another of the striped bourbons but the only one to have a very dark and intense crimson-purple striping on a background of lilac so pale as to be almost white. The extremely fragrant flowers open cupped, often with quartered petals, but these are so closely packed that the blooms can be rather marred by heavy rain. The midsummer flush is stupendous, that of the autumn less so. Growth is very vigorous to about 6 ft (1.8 m) and almost as much across. Black spot in the last few months of the summer is almost a certainty.

Finally, we come to the two most easily obtainable of the few remaining Portland roses, singled out and retained on their lists by nurseries over the years because they were probably the two best. However of this pair, 'Comte de Chambord' is in fact, a considerably better rose than 'Jacques Cartier', at least in its flower form and the reliability of its second crop of blooms.

'Comte de Chambord' appeared in 1860, introduced by Moreau-Robert, a sturdy, upright grower with strong canes reaching about 4 ft (1.2 m) and arching out quite widely under the weight of the many-petalled, deep-pink blooms, which have a tendency to open rather untidily but are sweetly scented. It is rare during the summer months for there to be no flowers on the bush and there is a second main flush in the autumn.

'**Jacques Cartier**' from the same raiser six years later was very similar and not really, as I have indicated, an improvement. The quite strong pink of the blooms pales in this case to blush-pink at the petal edges, which is attractive, but the autumn flowering is unreliable. The light-green, rather pointed leaves, are typical of this small group, which has perhaps an increasing value in these days of ever smaller gardens.

CHAPTER 10

The Hybrid Perpetuals

When giving a broad outline of the different groups of roses in Chapter 2, I described how it was difficult to pinpoint which was actually the first variety in any one group. As an example I mentioned the earliest hybrid tea 'La France' and the fact that it was initially classed as a hybrid perpetual. Well, there is the same vagueness about the early days of the hybrid perpetuals, no actual 'first' variety having ever emerged, and it even seems far from certain exactly when the new class name came into being. And a rather misleading one it was, in that none of the roses were perpetually in flower and some did not even have a second flush of bloom in the autumn or at best only managed an odd flower or two. One must, however, look at them in the context of what had gone before as we are still in an era when any rose that flowered more than once was a novelty.

The hybrid perpetuals were very largely developed in France and the name of the French nurseryman, Laffay, will always be especially associated with them as he was responsible for so many of the best. They resulted largely from crosses first of all between the bourbons and to a lesser extent the Portland roses (which it may be remembered from the last chapter are none too fertile as breeding stock) and hybrid China roses, and later on with teas.

The result was very vigorous bushes, in general growing reasonably upright, but tending to be over-tall and in many cases outright leggy. It was the habit with many of them for very long flowerless shoots to be sent up in the second half of the summer which, unless dealt with in some way, would thrash violently about in the winds of winter, their thorns causing much damage to neighbouring roses. Two options were open to the Victorian gardeners; to cut these shoots right back, which meant that much of the plant's strength was going to nothing, or to peg the shoots down. This meant that the long late-summer growths had only their soft tips removed in autumn and were then bent gently but firmly over until their ends could be tied in to pegs pushed into the ground. In the spring, instead of flowers and leaves forming only at the tips of these shoots, which could be 4 to 5 ft (1.2 to 1.5 m) long, dormant buds all along them would break and produce flowering side shoots. The effect was just the same as that achieved when climbing roses are fanned out and trained along horizontal wires, rather than allowed to go straight up and produce blooms only in the neighbourhood of the bedroom windows. If a number of hybrid perpetuals were planted together in the same bed, the pegged-down shoots of the different roses could be intermingled with great effect. For a complete bed, a frame of galvanised wires, criss-crossed horizontally between short stakes and about 10 in (26 cm) above the ground was an alternative to individual pegs. The shoots could be tied to the wires, and this method of growing roses can still, of course, be used today and need not be confined to the hybrid perpetuals. You can carry out pegging down with any lanky varieties provided that the shoots are reasonably flexible, or you can carry it out with many of the less vigorous modern climbers if you wish to grow them as shrubs. But whatever rose you choose, gentleness in the bending is essential. It is all too easy to kink a shoot or even to snap it off altogether. If necessary, carry out the bending over several weeks, progressing a little each time, though you may feel that if so much trouble has to be taken the rose is not a candidate for pegging down at all but one, if I dare say it, for the bonfire.

The flowers of the hybrid perpetuals, particularly the early ones, are not dissimilar to those of the bourbons in form, being large like the bourbons and mainly with many petals, and globular in shape. The colours are those of the old roses but with very few exceptions they are pure, unshaded reds or pinks, maroons or purples, and lack the subtleties of earlier families in which colours changed as the blooms aged or a lighter tone blended harmoniously into a darker tone in the same bloom. They were roses beloved of exhibitors of their day, for they came into existence at about the time when rose shows were beginning to be popular and the large, firm, regular HP blooms stood up to the perils of getting them undamaged to the show bench and they lasted a long time in water. With a number of notable exceptions (some of which are included in the selection which follows) they are not, largely because of their rangy habit of growth, the easiest of plants to use well in the garden. This did not, it may be said, stop people from growing them in their heyday. *Cultivated Roses*, edited by T.W. Sanders and published in 1899, lists 826 hybrid perpetual varieties, the majority of which one imagines must have been available from

63

nurseries somewhere, even though it was not unknown at that time for the same variety to be put out under different names by different nurseries – not, it may be said, always intentionally.

Some of the best of the hybrid perpetuals still on the market are:

'Baron Girod de l'Ain', introduced as a sport of 'Eugene Furst' by Reverchon in 1897, is something of a novelty, in that it is one of only two roses, both deep-crimson, that have irregular scalloping of the petals, which are also edged and flecked with white. The other rose is 'Roger Lambelin', also a sport, though this time of a completely different hybrid perpetual called 'Fisher Holmes'. I feel there may be some doubt about this declared parentage in that the two roses are so very similar, the only real difference being that 'Roger Lambelin' is generally considered to be the less vigorous of the two and to hold its colour rather better. The large-cupped, sweetly scented blooms of 'Baron Girod de l'Ain' do in my experience take on what I can only describe as a rather dusty look after a few days, while the petals of 'Roger Lambelin' glow till they drop. Both roses have 'Général Jacqueminot' (see below) some few generations back in their family tree, which is the only link I can find between these two very distinctive and very similar roses. 'Baron Girod' will only reach 5 ft by 3 ft (1.5 m by 90 cm) and so it is not one of the really lanky HPs, while 'Roger Lambelin' will be perhaps 1 ft (30 cm) less all round, and its leaves a lighter green. Both are recurrent.

'Baronne Prévost'. Dating back to 1842, when it was introduced by Deprez, this is, I believe, the earliest HP that is still available – if only from specialist nurseries. The large (4-in or 10-cm), very double, rose-pink blooms, sometimes quartered and each centred by a button eye, may have been equalled but have never been surpassed by later members of the group. They are carried with great freedom and a good continuity on a sturdy bush that will stay reasonably compact at about 4 ft (1.2 m). At one time this rose seemed to have disappeared from cultivation in Europe but it was fortunately rediscovered in America.

'Empereur du Maroc' comes from the middle period of hybrid perpetuals, from 1858, and was introduced, almost needless to say, in France by Bertrand-Guinoisseau. Graham Thomas tells us that it was the first of the dark-red roses to have none of the rather unattractive purple shadings in its colourings. Certainly the dusky-crimson is very striking and makes the rose worth growing for the colour alone – even without its lovely fragrance. The blooms in this case follow early precedent and open quite flat. The plant may at first glance seem to lack robustness – certainly it is small for an HP – but it is natural for it to be rather spindly and this does not mean that it is not growing quite happily. Its ultimate height is likely to be 4 ft (1.2 m).

'Frau Karl Druschki' is a German rose, introduced by Peter Lambert in 1901, just in time for it to run into nationality trouble in the very jingoistic early part of the First World War. At one time it had been tentatively called 'Snow Queen' and this was the name under which it was sold in the UK in order to disguise its country of origin. The Americans called it 'White American Beauty', but somehow the original name of 'Frau Karl Druschki' is the one that persists. From the turn of the century it really is a transitional rose, halfway between the hybrid perpetual and the hybrid tea, and its parents were actually one of each, 'Merveille de Lyon' × 'Mme Caroline Testout'. The high-pointed centres of the large, very double, pure-white and unfortunately completely scentless blooms of 'Frau Karl', which strangely come from pink-tinted buds, are typically HT, but the tall leggy growth to about 5 ft (1.2 m) and the light-green leaves are hybrid perpetual. For a long time this was considered, and is still considered by some, to be the best white rose ever raised, but the flower buds grow far too close together at the ends of the canes for perfection and this is a rose that really has to be debudded. Mildew is more than likely in late summer when the second crop of blooms appears after a considerable pause.

'Général Jacqueminot'. Roussel, 1853. One of the landmarks in rose breeding because it was this wonderful variety that passed on its many qualities and colour to most of the red and crimson varieties that we grow today. So many are descended from it and so much was it used in the nurseries as a breeding rose that it achieved the ultimate accolade of popularity, a nickname, 'General Jack'. The very fragrant blooms are what might be described as globular HT type, though they open out later and some become cupped. The first flush at midsummer is probably better than the later one, but it is a bush of excellent constitution, upright and reasonably compact to about 4 ft (1.2 m).

'Georg Arends', introduced by Hinner in 1910, might almost be a modern rose from its flower, which has a scrolled, pointed bud and a classic high-centred shape when it develops, but the habit of growth with long shoots reaching to at least 6 ft (1.8 m), coupled with a lack of bushiness, is pure HP. The technique of pegging down might have been created for this rose if the dates had been right. The blooms are a soft rose-pink with hints of cream, particularly in the petal reverses.

'Mrs John Laing' came from the famous raiser Henry Bennett comparatively late – in 1887 – so as with the last two roses described, the tea influence is predominant, not only in the large, high-centred, fragrant, bright silver-pink flowers, but also in the fact that this is one of the most recurrent of all the hybrid perpetuals. If I could grow only one, this would be it, compact at 5 ft by about 3 ft (1.5 m by about 1 m) and with attractive bright-green leaves.

'Paul Neyron' was also a fairly late-comer introduced by Levet in 1869, but there is no tea nonsense about this one. Where 'Mrs John Laing' shows the utmost refinement in its immaculate flowers, those of 'Paul Neyron', one is almost tempted to say, are blowsy, but that is not really right. Deep pink with a rather lighter petal reverse, they open informally like gigantic paeonies and will certainly reach 5–6 in (13–16 cm) across. Unfortunately, they lack scent, but otherwise they make the perfect cut flower, and an economical one, too, as so few blooms are needed to fill a vase. There is a good second show in the autumn and the long strong canes mean a height of something like 6 ft (1.8 m) on good soil.

'Prince Camille de Rohan' of 1861 is included in this section purely on the strength of its medium-sized, richly scented, very dark, velvety flowers. If you want these – and once you have seen them you will – you must be prepared for a poor autumn performance accompanied by mildew and possibly rust. Not too vigorous a grower up to about 4 ft (1.2 m), it should just the same be in every HP collection, but not if you only have room for one.

'Reine des Violettes' was a seedling put on the market by Millet-Malet in 1860 from an HP called 'Pius IX', but anything less like an HP is difficult to imagine. The double flowers more closely resemble those of a gallica, opening flat and often quartered. They have cerise tints at first but the colour settles down to a violet-purple which fades to some extent after a while. At all stages they are very beautiful and they are carried in clusters with great freedom and continuity on a freely branching, spreading, arching bush which can easily top 5 ft (1.5 m) and closely resembles a bourbon rose in habit. The leaves, greyish-green, are probably a little on the sparse side. Good soil and good cultivation are really essential if this rose is to give of its best.

'Souvenir du Docteur Jamain'. Lacharme, 1865. This is one of the first generation offspring of 'Général Jacqueminot' as the fragrant, cupped, wine-red flowers testify clearly. Many HPs are at their best in fairly cool conditions and the blooms do suffer and lose their sparkle in hot sunlight. This is one of them, so a position out of the middday sun – but not, of course, out of the sun altogether – is advised. It should also be in a site where the lanky 6 ft (1.8 m) canes can be accommodated, as this will almost certainly be a candidate for pegging down. Quite a good repeat in the autumn.

CHAPTER 11

Tea Roses

Most rose books ignore tea roses completely, except perhaps when describing how the hybrid teas came into existence. Then what seems to me to be a completely mythical reason for the name 'tea roses' is always trotted out: that they smell of, variously, newly opened packets of tea, newly opened tea chests, drying leaves of the tea plant and so on. I have never been able to detect any fragrance in any of them remotely resembling tea in any of its periods of transformation (as far as my rather limited experience of them goes) from bush to packet, though, mind you, I have no alternative theory to substitute. So I am knocking down without building up again which is not very constructive.

The reason rose books so neglect the teas is that they are not generally considered to be hardy in a climate such as that of the United Kingdom. Well, one does not grow orchids in the open on a Scottish ben, but that does not mean that nobody in the rest of the UK – or for that matter in the Irish Free State – should not grow them in suitably protected sites or under glass. One could say the same for tea roses, for they have a charm and interest all their own and some at least, particularly in their climbing versions, are perfectly capable of existing out of doors, at least in a reasonably mild climate, even if it is best to think of them in general as a group of roses for the greenhouse or conservatory.

Before deciding to try some tea roses – and all those I either describe in some detail or simply list are available at specialist old rose nurseries – do not equate them in your mind with hybrid teas. With some exceptions they will be much more slender and less robust in growth, and the flowers of many of them, with their long pointed buds, may seem insubstantial by modern standards. Others will have blooms that are very double and perhaps quartered – a throwback to earlier generations – and the typically weak foot stalks or pedicels mean that they are likely to hang their heads. There will be no strong, bright colours, and it does seem from the descriptions one reads of these roses in their heyday that those we still have are by no means what they were in general vigour and robustness. However, they are still well worth growing by anyone who really loves the rose in all its forms and for details of the cultivation of those which really will not thrive out of doors I would refer you to the section of Chapter 20 which covers growing roses under glass.

It is believed that the first tea roses came from China to Sweden in the middle of the eighteenth century, but there is no record of what happened to them and it does not seem that their potential as breeding material was used in any way. The first of what have become known as the 'stud' Chinas was 'Hume's Blush Tea-scented China', received in England by Sir Abraham Hume from an agent of the British East India Company in Canton in 1810. It was given the specific name *R. odorata* because of its scent and its import was followed in 1824 by John Dampier Parks, collecting plants in China for the Royal Horticultural Society, bringing back with him the pale-yellow rose that became known as 'Parks' Yellow Tea-scented China'. This, though actually the second tea to arrive in the UK, was actually introduced as the first tea rose and it was a much more prolific parent than Hume's rose. Teas of European origin soon began to appear, especially in France, even if the lineage was by no means always certain. A variety called 'Allain', very beautiful and lilac-pink, is generally thought of as the first Western tea for which any sort of claim for a pedigree can be made, in this case reputedly 'Hume's Blush' and the original bourbon rose. The first rose actually to be hand-pollinated by Beauregard and the parents fully recorded (lilac-pink bourbon 'Mme Desprez' and 'Parks' Yellow') was the deep-saffron 'Safrano'. 'Hume's Blush' is still in existence, but 'Parks' Yellow' (featured in Redouté's *Les Roses* as *R. sulphura*), unfortunately vanished many, many years ago. The tea roses with their long petals were instrumental, as has been mentioned earlier, in completely changing the shape of the rose flower until the high, pointed centre of our prized exhibition blooms emerged.

Below I describe the few varieties of tea that I know reasonably well and have some experience of. The much more extensive list that follows is of tea roses that are available from specialist nurseries.

'Catherine Mermet'. Guillot Fils, 1869. Very definitely one for the glasshouse because, apart from any aspect of hardiness, the soft petals just crumple in the rain. At its best, however, the flower is very shapely, fragrant and, before it fades to an overall blush-pink, of a delicate flesh-pink, blending to lilac-pink at the petal edge. Quite a strong grower and a rose that was used very extensively for many years by the cut-flower trade on both sides of the Atlantic. An almost equally popular white sport from it was called 'The Bride' but this does not now seem to be available.

'Devoniensis'. Foster (or Forster?), 1841. 'Elinthii' × a yellow China? A rose of somewhat doubtful origin, as can be seen by the two question marks. It does, however, seem certain that it came from the county of Devon (hence its name) and that it was the first British-raised tea rose. Nowadays the original bush form has vanished, but it is available as a quite vigorous climbing sport to 10 ft (3 m) or so on a warm, sheltered wall. Sometimes known as the 'Magnolia Rose', the flowers are very large and creamy-white, with an occasional pink flush. Fragrant.

'Duchesse de Brabant' ('Comtesse de Labarthe'). Bernede, 1857. Parentage unknown, but something gave this one toughness, for it is one of the hardiest and it can certainly be grown outside, at least in the climate of southern England. It will make a fairly lax, spreading bush about 3 ft by 3 ft (90 cm by 90 cm) with very double and very fragrant bright rose-pink blooms which open cupped and repeat well.

'Général Schablikine'. Nabonnand, 1878. Nowadays quite a short grower, whatever it may have been in the past, rarely exceeding 3 ft by 2 ft (90 cm by 60 cm). One of the teas with un-tea-like flowers, for they open very double and are often quartered. The colour is a coppery-red and there is a good repeat.

'Lady Hillingdon'. Lowe and Shawyer, 1910. 'Papa Gontier' × 'Mme Hoste' is the parentage given, but it appears there is some doubt. At any rate, this late-comer on the scene is quite hardy, both in bush and in climbing form, though it is as a climber (dating from 1917) that one most often sees it nowadays. The flowers are some of the most beautiful, long and pointed and of a very pleasing apricot-orange and with a sweet scent. Plum-coloured shoots and attractive grey-green leaves. As a bush 3 ft by 2 ft (90 cm by 60 cm) and as a climber up to 12 ft. Despite its hardiness, choose a warm wall for preference and you will get blooms over a long period.

'Maman Cochet'. Cochet, 1893. 'Marie van Houtte' × 'Mme Lombard'. One of the very best of the teas, vigorous to 4 ft by 3 ft (1.2 m by 90 cm) with very large (4 in or 10 cm) double, high-centred, fragrant blooms of pale-pink, deepening in the heart and with the base of the petals lemon-yellow. This was a star exhibition rose for many years and no wonder, although in America its popularity was exceeded by 'White Maman Cochet' (which I have not seen), a sport introduced by John Cook in 1896. Very few thorns on the stout canes.

'Niphetos'. Bougere, 1843. Parents unknown. I have hesitated about including this one in my selection, but it was in its day considered the finest white rose there was and it was extensively used by the cut-flower trade. It achieved great popularity and cannot be ignored in the story of the teas as a whole. All this despite the fact that the blooms, immaculate in shape on opening, only hold their shape, if one may exaggerate a little, for about 30 seconds before the petals flop all over the place. The long, pointed buds, as Jack Harkness indicates in his book *Roses*, were still a great novelty when 'Niphetos' was introduced, for this was one of the earlier Western teas.

'Safrano'. Beauregard, 1839. Semi-double, pointed flowers in the bud though less shapely when open, but it was colour rather than flower form, plus its reputation for free-blooming, that gained this rose such a reputation in its day. Its saffron-yellow to buff-apricot tones (though they fade fairly soon) were a great novelty and this was a rose that probably appeared in more French buttonholes in its early bud stage than any rose in history. Is is still free-flowering and repeats very quickly and will make a bush of about 4 ft by 3 ft (1.2 m by 90 cm).

'Sombreuil'. Robert, 1850. 'Gigantesque' seedling, and in case you wonder, as I did before I looked it up, what on earth 'Gigantesque' could be, it was a deep-pink HP introduced by Odier in 1845 and with no parentage known. Quite how this makes 'Sombreuil' a climbing tea rose – except that it has a lot of the attributes of the teas – I do not know, but that is how it is classified. In fact, it can be grown as a lax shrub as well as a climber, but in the latter form will reach 8 ft (2.4 m) or so, preferably on a protective wall, though it seems reasonably hardy. The flowers are quite large, double and open flat. The colour is a creamy-white and sometimes there can be a pink flush.

'William R. Smith' ('Blush Maman Cochet', 'Charles Dingee', 'Jeanette Heller', 'Maiden's Blush', 'President Smith', 'President Wm. R. Smith'). Bagg, 1908. 'Maman Cochet' × 'Mme Hoste'. It hardly needs saying that a rose with so many alternative names was a rose of considerable popularity and it is still a good tea to grow. Long, pointed buds open to reveal shapely double flowers in a blend of pale-pink and creamy flesh-pink with a golden-yellow base to the petals. A vigorous grower with stronger stems than some to about 4 ft (1.2 m) with tough, leathery, semi-glossy leaves. Reasonably hardy.

Other Tea Roses Available

'Adam' (climbing). 1870. Peachy-pink.
'Anna Olivier'. 1872. Flesh-pink and deep-rose.
'Archiduc Joseph'. 1872. A pink, purple and orange mixture.
'Dr Grill'. 1886. Pink and copper.
'Freiherr von Marschall'. 1903. Carmine-red.
'Gloire de Dijon'. 1853. Buff to orange. See fuller description in Chapter 16.
'Homère'. 1858. Pink with white centres. Hardy.
'Lady Plymouth' 1914. Creamy-white.
'Marie van Houtte'. 1871. Pink, orange and creamy blends.
'Mme Berkeley'. 1899. Salmon-pink, cerise and gold.
'Mme Bravy'. 1846. Creamy-white flushed pink.
'Mme Scipion Cochet'. 1873. Mauve-pink.
'Mme Jules Gravereaux' (climbing). 1901. Yellow, peach and pink blends.
'Mme de Tartas'. Blush-pink.
'Mme de Watteville'. 1883. Lemon-yellow.
'Mons. Tillier'. 1891. Blood-red.
'Papa Gontier'. 1883. Bright-pink.
'Perle des Jardins'. 1874. Sulphur-yellow to buff. Hardy.
'Rosette Delizy'. 1922. Rose-pink, buff and apricot.
'Souvenir d'Elise Vardon'. 1855. Coppery-cream.
'Triomphe du Luxembourg'. 1839. Salmon-pink.

CHAPTER 12

Large-flowered Bush Roses (Hybrid Teas)

1867 was, as we have seen, the date of introduction of the first officially recognised hybrid tea, 'La France'. The HP 'Mme Victor Verdier' and the tea rose 'Mme Bravy' are often given as its parents, which would be quite acceptable if true, but rose breeding in the first part of the nineteenth century was a very haphazard affair, nurserymen as often as not simply planting two different varieties next to each other and hoping for the best. Such was the case when 'La France' came into existence and it is rather ironical, in view of the other and sometimes apparently better-documented claims to have been the first, that even 'La France's' raiser, Henri Guillot, was by no means prepared to swear as to the varieties that produced his own winner. In 1859, for instance, the nurseryman Lacharme of Lyon brought out a rose called 'Victor Verdier' (not to be confused with 'Mme Victor Verdier' above) which was enormously popular in its day and he gave the parents as the HP 'Jules Margottin' and tea rose 'Safrano'. A hybrid tea if ever there was one, but it was to remain a hybrid perpetual all its life, and really one must look on the whole question as to which rose was first as a puzzle from the past which is most unlikely to be solved at this late date.

Things became much more controlled when Henry Bennett in England began what appears to have been the first properly planned and recorded breeding programme of hybrid teas. He produced many notable roses, among them the wonderful pale-pink 'Lady Mary Fitzwilliam', which appears, it is said, in the family tree of some 1300 later varieties. His 'William Francis Bennett' was probably the first hybrid tea to reach America from Europe and was enormously popular there for many years.

Careful selection has made the HT what it is today. In many of the early varieties the flowers were lacking in petals and opened rather formless. 'Betty Uprichard' and 'Mme Edouard Herriott', both enormously popular in the 1920s, were examples of this, and during the same period a number of single-flowered HTs, such as 'Mrs Oakley Fisher', 'Irish Fireflame' and the supremely beautiful 'Dainty Bess', were put on the market. The singles, however, never really caught on with gardeners. What did catch on were the roses in the new colours just arriving on the market, and for the story of these we must go back a little way to just before the turn of the century.

Apart from a few wild roses from the Middle and the Far East, which probably were only to be seen in the collections of specialist growers, there were no bright-yellow, orange or flame-coloured roses in the gardens of the West. The nearest one got were some tea roses in a pale creamy-yellow, but few of them could be grown out of doors. They were pot plants for the conservatory.

However, a dramatic change was coming, and if the French nurseryman Joseph Pernet-Ducher was probably not the only person working to produce true yellow garden roses, he was certainly the first to succeed. His success was the result of years of patient effort, for the rose he chose to work with was the Persian species *R. foetida* ('Austrian Yellow'), perhaps the brightest yellow rose there is, and its two sports (or forms?), *R. foetida bicolor* ('Austrian Copper') in red and yellow and the double-flowered yellow *R. foetida persiana* (the 'Persian Yellow'). These he interbred with various hybrid perpetuals and in 1900 was able to put on the market the first really worthwhile result of all his painstaking work. This was 'Soleil d'Or', the result of a cross of the 'Persian Yellow' and the HP 'Antoine Ducher' and had double flowers of the HP type in a rich orange-yellow, sometimes with red streaks on a few petals. It could not be called a true yellow but this was to come with 'Rayon d'Or' in 1910.

Some people hold that all our bicolour roses are descended from *R. foetida bicolor*. There seems to be very little direct evidence for this, but it does seem possible that if the latter was a sport of *R. foetida*, the bicolour genes could have come out in later generations. At any rate, the yellow roses on their own (known at first as pernetianas) were quite enough to bring about a revolution. They coincided more or less with the coming of the HTs and all the old rose families were swept aside in the rush for the new, as the blood of the pernetiana roses was gradually intermingled with other roses. After a time they lost their separate identity and the name was dropped, but yellow garden roses had come to stay – and so, as a by-product, had black spot.

If you read a gardening book published before 1900, black

spot is hardly mentioned. It was there, but clearly not a great problem until *R. foetida* came along. Whatever it may have been like in its native home, in the West it was a martyr to the black spot fungus, and because its offspring the pernetianas were in their early days crossed with everything in sight except perhaps a hollyhock this susceptibility to disease was handed on with no thought to the future. Now there are few modern roses in the veins of which, however, diluted, its blood does not run.

The alternative names 'Austrian Yellow' and 'Austrian Copper' given above in parentheses derive from the fact that these Persian roses appear to have travelled westward from their homeland via Austria, where they seem to have rested, probably for a number of years. They must then have been thought by the uninitiated to be natives of that country in the same way that the early roses that came to Europe from China, having been given a break in their long voyage in India, were subsequently known as Bengal roses or *R. indica*.

An interesting and to me intriguing footnote is added to the story of the first yellow roses by this short quotation from Robert Louis Stevenson's *Prince Otto* of 1885, which he set in the vaguely Bohemian (Austrian?) kingdom of Grünewald. Writing about the Countess von Rosen he says: 'A glance, a loosened curl, a studied and admired disorder of the hair, a bit of lace, a touch of colour, a yellow rose in the bosom, and the instant picture was complete.' It is interesting to speculate what, at that date, the rose could have been as there does not seem to be any hint that a yellow rose was anything particularly unusual. Was it the 'Persian Yellow' if, like its two companions, it ever had an Austrian phase – which would make it right geographically? Or was it perhaps simply a tea rose in a colour we would probably describe today as creamy-yellow? We will never know, of course.

A selection of large-flowered varieties (HTs) is given below:

'Adolf Horstmann'. Kordes, 1971. 'Colour Wonder' × 'Dr A.J. Verhage'. Yellow blooms with a hint of bronze or perhaps deep-orange, together with some pink flushes. They are large and full but only occasionally of the immaculate shape needed for the show bench. Nevertheless they do last exceptionally well as cut flowers and the fragrance is pleasing if not outstanding. There have been reports that 'Adolf Horstmann' does not always flower as freely as it might, but this has not been my experience, and the plants' good health, especially notable in a yellow rose, would in any case make up for a good many failings. The leaves are semi-glossy and plentiful on a sturdy bush of medium height or a little more. It was awarded an RNRS (Royal National Rose Society) Trial Ground Certificate in 1972.

'Alec's Red'. Cocker, 1970. 'Fragrant Cloud' × 'Dame de Coeur'. Many claim that this is the best red bedding large-flowered variety produced for many years but though it has many fine qualities, I am not prepared to go all the way with that myself. In its freedom of flowering, compact and reasonably bushy growth to medium height, health and perhaps above all its fragrance, I would agree, but the blooms, of a bright light-crimson that really glows and never loses its brilliance, are rarely of classic shape. Occasionally, one sees the odd exceptional flower on the show bench but in general they follow the pattern of their second parent. This means they are round and globular, with the centre petals too short to give a high, pointed centre, and they sometimes spot after prolonged rain. The leaves are mid-green and glossy and, though generally unmarred by mildew, will not be completely proof against black spot. A winner of many awards, including the RNRS Gold Medal and the Edland Medal for fragrance.

'Alexander'. Harkness, 1972. 'Super Star' × ('Ann Elizabeth' × 'Allgold'). This is not a rose for bedding unless it can be carried out on the grand scale, for it grows to a height of 4 ft (1.2 m) that almost takes it into the shrub rose class. Although quite freely branching and making plenty of new growth from the base each year, it remains upright and quite compact so that it is an ideal candidate for a colourful hedge that does not take up too much room. The blooms, coming in the main in small clusters, are of a striking deep vermilion. Shapely at first, they open informally as they have not too many petals, but they are very freely produced over a long season with good continuity and last well in water. Scent is only slight. 'Super Star' gave this rose its colour – although the vermilion of 'Alexander' is deeper – but fortunately did not also pass on its proneness to mildew. 'Alexander' with its handsome deep-green, semi-glossy leaves, can be counted among the healthier roses on the market.

'Alpine Sunset'. Cant, 1974. 'Dr A.J. Verhage' × 'Grandpa Dickson'. In every way but one this rose can be said to be the ideal bedding rose. Its single drawback, and it is not a major one, is that there can be rather a long pause between the first and second flush of bloom. Growth is very sturdy and upright and on the short side, with a good coverage of healthy, deep-green glossy leaves. The blooms are most striking, very large and full and an attractive blend of creamy-yellow and peach tones, and, as is often the case, in the cooler autumn days the colours become richer. The scent is outstanding and weather resistance good. RNRS Trial Ground Certificate.

'Baronne Edmond de Rothschild'. Meilland, 1968. ('Baccara' × 'Crimson King') × 'Peace'. Large, high-centred, fragrant, deep rose-pink blooms with a silvery petal reverse distinguish this rose. Not everyone seems to like bicolours, but this is a very pleasing one and, if not perhaps as tall a grower as one might expect from a descendant of 'Peace', it is still very vigorous and branches freely. It does get its general good health from 'Peace' and its fine glossy, leathery leaves have the familiar 'Peace' look, too. It has won Gold Medals in Lyons and Rome and a fragrance medal from Belfast.

'Blessings'. Gregory, 1968. 'Queen Elizabeth' × seedling. This has long been regarded as one of the best bedding roses ever raised because it seems to produce more flowers (and produces them more or less non-stop) than any other large-flowered bush rose. They are big and open quite loosely as there are not all that many petals. The colour is a soft light-pink with salmon overtones, a most pleasing combination, but the scent is only slight. One would expect a rose with 'Queen Elizabeth' as a parent to be taller than average, but this has not happened here. On the other hand, 'Queen Elizabeth's' disease resistance may have helped on the health side. A member of roses in the salmon-pink range have a poor health record. 'Blessings' is an exception, not actually proof against either mildew or black spot – and what rose is? – but no more likely to be affected by them than most other varieties. It gained a Gold Medal in Baden-Baden and an RNRS Certificate of Merit in 1968.

'Bobby Charlton'. Fryer, 1974. 'Royal Highness' × 'Prima Ballerina'. 'Royal Highness' does not like rain and 'Prima Ballerina' positively welcomes mildew, but in this rose the best rather than the worst qualities of both parents seem to have been preserved. The flowers of 'Bobby Charlton' have every-thing an exhibitor could desire, as have those of 'Royal Highness', but they are much better in bad weather. Full and high centred, they are a lovely soft pink with the reverse of the petals a little lighter, and they have a scent that has come from 'Prima Ballerina'. Although a rose which is now a favourite for the show bench, it is one that is rewarding in the garden, too. It is a tall, upstanding bush with large, dark-green, semi-glossy leaves, and if it has a fault it is that it comes into bloom rather later than most others, no doubt a legacy from 'Peace' via 'Royal Highness'. Gold Medal from Baden-Baden.

'Bonsoir'. Dickson, 1968. The parentage is often given as 'seedling × seedling', which really means absolutely nothing unless one knows something about the seedlings. Anyway, an especially lovely rose has been the result of the cross, and it has remained very high in the popularity lists of both gardeners and exhibitors, despite the fact that it is quite hopeless in wet weather. For exhibitors there are bloom protectors which they can use, and with the help of these 'Bonsoir' has carried off award after award. It even received a Certificate of Merit from RNRS, in what one can only think must have been a spell of three consecutive dry summers, and a Gold Medal from Baden-Baden. Clearly gardeners other than exhibitors put 'Bonsoir' in the category of roses they cannot be without for they continue to grow it for the sheer beauty of its very double and finely shaped, peach-pink, delicately scented blooms. These are generally borne in small clusters so that some disbudding is needed if they are to reach their full potential. A moderately bushy grower to average height, I have had to spray it against mildew but rarely against black spot. Fine, glossy, very dark-green leaves.

'Camphill Glory'. Harkness, 1982. 'Elizabeth Harkness' × 'Perfecta'. With these parents, one gets what might be expected – flowers of large size and pointed form, creamy-pink with deeper pink flushes. It blooms very freely and stands up to rain well for so large a rose. A tall, strong grower, well branched and with healthy mid-green foliage, it can be used for bedding or as an alternative makes a very fine hedging rose. The name commemorates the work of the Camphill Village Trust, which provides sheltered communities for those who cannot live in a wider world, and the Trust receives a donation for each plant sold.

'Cheshire Life'. Fryer, 1972. 'Prima Ballerina' × 'Princess Michiko'. Once again Fryers have used 'Prima Ballerina' for breeding this rose (see 'Bobby Charlton' above), presumably in an attempt to pass on its fragrance, but this time it has not really worked. However, scent apart, a very good rose has resulted with outstanding, medium-sized, orange-vermilion blooms carried with great freedom and which are particularly good in weather that would finish many other rose blooms. The dark, leathery leaves are healthy, and the plant is a well branched and bushy grower to average height or a little less. A fine bedding rose of a striking colour.

'Chicago Peace'. Introduced by Johnson, 1962. A sport from 'Peace' and as the only difference between the two is in the colour of the flowers, the description of the rest of the rose can be found under 'Peace' itself. Here the huge blooms are in blends of coppery-pink with a yellow petal reverse, quite strong colours which to many people are more appealing than those of 'Peace' itself. The sport occurred in Chicago, which is the reason for the rather strange name.

'Congratulations' ('Sylvia'). Kordes, 1978. 'Carina' × seedling. There are and always have been a number of first-rate roses that never achieve the popularity they deserve. Those who do grow them know their qualities and may wrinkle their brows over why this should be so, but probably the reason is quite simple: there are too many new varieties introduced each year. And even if there were not, it is also not unknown for a striking and garish novelty to edge out a much better but less exuberantly coloured variety. One such is 'Congratulations' from the German raiser Kordes, which is a rose of great elegance. The bush is tall and slender in habit and the medium sized, shapely blooms in soft rose-pink come mainly in small clusters on long and practically thornless stems, which make them first rate for cutting. As a hedge this rose is delightful but not showy, and it otherwise looks best in a small rather than in a major bedding scheme. Health and weather resistance are both good, but scent only moderate.

'Doris Tysterman'. Wisbech Plant Co., 1975. 'Peer Gynt' × seedling. One of the better coppery-orange varieties of which a considerable number of varying quality (particularly regarding health) were introduced in the 1970s. 'Doris Tysterman' is very free-flowering with quite shapely, medium-sized blooms which come sometimes singly and sometimes in clusters on long, strong and almost thornless stems so that they are excellent as cut flowers for the house. If the scent was more noticeable they would be even better, as the plant itself would be if its bronze-tinted dark-green leaves did not need watching for mildew in the late summer. It is a tall, upright grower to about 3 ft (90 cm) which does not bush out a great deal, a point to bear in mind when using it as a bedding rose.

'Double Delight'. Swim and Ellis, 1977. 'Granada' × 'Garden Party'. Considering the quality of many of them, it is surprising how few American-bred roses make the grade in Europe (the reverse applies too). However, 'Double Delight' is one which has crossed the Atlantic (from west to east) and really made an impact. This is not solely because of its generally good qualities as a bedding rose (apart from a tendency to let mildew get a hold if given half a chance), but because of its unique and very lovely flowers. They are shapely, large, and have plenty of creamy-white petals, the edges of which are flushed cherry-red, though not by any means in a uniform way. Some have more red, some less, and the overall effect is indeed delightful, the other half of the double delight consisting of a strong, sweet fragrance. The blooms come freely and continuity is good. Growth is vigorous and freely branching to average height. The mid-green leaves are semi-glossy. This was an All-American Rose Selection (the top accolade in the USA) and a Gold Medal winner in Rome and Baden-Baden. It was not entered in the RNRS trials for a possible award in the UK.

'Dutch Gold'. Wisbech Plant Co., 1978. 'Peer Gynt' × 'Whisky Mac'. A yellow rose with a good scent is sufficiently rare to make it sought after on that score alone. When this is combined with good, vigorous, upright growth and large, full and usually very shapely bright-yellow blooms which hold their colour well, you have a rose that is being added to more nursery catalogues every year. The flowers are frequently of exhibition size and standard, but there are likely to be a number of split blooms, too, which does not matter particularly for garden display. The mid-green, glossy leaves are healthy on the whole, which, considering that the hypochondriachal 'Whisky Mac' is one parent, is quite remarkable. It was awarded a Gold Medal at The Hague.

'Elizabeth Harkness'. Harkness, 1969. 'Red Dandy' × 'Piccadilly'. Nobody knows better than a rose breeder how capricious nature can be, but I wonder if even Jack Harkness, who raised this rose, expected a red cluster-flowered variety and the red and yellow 'Piccadilly' to produce between them the very elegant ivory-white large-flowered bush rose he was to call after his daughter. There is sometimes a pink tinge to the petals and I have seen this become much more pronounced as the flowers age, although it does not always seem to happen. An attraction is that the blooms, carried both singly and in small clusters, come earlier than most and continuity from then onwards is well up to average. Not a great deal of scent, unfortunately, and weather resistance could be better. Although making a medium-sized and reasonably bushy plant, I would describe this as a rose of only moderate vigour, which was cut back badly in the extreme cold of the few nights during the winter of 1981-2 in the UK which provided a testing time for so many plants. The semi-glossy, mid-green leaves are of average health. An RNRS Certificate of Merit was awarded in 1969.

'Ernest H. Morse'. Kordes, 1965. Parentage unknown, or at any rate, not given. Quite an old-timer, this rose is deservedly still very popular as a bedding variety, although one can perhaps detect the first signs of a decline in its constitution in that, always considered one of the healthiest of roses, there is now more likelihood of mildew getting a hold in the autumn. But then that happens with many much newer roses which have not got all the plus qualities still possessed by 'Ernest H. Morse'. The flowers, generally in small clusters, are produced with the greatest freedom and with scarcely a pause between the flushes. They can be very large and shapely, but if one is tempted to try them at a show, timing will be very important because they do not hold their shape for long and open wide. I am not quite sure what turkey-red is, but that is the colour usually attributed to this rose. It does not seem to me to be all that far from crimson, and it really glows for the first day or two after the flowers open. Then it dulls a little but is still attractive, and there is always a fine scent. This is a very robust, compact, upright grower, making plenty of strong new shoots from the base each season and which will grow to average height. It has dark-green, semi-glossy leaves. It is a rose with an RNRS Gold Medal, RHS Award of Merit and an outstanding fragrance award from The Hague.

'Evening Star'. Warriner, 1974. 'White Masterpiece' × 'Saratoga'. White roses come and go with disconcerting rapidity. Today's white wonder is forgotten tomorrow and there have almost always been two reasons for this. In the first place, a number of people do not like white flowers, which I suppose is their prerogative and certainly their loss. This means that white roses – and, for that matter, most roses in the softer, pastel colours – are never reckoned on to be particularly good sellers, even without the white varieties' almost universal weakness, a dislike of rain. In recent years the only white large-flowered rose that has lasted any time at all is 'Pascali' and its flowers are rather small for the class and not absolutely pure white. Most of the other introductions have had blooms that either refused to open in rainy weather or else, if they had managed to open before the rain came, collapsed into sodden and most depressing lumps preparatory to setting the seal on an inglorious end by turning brown. So how does 'Evening Star' from America stand in all this?

It was introduced in America in 1974, but as it has only been on the market in the UK much more recently it is probably too early to make any positive pronouncements as to how it will perform in such a different climate. However, one can, I think, say that things look promising. A rose that wins a Gold Medal in the Belfast trials, as 'Evening Star' did, must have survived a wet day or two with credit, and it received an award there for fragrance as well, which is more than 'Pascali' would have done. The blooms are large and can be of exhibition standard. They come singly and several together on a strong, upright bush that is on the tall side for bedding, as it usually reaches about 3 ft 6 in (just over 1 m). The dark-green leaves are semi-glossy and as healthy as most.

'Fragrant Cloud' ('Duftwolke', 'Nuage Parfume'). Tantau, 1963. Seedling × 'Prima Ballerina'. This is a rose that would be counted as being among the all-time greats were it not for the fact that after the comparatively short period of 20 years it has changed in the fairly recent past from a variety of outstanding health to one which must be watched for both mildew and black spot. Until this happened, its only failing was an instability in the colour, the bright geranium-red of the blooms taking on much duller tones fairly rapidly, although this did not mean they became much less pleasing to look at. They were different, that was all.

So much for the minus side, but what was it that made it such a great rose? A fine constitution, a sturdy habit with free branching that meant that all the blooms were not carried just at the top of the bush – and what blooms they were and still are. They start early and then come with such freedom and continuity that in Germany, its country of origin, 'Fragrant Cloud' is classed as a cluster-flowered variety rather than a large-flowered rose, even though many blooms may be 5–6 in (13–16 cm) across and of exhibition standard. However, fine as these are to look at, it is their rich deep fragrance, unsurpassed by any other modern variety, that has really made and maintained this rose's reputation. The bush is of average height and the leaves cover it well. They are dark-green and glossy. This rose has won an RNRS gold medal and an RHS Award of Merit.

'Golden Times'. Cocker, 1972. 'Fragrant Cloud' × 'Golden Splendour'. At least some, though certainly not all, of 'Fragrant Cloud's' scent has been passed on to 'Golden Times', which makes it one of the growing number of scented yellow roses. The flowers, a pure pale gold, are carried with great freedom and good continuity and, though shapely, do not really have sufficient substance to make good exhibition blooms. For garden display, however, they make a fine show and they last well when cut for the house. The bushes are quite tall, but branch well and have plenty of dark-green, leathery leaves. Resistance to disease is well up to average and rain resistance, as is the case with most yellow roses, well above it. The autumn performance is especially good.

'Grandpa Dickson' ('Irish Gold'). Dickson, 1966. ('Perfecta' × 'Governador Braga de Cruz') × 'Piccadilly'. An RNRS Gold Medal, an RHS Award of Merit, and Gold Medals at both Belfast and The Hague should be indication enough that 'Grandpa Dickson' is something special – and it is. It is one of those not too common roses that perform equally well for both the exhibitor and the average gardener, in that almost every one of the large double blooms is of classic form, but at the same time they come with such freedom and are so tolerant of rough weather that this is an almost unbeatable variety for bedding. Only 'almost' because the short, very upright bushes could really do with more of their small, dark-green, glossy leaves, especially as these are outstandingly disease-free, and also because it is not really happy in dry sandy areas. This latter point could be made, of course, about most roses, but 'Grandpa Dickson' does seem to need good soil and cultivation more than most. For bedding, closer planting than usual will be needed as the bushes are unlikely to spread out much. The colour is a soft, pleasing yellow with occasional pink flushes on the petal edges, especially late in the season. Little scent.

'Honey Favorite'. Von Abrams, 1962. 'Pink Favorite', of which this is a sport, is in countless nursery lists. 'Honey Favorite' appears much more rarely, which is strange as I am not alone in thinking that it has much the most attractively coloured flowers of the two, a light-pink flushed with peach tones. Otherwise the roses are virtually identical and for a more detailed description, the reader can refer to the entry for 'Pink Favorite' later in this list. It could just be added here that where the latter is always cited as just about the healthiest bedding rose there is, 'Honey Favorite' is every bit as good.

'John Waterer'. McGredy, 1970. 'King of Hearts' × 'Hanne'. This is also a rose that should be in more nursery lists than it is, for it is an absolutely first-rate deep-crimson bedding rose, of good growth habit, profuse in bloom, and the dark-green, matt foliage is well up to the average in its resistance to disease. Perhaps the reason that it is not better known is that a red rose that has little if any scent will probably be looked at sideways by many people, and this is the case with 'John Waterer'. Otherwise, however, the large shapely blooms, singly to a stem or in small clusters, lack nothing. The bushes are strong-growing and upright to average height or a little more. An RNRS Certificate of Merit was awarded in 1969.

'Just Joey'. Cant, 1973. 'Fragrant Cloud' × 'Dr A.J. Verhage'. Here is one that, such is its popularity, you could not keep out of the nursery lists if you tried, and 'Just Joey', bracketted (I would say) with 'Silver Jubilee' (which see), could fairly be described as *the* roses of the 1970s, one ushering in the decade in great style and the other seeing it out, although both are still going from strength to strength. The large blooms of 'Just Joey' are for the flower arranger rather than the show bench, for although they can be shapely in the bud they quickly open wide with attractively waved and ruffled petals, sometimes singly to a stem and sometimes in small clusters. Flowering carries on with the greatest freedom well into the autumn months and seems quite unaffected by rain. In colour this rose is a delightful coppery orange-pink which lightens towards the petal edges. There is some scent even if it is not strong. The bush is robust and well branched, reaching average height for a bedding rose, and the matt, dark-green leaves, red-tinted when young, have a good health record. Despite the especially fine qualities that have perhaps only revealed themselves when the rose has actually been planted out in gardens, in 1971 'Just Joey' received just a Trial Ground Certificate from the RNRS, not in itself a bad thing to get, but one would have expected a little more. Perhaps more surprisingly, it received a fragrance award at the The Hague.

'La France'. Guillot, 1867. Possible parentage is discussed in the introduction to this chapter. I am by no means suggesting that this should nowadays be considered for a modern bedding scheme. For one thing, if pictures and descriptions are to be relied on, it is, perhaps not surprisingly, not the rose it was. However, as the first hybrid tea ever, using in this instance the old class name which was invented specifically for it and its contemporaries, we are lucky that it exists at all and that we can still grow it, even if only as a novelty. Although it seems to have been taller in the past, modern strains seldom exceed average height and the bush is actually none too robust. The blooms, however, are still lovely, china-pink, large and double, with shell-like petals. They usually remain globular and do not open out fully. For their size and type they are remarkably resistant to rain and are very fragrant. It has matt, medium-green and rather dowdy-looking foliage, not proof against the usual rose ills.

'Lakeland'. Fryer, 1976. 'Fragrant Cloud' × 'Queen Elizabeth'. Because a variety has not won any awards from the various international trial grounds, it does not mean that it is not a first-class rose. At the same time, it does not mean that it is, and an award does give a prospective buyer some reassurance that he is getting something good. But then all good roses are not, for one reason or another, entered for trials, or a rose may take a number of years of being grown in gardens to reach, or at least to reveal, its full potential. It may have made no particular impression, even in trials lasting over three years, as those of the RNRS do. Some roses, like some humans, are late developers. 'Lakeland' won no awards but is turning out to be a very good rose, which might have been expected when one looks at its parents, even if it is not really in the least like either of them. Vigorous to average height and very free-flowering for a rose whose blooms will reach exhibition size and standard, it performs well enough in wet weather to make it a successful garden rose. The fragrant blooms are a soft pale-pink and the mid-green, semi-glossy leaves have a good resistance to disease.

'Midas'. Le Grice, 1980. 'Grandpa Dickson' × 'Dr A.J. Verhage'. There is nothing particularly sensational about 'Midas'. It is just a thoroughly good and very reliable bedding rose of medium height and excellent health. The flowers are produced with great freedom and reasonably continuously. They range from medium to large in size, full and rather rounded, lemon-yellow in colour, but they are not strongly scented. Long-lasting when cut for the house.

'Mischief'. McGredy, 1961. 'Peace' × 'Spartan'. This is one of the great survivors, which may not sound as complimentary as it is meant to be. Put another way, this is a rose that has remained a favourite for over 20 years and still, unless you live in a district where rose rust is likely to be problem, in which case it is best avoided, takes a lot of beating for continuity and the sheer number of high-centred blooms of classic form that it produces. Unless some disbudding is done, these will be on the small side, but if they are confined to one or two to a shoot, exhibition size and standard will be reached. The colour, which varies to some extent, can best be described as coral-salmon. Little scent, but good rain resistance. Growth is strong and bushy to average height and the light-green leaves may need watching for mildew, as well as for possible rust. It was an RNRS Gold Medal rose in 1961.

'Mister Lincoln'. Swim and Weeks, 1964. 'Chrysler Imperial' × 'Charles Mallerin'. The perfect really dark red rose – deep-crimson with blackish shadings – has yet to be produced. 'Josephine Bruce' is pretty good, but it does sprawl and, like so many in this colour, including 'Papa Meilland', and the two parents of 'Mister Lincoln' itself, it embraces mildew with the greatest enthusiasm. However, there is not too much doubt that 'Mister Lincoln' is the best so far from the health point of view, and the dusky-red petals do not 'blue' with age like so many of its kind. In fact, what happens is that in strong sunshine they turn a much brighter and lighter crimson and, though the blooms will have been shapely at first, they soon open cupped, showing the golden stamens. They are very fragrant, which is a plus, but they do tend to come in small clusters at the end of strong, 3–4 ft (90 cm–1.2 m) canes, not too well provided with this rose's very dark green leaves. This is a minus, particularly for bedding, but it is a good enough rose to have been an All American Rose Selection. It did not go through many trials in Europe.

'Mme Butterfly'. Hill, 1918. Sport from 'Ophelia'. What, it may be wondered, is a rose from so many years back and which has no great significance historically (though its parent could be said to have) doing in a list of roses recommended for modern gardens? The answer is quite simple: there has been nothing since that could better it in its own particular way.

Although 'Mme Butterfly' will grow to medium height, it might as far as the blooms are concerned be called a half-size hybrid tea. These flowers are borne with the greatest freedom, sometimes in quite sizeable clusters, are always of immaculate shape with the most beautiful high, coiled centres, but are, with rare exceptions and only then if a lot of disbudding has been carried out, quite small. The colour is a delicate flesh-pink and the fragrance good. The matt green foliage is about average in its resistance to disease, but there is one thing that 'Mme Butterfly' and others of its family does suffer from particularly. Thrips, or thunderflies as they are also known, do nibble the petal edges of the early buds if precautions are not taken, particularly in spells of hot weather.

The 'family' referred to above consists entirely of sports of 'Ophelia', which was introduced by Paul in 1912. A sport occurs when a rose wither produces a shoot with flowers different from those on the rest of the bush, or else the same flowers, but shoots so long and vigorous that a climbing sport is created. In both cases it is probably some throwback to previous generations which produces a genetic change and the shoots which are affected can be propagated from so that a new variety has been created. Some sports are prone to revert to the original, while others are relatively stable. 'Ophelia' produced many sports, and varieties like 'Mme Butterfly' have themselves sported other roses. 'Lady Sylvia' of 1927 in light pink is probably the best known of them, and is in every way as good as its parent.

'Mullard Jubilee' ('Electron'). McGredy, 1970. 'Paddy McGredy' × 'Prima Ballerina'. This is, I think, the fourth rose in this comparatively brief selection of large-flowered varieties to have 'Prima Ballerina' as a parent. Why then, if it is such a good rose, is 'Prima Ballerina' not in this list of recommended roses? As far as I am concerned, as I have already said when describing 'Bobby Charlton', it is because of its disfiguring mildew, but it is its wonderful scent that has tempted breeders to keep on using it in the hope that this will be passed on.

Having said that, it must also be said that 'Mullard Jubilee', a fine deep-pink bedding rose with very large full blooms (which open too quickly and loosely for exhibition), has not inherited the mildew but neither has it inherited 'Prima Ballerina's' remarkable scent. There is some fragrance but that is all. Rain resistance is good. The bushy, vigorous plant, which will reach average height, is extremely thorny, which can present painful problems when cutting for the house, for which this rose is otherwise very suitable. The dark-green leaves are of average disease resistance. It has won RNRS, Belfast and The Hague Gold Medals and was an All-American Rose Selection, a signal honour for an overseas variety.

'National Trust'. ('Bad Nanheim'). McGredy, 1970. 'Evelyn Fison' × 'King of Hearts'. An endless succession of impeccably-shaped, bright-red blooms, usually in fairly large clusters, make this one of the best bedding roses there is. Although they have many petals (which helps them to hold their shape well when cut for the house), the flowers stand up to rain well. They are never very large, even with disbudding, and it is a pity that they are practically without scent. A fine bushy grower to perhaps a little below average height, it has matt, dark-green leaves which should present no particular health problem. It has been awarded an RNRS Trial Ground Certificate.

'Pascali'. Lens, 1963. 'Queen Elizabeth' × 'White Butterfly'. Under the entry for 'Evening Star', I discussed some of the problems usually associated with white roses. As I mentioned, 'Frau Karl Druschki' (see Chapter 10, page 65) was for many, many years considered the best white rose that had flowers of any size and in the modern idiom, and there are those who still hold this view, which either says a lot for this veteran variety or not very much for those that have come after it. Although there were one or two show-bench white roses over the years, only the two French roses, Mallerin's 'Virgo' of 1947 and Meilland's 'Message' ('White Knight'), which had a double dose of 'Virgo' in its parentage as well as the redoubtable 'Peace', achieved any real popularity with gardeners and both of them looked a sorry sight after rain and were ready victims of rose mildew. It was not until 1963 and the appearance of Louis Lens's 'Pascali' from Belgium that a white rose could hold up its head in competition with other varieties in a wet summer, and was as healthy as any of them as well. As a matter of fact, if you examine the flowers of 'Pascali' closely, they are not pure-white, having pale creamy-buff tints in the centre, but for garden purposes it is white, and one only really notices that it is not when cutting some of the long, thornless stems for a vase. The beautifully shaped (if rather small) blooms last better than practically any other rose in water, possibly because the petals seem to be much more substantial in texture than most. This must help with the keeping qualities as well as with coping with rain. Not much scent and an upright rather leggy grower to a little above average height with mid-green glossy leaves. It has been awarded an RNRS Certificate of Merit, was an All-American Rose Selection and won the Golden Rose of The Hague Award which, it will by now be realised, is pretty good going for a white rose.

'Peace' ('Gioia', 'Gloria Dei', 'Mme A. Meilland'). Meilland 1942. Seedling × 'Margaret McGredy'. What can one say that has not been said already – *ad nauseum* – about the 'World's Favourite Rose'? So just a brief description will be given here for those few to whom it is less than familiar. To begin with, it is such a strong grower that, if lightly pruned as it always should be, it will easily reach 4–5 ft (1.2–1.5 m), spreading out well at the same time, which means that it is only for a fairly large bed, for use as a specimen, or perhaps as a hedging rose. The blooms are enormous, shapely at first and opening out like gigantic 5–6-in (13–16-cm) paeonies, pale-yellow with some pink flushes, the colour intensifying considerably in the last months of the year. For a rose which first saw the light of day in the breeder's nursery before the last war, there has been singularly little sign of weakening of the stock, but I suspect that what has always been considered one of the healthiest of roses, with fine, glossy deep-green foliage, is beginning to be a little more susceptible to the attacks of black spot than it was. One hopes that this is not the beginning of the end, but whatever happens 'Peace' will never be forgotten, not just because it has been without question the finest garden rose ever, but because it has been a parent to countless good roses, too. The only real B-mark is a lack of scent and a likelihood that there will be a number of blind shoots early in the summer. Oh, and it does come into flower a little later than most. It has an RNRS Gold Medal, and an RHS Award of Merit and was an All-American Rose Selection.

'Peer Gynt'. Kordes, 1968. 'Colour Wonder' × 'Golden Giant'. This is a rose very much for garden display for its continuity of bloom is first-rate. The flowers come mainly in clusters, are of medium size and rather globular at first, opening cupped and with the outer petals sometimes scalloped. They are bright-yellow, often with pink flushes, especially towards the petal edges. Very little scent. The plant is strong-growing and bushy to medium height, and the rather light green, semi-glossy leaves will almost certainly need to be sprayed against mildew. This is its biggest weakness and one which cannot be ignored, much as one would like to for the sake of the rose's good qualities. It gained an RNRS Certificate of Merit, though.

'Piccadilly'. McGredy, 1919. 'McGredy's Yellow' × 'Karl Herbst'. If ever there was a rose that deserved Gold Medals all round it was this one and it did get them in Rome and Madrid. The RNRS managed only a Certificate of Merit (which would have been pretty good for most roses) but the RHS did better with an Award of Merit. There have been many red and yellow bicolour roses since 'Piccadilly' was introduced over 20 years ago, but they have not lasted in the nursery lists. Not that 'Piccadilly' is perfect. The blooms are a little short on petals so that, shapely at first, they open right out rather quickly. And in anything but cool weather (in which it is superb) the red soon suffuses the whole flower so that it becomes blends of fiery coppery-orange rather than a two-colour variety. However, it is one of the earliest into bloom and keeps on and on with the greatest freedom, giving the gayest, brightest show imaginable. The leaves, too, are an attraction in themselves. At first deep-red and then bronze-tinted, they turn dark-green with such a glossy sheen that they seem polished. The growth is sturdy and bushy to medium height. Weaknesses? Yes, one: a watch must be kept for black spot.

'Pink Favorite'. Von Abrams, 1956. 'Juno' × ('Georg Arends' × 'New Dawn'). The spelling of 'Favorite' indicates this rose's American origin and the parentage indicates some original thinking and imagination in the breeder, Von Abrams, a hybrid tea crossed with a hybrid of a hybrid perpetual and a recurrent climber, but it is a combination that produced an outstanding rose. Outstanding primarily because with it black spot and mildew are almost unknown, a point already noted in the description of its sport 'Honey Favorite'. I would not myself have rated it right at the top otherwise even though its flowers have won many top awards on the show bench. They can be very large and very shapely, but they are by no means always so and considerable disbudding must be carried out for exhibition purposes. Even for garden display I find that they are too closely bunched to open properly unless some buds are removed and that the flower can be a trifle coarse. The bright rose-pink lacks the delicacy one finds in 'Honey Favorite' and the scent is only slight. Growth is exceedingly robust and upright however, medium to tall and with not a great deal of lateral spread. Many rate this a great rose, including the RHS, which gave it an Award of Merit. I do not go along with this, but would put up with a good many weaknesses in a rose that I do not have to spray against disease.

'Pot o'Gold'. Dickson, 1980. 'Eurorose' × 'Whisky Mac'. Of all the fragrant yellow large-flowered roses introduced during the last few years – and there have been quite a number – it seems likely that 'Pot o'Gold' may well turn out to be the most popular. As well as gaining a Certificate of Merit from the RNRS, it won the British Association of Rose Breeders (BARB) Award for 1980. This means that the members of the Association rated it the best of the year among themselves, and the way a nurseryman looks at a rose differs in some subtle and indefinable way from the way the rest of us do it. As well as assessing its more obvious good qualities, which all of us can do, some instinct, probably coupled with experience, tells him whether or not a rose is likely to sell. It does not always follow that what a layman considers is a good rose will top the sales charts, so a BARB endorsement such as 'Pot o'Gold' gained is a pretty useful pointer to a rose's future. It is a good clear yellow with nicely shaped flowers of a little over medium size, produced with great freedom and continuity. Growth is strong and bushy to average height, and all the qualities for a fine bedding rose are there in abundance, including above-average health and good weather resistance.

'Precious Platinum' ('Opa Potschke', 'Red Star'). Dickson, 1974. 'Red Planet' × 'Franklin Engelmann'. If you are looking for a really bright, shining red rose for bedding, this is the one. The flowers are large and carried mainly in small clusters on a fine, well-branched bush that will reach 3 ft (90 cm) in height and that has medium-green, glossy leaves. These are generally healthy but mildew cannot be ruled out. Not very much scent but good weather resistance. No awards for this one but it is nevertheless proving its worth in the garden and is increasing in popularity all the time. The only uncertain thing about it is why a red rose should have been given such a name.

'Pristine'. Warriner, 1978. 'White Masterpiece' × 'First Prize'. A lusty, tall-growing American rose that has acclimatised itself well to European conditions. The blooms come with satis-factory freedom and are large, moderately full and can be of exhibition standard. They are ivory-white with the most pleasing pink flush and a fine scent which gained them a medal for fragrance from the RNRS. The large, leathery leaves are dark-green and make a pleasing and contrasting background which shows the blooms off well. They are healthy on the whole.

'Red Devil' ('Coeur d'Amour'). Dickson, 1967. 'Silver Lining' × 'Prima Ballerina' seedling. Not in a way an easy rose to write about or to recommend as it is a combination of two extremes. On the one hand, it probably produces with the minimum of disbudding more large and perfectly shaped blooms, all of the highest exhibition standard, than any other rose. They are of a pleasing light-scarlet with a slightly paler reverse and have a fine strong fragrance. Time and again this rose has carried off the top awards at shows and even in a marquee in the baking sun they will maintain their perfect shape for several days. But they do not like rain and this would, with most varieties, remove them from any list of recommendations of roses for the garden. In this case, however, they do come with such freedom that damaged blooms are soon replaced and they represent such perfection during spells of sunny weather that an exception can legitimately be made. Growth is very vigorous and may go well above 3 ft (90 cm) and the large, glossy, dark-green leaves are exceptionally healthy. But, and here we come to the second area of doubt, despite its apparent robustness this is a rose than in my garden has been more seriously cut back by hard frosts than most. In the especially tough winter of 1981/82 in the UK I lost several plants completely, but, just the same, for my part the rewards 'Red Devil' gives outweigh the drawbacks. It gained an RNRS Certificate of Merit and Gold Medals in Belfast and Roeulx.

'**Rose Gaujard**'. Gaujard, 1958. 'Peace' × 'Opera' seedling. Raised well over 30 years ago, this was one of the earlier offspring of 'Peace' and inherited a great deal of its toughness, its strong, well-branched habit of growth (though it is not quite as tall) and its fine, dark-green, glossy leaves that are among the healthiest there are, though they are maybe a little more prone to black spot than they used to be. The blooms, however, are quite different from those of 'Peace'. Large and very shapely in the bud, they have many times won prizes at shows. In putting them on the show bench one is, however, taking a gamble for more often than not the flowers will open out with split centres, which is not a serious drawback for garden display but makes an exhibitor's toes curl. In colour the flowers are carmine-pink, contrasting strikingly with a silvery petal reverse. There is little if any fragrance but the petals shrug away the effects even of prolonged rain. A nice easy rose to grow that seems to put up with the worst of conditions. It has won an RNRS Gold Medal and an RHS Award of Merit.

'**Silver Jubilee**'. Cocker, 1978. ('Highlight' × 'Colour Wonder') × ('Parkdirektor Riggers' × 'Piccadilly') × 'Mischief'. This rose, winner of the RNRS President's International Trophy and a Gold Medal was launched amidst tremendous acclaim. I had seen and helped to judge it in the RNRS trial grounds at St Albans, but had only been on the judging committee during the rose's last year of its three trial years. I had given it the highest marks, but when I grew it in my own garden nothing but disappointment ensued. The flowers were fewer and smaller than they should have been and the growth was far from strong. I wondered whether it just could not cope with the poor sandy soil one encounters over so much of Surrey, but then I compared notes with another gardener who had had it longer than I had and was reassured. 'It's a slow starter', he said, and he was right; it took two years to settle down and perform as it should and I gather that this is quite typical. It is worth a lot of patience.

The shapely flowers, of medium size (though they can with disbudding be much bigger and be used for showing) are the most lovely blend of peach-pink and a coppery creamy-pink and come with quite incredible freedom and scarely a pause between flushes. There is not a great deal of scent unfortunately, although as usual some people seem to find more than others. Although the blooms will last well in water, you will not find very many of them with long stems. This is a very bushy grower to average height, freely branching and making plenty of new shoots from the base each year. Dark, very glossy leaves are strongly red-tinted early on and are exceptionally healthy. In other words, this is pretty well the ideal bedding rose.

'Silver Lining'. Dickson, 1958. 'Karl Herbst' × 'Eden Rose'. Large, light-pink blooms with a silvery-pink petal reverse give this rose an air of elegance. They are invariably well formed and extremely fragrant and come with considerable freedom on a well-branched bush of medium height. It has dark-green, glossy leaves that are likely to need watching for black spot, although mildew is seldom a serious problem. A useful bedding rose for those who appreciate the quieter colours. It won an RNRS Gold Medal.

'Summer Holiday'. Gregory, 1969. 'Super Star' × unknown. Vermilion became the rose colour to have when 'Super Star' was at its peak and before mildew began to cause its banishment from rose growers' catalogues. In a rather deeper, brighter vermilion, one of its offspring 'Summer Holiday' might have been expected to take its place and be equally popular, for it is a healthy, bushy grower to a little above average height. It has not, however, featured in as many lists as its good qualities warrant, for it is free-flowering, its full, fragrant blooms coming mainly in small clusters and with good continuity and rain resistance. The medium-green, semi-glossy leaves are as healthy as most. There is not very much scent. It was awarded an RNRS Trial Ground Certificate.

'Sunblest' ('Landora'). Tantau, 1970. Mathias Tantau is a German hybridist who has been responsible for some remarkable roses, among them 'Super Star' and 'Fragrant Cloud', but, unlike most breeders, he does not often reveal the varieties he has used as parents. They have never been given for 'Sunblest', which is a good but quite straightforward yellow bedding rose in which the blooms are of medium size and hold their golden-yellow colour well even in strong sunlight. There is little scent but they come freely, usually several to a stem. The mid-green, semi-glossy leaves are reasonably healthy and the habit of growth upright, bushy and compact to average height.

'Sutters Gold'. Swim, 1950. 'Charlotte Armstrong' × 'Signora'. An old favourite which still features in most growers' catalogues, although it probably held its place for so long on the strength of being the only predominantly yellow, large-flowered rose to have any real fragrance. In fact, the yellow of the flowers, which come very early in the year, is strongly flushed with red and, though they are quite full and shapely at the bud stage, they open rather quickly and there is some fading. They are nevertheless good for cutting as they come on long, straight and usually thornless stems and they last quite a while in water. The long stems do, in fact, reflect the general pattern of growth, for 'Sutters Gold' is inclined to be leggy and would certainly be improved as a bedding variety if there were more of the generally healthy, dark-green, glossy leaves. It will be interesting to see whether the many new, scented yellow roses now appearing will bring about the eclipse of this fine variety, which gained an RNRS Certificate of Merit, Gold Medals in Geneva and Paris and was an All-American Rose Selection.

'Tenerife'. Bracegirdle, 1972. 'Fragrant Cloud' × 'Piccadilly'. This is a variety that was bred by an amateur and there are very few such roses that achieve any real commercial success. To do so they have to be outstanding, for they are competing with those produced by professionals who have infinitely greater resources behind them and who are in any case producing far more varieties a year themselves than the market can comfortably accommodate. 'Tenerife' is not on every nursery list, but it is on a good many, and its large and very attractive salmon-red flowers, sometimes varying to apricot-orange, and having a peachy-yellow petal reverse, have won it many friends. Growth is strong and upright to average height for a bedding rose and the leaves are mid-green and glossy. They may need watching for black spot. It was awarded an RNRS Trial Ground Certificate.

'Troika' ('Royal Dane'). Poulsen, 1972. Parentage unknown. At last in 'Troika' we have a copper-orange rose that is not a martyr to die-back, black spot and all the other rose ailments. The colour is actually quite variable and on occasion scarlet veining can be seen on the petals of the large and very shapely flowers. Wet weather holds no menace but fragrance is not strong. The medium-green, glossy leaves are singularly disease-free and the bush is strong and upright to average height or a little more. Occasional blooms can be used for showing, especially those that come early, when they are generally one to a stem. Later there will be small clusters. It has been awarded an RNRS Certificate of Merit.

'Wendy Cussons'. Gregory, 1959. The parentage is often given as 'Independence' × 'Eden Rose', which looking at a bloom of 'Wendy Cussons' does not seem an impossibility, but as the raiser himself – the late Walter Gregory – was far from certain what the parents were, it is a puzzle as to where this information came from. However, whatever roses went into the creation of 'Wendy Cussons' they combined to great effect and produced what must in all ways save one be the ideal bedding rose. The only fault that can be found – if indeed it is a fault – is in the strong, unshaded, cerise-pink colouring which can make this a difficult rose to place in relation to others, particularly red varieties. Otherwise, here is a variety which makes a bushy spreading plant, its red canes carrying an almost unending succession of beautifully shaped, high-centred, strongly scented blooms in an unprecedented variety of sizes. At their biggest they are show roses, and rain, other than the most prolonged, does not seem to bother them. The dark-green, semi-glossy leaves may need watching for mildew, but on the whole are healthy. The wide-branching habit makes this a useful rose to grow as a standard. It has won RNRS and Rome Gold Medals, been awarded an RHS Award of Merit and been a Golden Rose of The Hague.

'Whisky Mac' ('Whisky'). Tantau, 1967. Another Tantau rose of which we do not know the parentage, but whether to do so in this case would be an advantage to anybody is a little difficult to say, for this rose is a puzzle. It is one of the top sellers and constantly in demand – and what is more, re-ordered by many people – yet, it suffers badly from die-back in frosty weather and has a health record that must make it the toast of fungicide manufacturers. However, its large, amber-yellow blooms are enchanting and come with the greatest freedom. They are not particularly shapely by show-rose standards and open cupped, but the plants are scarcely ever without them and the fragrance is strong and sweet. Growth is upright to medium height and the leaves are dark-green. I could not in all honesty recommend this rose – and yet . . .

CHAPTER 13

The Polyanthas

There are not too many of the true polyantha roses worth growing in the garden today, for although they were extremely popular for something like 50 years up to the early 1930s, they had certain very pronounced weaknesses. For one thing, perhaps through their rambler-type rose ancestry, they were martyrs to mildew, and secondly, they had a great tendency to sport, which could be a nuisance in the middle of a one-colour bedding scheme. As the immediate ancestors of the modern cluster-flowered (floribunda) roses, they are important histori-cally, and up to 1934 in America and considerably later elsewhere the cluster-flowered roses were known as hybrid polyanthas.

Remarkably, it was the French breeder of the first large-flowered (HT) rose, Henri Guillot, who also launched the polyanthas. It is thought that he probably crossed the Japanese wild rose *R. polyantha* (now known as *R. multiflora*), which has a habit of growth almost akin to a rambler and carries large clusters of white flowers, with one of the China roses, to produce in 1875 a small bush carrying its blooms in trusses and which he called 'Ma Paquerette'. However, it was a later variety of 1909, 'Orleans Rose', which really put polyanthas on the map, and the infinitely better floribundas, created by crossing polyanthas with hybrid teas, the aim being to increase the flower size and improve its form, that took them off again.

Nowadays the term 'polyantha' has rather lost its original meaning and few of those roses now listed as polyanthas are the genuine article. It is used, perhaps rather indiscriminately, to cover quite a large number of low-growing bush roses that carry their small flowers in clusters and most of them have little more than a nodding acquaintance with the true polyanthas. It can, I think, be quite convincingly argued (I have done it myself) that 'Cécile Brunner' is a polyantha, but it can also be argued equally convincingly that it is a China rose (which is the heading under which it appears in this book) and the smaller China roses do have quite a lot in common with some of the polyanthas.

Of the descriptions of the roses that follow, only four are true polyanthas. I have already said that few are worth growing, but these varieties certainly are.

It could be asked, what is the difference between these and some of the larger so-called miniatures that are now being put on the market as roses suitable for patios. And it could be answered, what indeed?

Here is my selection:

'Ballerina'. Bentall, 1937. Even though the parents are un-known, there are those who will take me to task for including this among the polyanthas, although the RNRS *Rose Directory* does so as well. Traditionally it is listed as a hybrid musk, but seemingly only because it happened to come (after his death) from the nursery of the Rev. Joseph Pemberton who raised and (misleadingly) named this particular group of shrub roses. It was actually put on the market by Pemberton's foreman, who continued to run the nursery for a while, but nobody knows whether 'Ballerina' was an offshoot of his hybrid musk programme or the beginning of a completely new line. A possible answer is suggested in Chapter 15. With its huge corymbs of very small apple-blossom-pink and white single flowers and its short but spreading habit of growth (perhaps 3–4 ft (90 cm–1.2 m) each way there is a lot of the polyantha in 'Ballerina's' overall appearance. Very good continuity is a feature, together with bright-green glossy foliage. It makes a most effective standard. Pretty well scentless.

'Cameo'. Introduced by de Ruiter, 1932. Sport of 'Orleans Rose' and hence a genuine polyantha. It makes a nicely compact and bushy shrub seldom more than 1 ft 6 in (45 cm) tall. The clusters of flowers are salmon-pink. The blooms themselves are semi-double and open cupped; they are borne freely over a long period and there is a good repeat. Only a very slight fragrance detectable.

'Little White Pet' ('White Pet'). Introduced by Henderson in 1879 as a sport from the rambler 'Félicité et Perpétue', itself a sport of *R. sempervirens*. As is not uncommon with sports from once-flowering ramblers, this rose is fully recurrent and in fact blooms almost continuously. The flowers are very double and carried in tremendous profusion in both small and large clusters, literally covering the cushion-forming mound of a bush, which will be some 2 ft (60 cm) tall and the same across. They are creamy-white with sometimes the faintest pink blush, but there is little if any scent. It is good for foreground planting or lining a path, in clumps of three or four on their own in a border, or for making a most attractive and unusual standard, in which form several nurseries are now supplying it.

'Marjorie Fair' ('Red Ballerina'). Harkness, 1978. 'Ballerina' × 'Baby Faurax'. The description of 'Ballerina' fits this one like a glove, except that the flowers are carmine-red with a striking white eye.

'Nathalie Nypels' ('Mevrouw Nathalie Nypels'). Leenders, 1919. 'Orleans Rose' × ('Comtesse du Cayla' × *R. foetida bicolor*). A true polyantha even if it has a rather strange mixture of other blood. Roses with the 'Austrian Copper' as a declared parent are not all that common and 'Comtesse du Cayle' is, of course, a China. Still, there it is, and the mixture has produced something charming and very good but really quite conventional. A typical polyantha in habit, about 2 ft by 2 ft (60 cm by 60 cm) and bushy, with dark-green leaves. The clusters of flowers come with a continuity obviously due to the China rose influence. They are semi-double and open cupped, rose-pink at first but fading almost to white without losing much of their appeal. A fine scent, which gives it an edge over most low-growing cluster-flowered varieties.

'Paul Crampel'. Kersbergen, 1930. It is, even though its parentage is not known, a true and typical 1930s polyantha, mildew and all, and is included here largely for its colour, an orange-vermilion which predated that of 'Super Star' by a great many years, even if it did not have the latter rose's luminosity. There are large trusses of globular to cupped double blooms and the bush will reach about 2 ft (60 cm) in height.

'The Fairy'. Bentall, 1932. A sport from the Wichuraiana rambler 'Lady Godiva', in its turn a sport from 'Dorothy Perkins', so once again we have, as was the case with 'Little White Pet', a recurrent bush sport from a once-flowering rambler. Seldom going over 3 ft 6 in (75 cm) in height, this dimension can be exceeded in width, for 'The Fairy' is a spreader, ideal for a low hedge or for bordering a path or formal pool. Bright-green glossy leaves (not entirely proof against black spot) show up well the large trusses of soft-pink, double, globular and scentless blooms, which last well unless there is very prolonged rain, when they can turn brown and not fall cleanly. There is fair continuity throughout the summer and an autumn main flush as good as the first just after midsummer.

'Yesterday'. Harkness, 1974. ('Phyllis Bide' × 'Shepherd's Delight') × 'Ballerina'. Not by ancestry a polyantha but could be said to be one by habit as it will make a light, airy, freely branching bush not often topping 3 ft (90 cm). The flower clusters are profuse and very recurrent, the individual blooms semi-double, opening flat, and of a deep lilac-pink, paling in the centre. The scent is good. Although a modern hybrid, it could easily be mistaken for one of the older China roses and it has all their delicacy and elegance. It has been awarded an RNRS Certificate of Merit.

'Yvonne Rabier'. Turbat, 1910. *R. wichuraiana* × a polyantha. Large trusses of small, semi-double, fragrant white flowers with yellow tints at the centre of each. Vigorous to about 3 ft 6 in (107 cm), the bush has very rich green glossy leaves and it is fully recurrent.

CHAPTER 14

Cluster-flowered or Floribunda Roses

Rose breeders, being for ever curious as to what will happen if they cross this with that, soon began to cross polyantha roses with early hybrid teas, and even with some of the hybrid perpetuals, which still appeared in many nursery catalogues. The result was a number of roses that had bigger blooms than the polyanthas, which is what they were aiming for, but few of these early ones survive today. 'Gruss an Aachen' of 1908, which has clusters of quite large creamy-white very double flowers in the old rose style, is sometimes quoted as being the first of what came to be known as hybrid polyanthas, but there were in fact, earlier ones such as 'Mlle Bertha Ludi' and 'Annchen Muller'. In any case, 'Gruss an Aachen' had the hybrid perpetual 'Frau Karl Druschki' and a hybrid tea called 'Franz Deegen' as parents, so in no way could it be classed as a hybrid polyantha, even if it conformed to the polyantha pattern of growth. It is the only one of those I have mentioned that is reasonably easy to buy nowadays and is, after a number of years when it was practically forgotten, being recognised once more as a very fine bedding rose.

It was the Danish breeder, Svend Poulsen, who really put the hybrid polyanthas on the map early in this century, first with 'Red Riding Hood' in 1912 and then in 1924 he began the famous series of roses bearing the Poulsen name, starting with 'Else Poulsen'. Other notable varieties like 'Donald Prior' and 'Betty Prior' were produced in England.

A dwarf bush sport of the rambler 'Tausendschön' was named 'Echo', and this, crossed with the hybrid tea 'Rev. F. Page-Roberts' in 1934, resulted in a rose with buff flowers with an orange-carmine reverse that was called 'Rochester'. This was the first to bear the class name 'floribunda' which, because it is not botanically valid, caused the establishment a few heartaches before it was finally adopted in the United Kingdom some ten years after it had been initiated in the United States.

Le Grice in the 1940s was another important name in the

story of the floribunda – or cluster-flowered rose, as I had better begin calling it – and during that decade this Norfolk breeder launched his well-known 'Maid' series, beginning with 'Dainty Maid'. In America a little later, Eugene Boerner brought new flower forms and new colours to cluster-flowered roses with varieties like 'Masquerade', 'Fashion' and 'Spartan'. Others were crossing large-flowered roses with these new cluster-flowered ones, and the result was ever-bigger flowers with often fewer in the truss. These were sufficiently different to be given a new designation, the incredibly clumsy group name of 'flori-bunda hybrid tea-type' in Britain, while the taller of the large-flowered cluster-flowered roses (if you are still with me), which started with 'Queen Elizabeth', became 'grandifloras' in the USA and several Continental countries. So a stage was reached, and it is still with us, when it was getting progressively more difficult to tell cluster-flowered roses with big flowers from large-flowered roses with comparatively small ones. We, as members of the World Federation must do something about it, but meanwhile we have varieties like 'Sunsilk', which I have put with the cluster-flowered varieties, but could equally well have been among the large-flowered ones.

It is to be regretted that the majority of cluster-flowered varieties are scentless or nearly so. This was touched on briefly in the chapter on damask roses, and although *R. polyantha* (from which the polyanthas come) has fragrance, it seems likely that the other China rose parent did not. At any rate, the true polyanthas, as opposed to a number of the roses that I included in the polyantha chapter, were notable for their lack of scent and seem to have passed on this characteristic to most of the cluster-flowered varieties.

Apart from getting ever bigger blooms, where is the cluster-flowered rose going now? The latest development has been the production by Sam McGredy of what, with his usually astute eye for a good publicity phrase, he has chosen to call his 'hand-painted' varieties, starting with 'Picasso' in 1971. The flowers of these have a variable patterning of carmine, orange-vermilion and, in some cases, pale-pink on a silver-white background. And new colour combinations are on the way.

Here is a selection of cluster-flowered roses that I would recommend for growing:

'Allgold'. Le Grice, 1956. 'Goldilocks' × 'Elinor Le Grice'. It received an RHS award of merit and an RNRS gold medal in its year of introduction and has, ever since that time, been considered by most people to be the best yellow cluster-flowered bedding rose. It has many qualities that support this view: it is exceptionally healthy; the bright-yellow flowers do not fade in the way that practically every other yellow of the period was prone to do; continuity is first-rate, and it is a short and compact grower which is an asset in smaller gardens. Speaking for myself, though, I have always found that there is a reluctance to send up new shoots from the base, and a tendency for individual bushes to become unbalanced as not enough new wood is made after pruning. There could also be a good many more of the dark-green glossy leaves, and there have been signs in the last few years that perhaps this notable variety is at last in the decline as the foliage seems less resistant to fungus attacks than it used to be. It is still worth growing, however, at least until the lasting potential of new roses such as 'Korresia' and 'Amanda' (which see) is established. As this looks like happening, 'Allgold' is perhaps headed for an honourable retirement before too many years have passed.

'Amanda'. Bees, 1980. 'Arthur Bell' × 'Zambra'. It was awarded an RNRS Trial Ground Certificate in 1980. The large, shapely blooms are of a very deep pure-yellow and are carried on a medium to large truss. An upright grower to 2 ft 6 in (75 cm) or so that branches reasonably freely and carries mid-green, semi-glossy leaves of above-average health. This quality must certainly have come from 'Arthur Bell' and not that well-known invalid 'Zambra', but it is a pity that 'Arthur Bell' did not hand on its scent, too. However, this is a rose of great promise.

'Anna Ford'. Harkness, 1980. 'Southampton' × 'Darling Flame'. A first-rate cluster-flowered rose crossed with a first-rate miniature has produced this RNRS Gold Medal winner which is a difficult one to fit into any of the existing rose classes as it is halfway between two of them. Seldom exceeding 12–18 in (30–45 cm) in height, the bush carries small, semi-double flowers mostly in large clusters. They are of a striking deep orange-red which fades a little after a while. There are plenty of dark-green, glossy, healthy leaves on this freely-branching plant that is ideal for edging or for planting in troughs or tubs on a patio.

'Anne Cocker'. Cocker, 1971. 'Highlight' × 'Colour Wonder'. Those who remember the flowers of the 1958 Poulsen variety 'Rumba' will know what I mean when I say that the compact many-petalled rosette blooms of 'Anne Cocker' much resemble them both in form and colour. Those who do not remember 'Rumba' will not know, and must exercise their imaginations rather more. The flowers are a light-vermilion without 'Rumba's' yellow highlights, and an outstanding quality is the time they will last when cut for the house or for exhibition. Although there are quite a number of blooms in each truss, the individual flower stalks are exceptionally long. The bush is tall and upright and the possibility of mildew cannot be dismissed on the deep-green leaves. It is rather late into bloom and has little if any scent.

'Anne Harkness'. Harkness, 1980. 'Bobby Dazzler' × [('Manx Queen' × 'Prima Ballerina') × ('Chanelle' × 'Piccadilly')]. Like 'Anne Cocker', it is late into bloom, but this can be an advantage as it means that the months immediately following midsummer will be more colourful than they would otherwise have been. Not that 'Anne Harkness' is the dazzler that one of its parents might have indicated, for the double, medium-sized blooms are a very pleasing soft buff-yellow. They are borne in very large trusses on a tall, upright, but nicely branched plant, and they last exceptionally well when cut. A rose that exhibitors are welcoming enthusiastically and that was awarded an RNRS Trial Ground Certificate and, judging by its subsequent performance, might well have been of Gold Medal standard. It makes an excellent hedging rose and I have seen it standing, clean as a whistle, like a lighthouse in a sea of other mildewed varieties.

'Apricot Nectar'. Boerner, 1965. Seedling × 'Spartan'. An All-American Rose Selection, but despite the fact that the RNRS also awarded it a Certificate of Merit, the true worth of this fine rose has never been recognised in the United Kingdom. Best, if rather imprecisely, described as a pinkish, buffish apricot, the flowers are large and moderately full, carried in trusses of four or five, and they have a delicate, pleasing fragrance. The height is medium to tall and, if it is grown well, this can make a good hedging rose. Health is probably above average, but in the United Kingdom mildew appears to be more likely than it is in its country of origin.

'Arthur Bell'. McGredy, 1965. 'Cläre Grammerstorf' × 'Piccadilly'. The flowers of this rose come in medium-sized clusters, are very large, and are somewhat halfway between semi-double and double. The bright-yellow blooms with their large petals stand up to wet weather well and, in common with a good many yellow roses, are particularly good in the autumn. At that time they probably hold their colour better, for in the summer they quickly fade to a creamy-yellow. Chameleon-like, they could then be said to have become another and equally attractive rose and one still with the strong, sweet scent of the original. A tall grower, the bush branches satisfactorily and carries plenty of large, leathery and generally very healthy leaves, an attribute which no doubt helped it to gain an RNRS Certificate of Merit.

'Bonfire Night' ('Bonfire'). McGredy, 1971. 'Tiki' × 'Variety Club'. Medium to large trusses of medium-sized double flowers in a mixture of orange-scarlet and yellow make the reason for this rose's name plain. It really does light up a garden, but it must be said that a number of people find it too garish and reach for their dark glasses. It is a strong, bushy grower of average height, with dark-green, semi-glossy leaves that are as healthy as most. It has little if any fragrance.

'Bright Smile'. Dickson, 1980. 'Eurorose' × seedling. A happy name for a happy little rose, very suitable and attractive for a small bed, for patios, or for edging beds of larger varieties. A bushy grower that will not go much over 2 ft (60 cm), it carries the most enchanting flowers. They come in small to medium clusters and with good continuity, are semi-double and the brightest yellow on opening, softening slightly after a while but always maintaining the kind of freshness one associates with early primroses. The healthy, mid-green leaves cover the plant well.

'City of Belfast'. McGredy, 1968. 'Evelyn Fison' × ('Korona' × 'Circus'). An RNRS Gold Medal winner and also named as the Golden Rose of The Hague, 'City of Belfast' has gained an enviable reputation as a first-rate and very reliable and healthy bedding rose of perhaps a little below average height but making a fine, bushy plant. When young, the leaves are a striking red, maturing to a glossy mid-green. The flowers are pure scarlet, fairly full, and come in good clusters with exceptional continuity, but there is little scent. However, good as this rose is, one would be taking something of a chance in growing it in a cold climate, where die-back would almost certainly strike.

'City of Leeds'. McGredy, 1966. 'Evelyn Fison' × ('Spartan' × 'Red Favourite'). Certainly this is one of the outstanding roses of recent years and worthy of the Gold Medal the RNRS gave to it in 1965, the year before it came on the market. The salmon-pink blooms are large and carried in medium-sized trusses in great profusion, and they repeat so quickly that one can forgive this variety's single fault – some spotting after prolonged rain. Perhaps the dark-green, semi-glossy leaves could be a little larger, too, but the mass of flowers pretty well hides this deficiency. A bush of medium height which will grow practically anywhere.

'Coventry Cathedral' ('Cathedral', 'Houston'). McGredy, 1973. ('Little Darling' × 'Goldilocks') × 'Irish Mist'. Large clusters of medium sized, moderately full blooms in blends of orange-red to salmon, a pleasing combination and certainly not as strident as it may sound. A strong bushy grower to medium height, with mid-green leaves on which the possibility of black spot cannot be ruled out. There is some marking of the petals with age. An RNRS Trial Ground Certificate was given in 1971.

'Dame of Sark'. Harkness, 1976. ('Pink Parfait' × 'Masquerade') × 'Tablers' Choice'. A good rose for a large bed or for a hedge as it is a tall and quite bushy grower and almost constantly in flower. It is also very resistant to disease. The blooms are large and double and carried in medium-sized trusses on strong canes. Little scent, but fine mid-green, glossy leaves that show off well the bright orange-red blooms which have a yellow base to the petals and a yellow reverse. It has been awarded an RNRS Trial Ground Certificate.

'Dearest'. Dickson, 1960. Seedling × 'Spartan'. An RNRS Gold Medal rose that also gained an RHS Award of Merit and then went on to become the top-selling pink cluster-flowered variety of the 1960s, the 1970s and the early 1980s. It is still immensely popular, but if its star is beginning to wane a little, this may be due to an apparently increasing susceptibility to black spot and, in the eastern parts of the UK, to rust. Nevertheless it is difficult even now to name a pink rose to replace it. 'City of Leeds'? Very good, certainly, but it lacks the camelia-like charm of the flowers of 'Dearest', even if its blooms are much better able to withstand wet weather. 'Dearest' has never been rain-proof but nobody has seemed to mind, and the flowers seem quite unaffected by a damp, misty autumn. The appeal of the soft, salmon-pink is immense and there is a fine fragrance, which is, of course, a great plus in this group of roses. The leaves are plentiful, dark-green and glossy, and the bush is sturdy and compact to medium height.

'Donald Prior'. Prior, 1934. Seedling × 'D.T. Poulsen'. An old variety now, but still highly rated, particularly in the United States, where it has been a great favourite for growing in pots in greenhouses and conservatories. It is, however, equally good as a garden rose, the large, bright-crimson, semi-double blooms being carried in big, well-spaced clusters. Growth is vigorous and bushy to a little below average height. Very little scent.

'Elizabeth of Glamis' ('Irish Beauty'). McGredy, 1964. 'Spartan' × 'Highlight'. To me, with its beautiful, large, soft salmon-orange, sweetly scented blooms, shapely and high-centred at first and then opening wide, this is probably the loveliest cluster-flowered rose ever raised. An RNRS Gold Medal and an RHS Award of Merit would appear to show that I am not alone in thinking this, though neither is, of course, given for beauty alone. In my garden with its dry sandy soil that is so typical of much of the county of Surrey, 'Elizabeth of Glamis' has always thrived, making sturdy, upright plants of average height with dark-green, semi-glossy leaves which are no more prone to mildew or black spot than any other variety. It seemed to revel in the exceptionally hot dry summers of 1976 and 1983 in the UK but, and I am afraid that with this rose it is a rather large 'but', my experience of this variety is not shared by gardeners with heavier colder soils. Some nurseries even refuse to stock it as they say it does not transplant well, meaning, I suppose, that it will only transplant well to situations that suit it. In the wrong place, diseases of all sorts will strike and die-back is likely to be a problem, but I know friends that still persevere with it, even on heavy clay. They just do not want to be without it even if they have to spray for 26 hours a day.

'Escapade'. Harkness, 1967. 'Pink Parfait' × 'Baby Faurax'. A cluster-flowered rose that cannot be mistaken for any other, for its colouring is unique. The large, semi-double, fragrant flowers open wide to show the white eye in the centre of the soft rosy-lilac petals. They are carried in sizeable trusses with a good repeat. Continuing strong sunlight will cause some paling of the colours, and it is not unknown for there to be individual pure-white blooms in a cluster, though this adds to this lovely variety's novelty rather than detracting from it. The bush grows sturdily to average height, freely branching and making plenty of new wood from the base. The glossy leaves are a light bright-green. A good rose for cutting and exhibition as it lasts particularly well in water, though for showing I would avoid trusses with white flowers in them as this is an eccentricity the judges would frown on. It is worthy of its RNRS Certificate of Merit and Gold Medal at Baden-Baden.

'Europeana'. De Ruiter, 1963. 'Ruth Leuwerick' × 'Rosemary Rose'. Enormous clusters of closely packed, rosette-shaped, very double, deep-crimson blooms distinguish this rose. That and its unfortunate lax habit, for the weight of the clusters of flowers bow down the shoots that carry them, particularly after rain, when a well-grown 'Europeana' must harbour a good many pints of water. Keep it well back from the edges of paths, plant it close so that neighbouring bushes to some extent support each other, and in anything other than an exceptionally wet season it will reward you handsomely. It makes a noteworthy cut flower and time after time I have seen it win awards at shows, although not, unfortunately, for fragrance. Spray the dark, bronze-tinted leaves regularly for mildew and you will have a variety which, despite some marked weaknesses, has a good many moments of glory. How else would it have gained an RNRS Certificate of Merit, an RNRS Award of Merit, an All-American Rose Selection and a Gold Medal at The Hague?

'Evelyn Fison' ('Irish Wonder'). McGredy, 1962. 'Moulin Rouge' × 'Korona'. There have been so many bright-red cluster-flowered bedding roses produced over the last 25 to 30 years that it is by no means easy to pick the best, but on anyone's list 'Evelyn Fison' must surely come near the top. The scarlet of the blooms is generally quite unfading, although day after day of brilliant sunshine such as we had in the UK in 1983 does affect them a little. They appear to be rain-proof as well and the only thing they lack is scent. They come on medium-sized and occasionally very large and well-spaced trusses on a vigorous, bushy plant of medium height. The foliage is dark-green and very glossy, with a reputation for being extremely healthy which in my experience is not entirely justified as I have had to deal with black spot in most seasons. The leaves might perhaps be more plentiful, but this is a rose that well deserved its RNRS Gold Medal and an RHS Award of Merit, for it is still after 20 years as good as ever it was.

'Eye Paint'. McGredy, 1976. Seedling × 'Picasso'. This is one of those roses that would be equally (or possibly more) at home if it were categorised as a shrub rather than a cluster-flowered variety. It is very bushy and free-branching and will certainly reach 4 ft (1.2 m) or so in height and 3 ft (1 m) across, well

clothed with its dark-green semi-glossy leaves. The flowers
appear in great profusion in large clusters all over the bush,
each individual one small, single, and the brightest scarlet with
a white eye and white reverse to the petals. Overall they make a
most striking effect and many people on first seeing this variety
have said: '– but surely this is not a rose?' Descended from
'Picasso', I suppose 'Eye Paint' must be classed among the
'hand-painted' varieties from its Irish breeder although it does
not much resemble the others except in its proneness to attack
by the black spot fungus. If you do not mind this, try it as a
hedging rose.

'Fragrant Delight'. Wisbech Plant Co., 1978. 'Chanelle' ×
'Whisky Mac'. The colour of this rose is very difficult to do
justice to in words; 'light orange-salmon' is how the RNRS *Rose
Directory* describes it; others say coppery-salmon with yellow
shadings. I will not attempt to better these two and would only
add that if you know the two parent roses and can imagine a
colour combining the two, you will not be far out. Better still,
try to see the rose growing, for it is a singularly lovely one, and
its habit – bushy and of average height or a little above it –
makes it fine for bedding. The flowers have the classic high-
centred shape in the bud, but not having too many petals they
open more loosely. They are exceptionally fragrant. The leaves
make a good foil, bronze-tinted when young and maturing to a
glossy mid-green. It was awarded an RNRS Trial Ground
Certificate and a special medal for fragrance.

'Glenfiddich'. Cocker, 1976. 'Arthur Bell' × ('Sabine' ×
'Circus'). A rose that has a reputation for being much more at
home in its native Scotland and in the cooler northern counties
of the United Kingdom. There it is widely grown and very
popular, but when it tries to acclimatise itself to a warmer, drier
climate something seems to go missing and even the warm
amber-yellow of the flowers is paler. The blooms come in well-
spaced trusses, moderate in size and shapely in the bud.
It is moderately scented, but performance in the autumn is
particularly noteworthy and the flowers do not mind rain.
Growth is strong and bushy to medium height, and the leaves,
healthy on the whole, are dark-green and glossy.

'Grace Abounding'. Harkness, 1968. 'Pink Parfait' × 'Penelope'. Interesting parentage (not unexpected with this breeder)
in that 'Penelope' is one of the hybrid musk shrub roses, a
group recommended for their scent and presumably it was

hoped to capture some of this quality. Little fragrance here, though, which is a pity for 'Grace Abounding' looks very much the sort of rose that should have it, a very dainty, winning variety with prolific, wide-spreading trusses of semi-double, medium-sized, creamy-white blooms. The height of the bushes is about average for bedding and there is good continuity. Although not very widely grown, this variety has stayed in the more discerning nursery lists longer that I thought it would when it first came out, for it is in one of the quieter colours which, as I mentioned earlier, are supposed not to sell. Long may it continue to do so. It was awarded an RNRS Trial Ground Certificate in 1970.

'Iceberg' ('Fée des Neiges', 'Schneewittchen'). Kordes, 1958. 'Robin Hood' × 'Virgo'. What new can one say about a rose which has so often been described? Not much, but I will try. Like those in the pastel colours, white roses rarely top the best-seller lists and not, I think, solely because so many of them have behaved dismally in the rain. I never cease to be surprised at the number of people who say to me: 'I don't much like white flowers', and yet here is a white cluster-flowered rose which for something over a quarter of a century has topped the popularity charts and outsold all the others of whatever colour. Why? Well, I doubt if anybody could put their hand on their heart and say: 'This is the reason', but it can be said with a good deal of confidence that it would not have lasted at the top – nor reached it – if it had not been an outstanding rose in every way – despite its colour.

'Iceberg' is best if only lightly pruned so that it will build up over two or three years into a sizeable shrub, up to 4 ft (1.2 m) tall. Its slender and almost thornless shoots will then bear sprays, sometimes of enormous size, of white, gardenia-like flowers at all levels and not just at the top in the conventional cluster-flowered fashion. This is a very great attraction if you use the rose for a specimen planting, but it is equally effective in a large bed, for a hedge, for cutting and for the show bench, which means it lasts well in water. The leaves are glossy and mid-green and rather pointed in shape. Reports have come in in recent years that they are more likely to be affected by black spot than they used to be and I have seen some evidence of this myself. I would still buy it, though. It will be a long time yet before we are holding a memorial service to 'Iceberg'.

'Kerryman'. McGredy, 1970. 'Paddy McGredy' × ('Mme Léon Cuny' × 'Columbine'). This is not a rose that you will find in very many nursery lists, but it is well worth a try if you like to have something away from the run of the mill. The flowers are carried in large clusters and are themselves large with many petals which open wide, light-pink in the centre and a much deeper pink towards the edge. No fragrance, unfortunately, and rain resistance could be better, but a most striking variety when given a modicum of sun to bask in. The leaves are a glossy mid-green and the growth bushy and vigorous to medium height. Better watch for black spot, but this is an RNRS Certificate of Merit rose.

'Korbell' ('Anabell'). Kordes, 1972. 'Zorina' × 'Colour Wonder'. This one is near the top of many exhibitors' lists as it lasts well in water. The attractive, salmon-pink blooms are of some substance and are quite large, shapely at the bud stage, and they do have some fragrance. The bush is upright and compact to average height, with mid-green leaves. It has been awarded an RNRS Trial Ground Certificate.

'Korp' ('Prominent'). Kordes, 1970. 'Colour Wonder' × 'Zorina'. Notice the parentage, the same as 'Korbell' but with the roles of seed and pollen parent reversed, this time producing an equally good show rose and one that does exceptionally well when pot-grown in the greenhouse to produce early-in-the-year buttonhole roses to surprise your friends. The sprays are not large, often carrying no more than four or five of the very double blooms, but nevertheless they catch the eye for they are of the most vivid orange-scarlet. Growth is tall and upright and health well up to average. Little if any scent. It has been awarded an RNRS Certificate of Merit.

'Korresia' ('Fresia', 'Friesia', 'Sunsprite'). Kordes, 1974. 'Friedrich Wörlein' × 'Spanish Sun'. I mentioned 'Korresia', you may remember, when discussing a possible successor to 'Allgold' as the best yellow cluster-flowered bedding variety. Nine pages later I see no reason to revise this opinion, for here is a rose with bigger flowers than the earlier variety, shapely in the bud and holding their colour well, with good continuity and fragrance to boot. The trusses are not particularly large, but there are plenty of them on a good strong bush that will branch freely and reach average height. The mid-green leaves are plentiful and glossy and outstandingly healthy. A Gold Medal was awarded at the Baden-Baden trials to 'Korresia', and it is difficult to see how it was apparently passed over in the RNRS trials. It seems at least possible that the wrong rose was sent to St Albans.

'Lilli Marlene'. Kordes, 1959. ('Our Princess' × 'Rudolph Timm') × 'Ama'. A long-time favourite and probably still as good as any of the deep dusky-scarlet, cluster-flowered roses that came later. Growth is fairly slender and there are few thorns, but the plant does bush out quite well to medium height. The shoots are plum-red. The leaves are dark-green with bronze-red tints when young and are an attractive feature of the rose at all stages. Mildew can attack them and I have recently seen black spot on 'Lilli Marlene' for the first time, but in past years its health record has been well above average. I would hesitate to say on the evidence of this one year that the pattern in changing, but the fact that there has been a variation will be noted at the back of my mind. The blooms, which come from blackish buds and in the main in quite large clusters, are more or less rain-proof and only the hottest of sun will bleach them at the petal edges. You have to be pretty determined to detect any scent. It was awarded an RNRS Certificate of Merit, an RHS Award of Merit, and a Golden Rose of The Hague award.

'Living Fire'. Gregory, 1973. 'Super Star' × unknown. This is a variety which, though over ten years old, is only just beginning to reach the catalogues of growers other than that of its raiser. It is such a good one that this can only be explained, I think, by the fact that there was an unusually large number of roses in the same general colour range introduced at about the same time and nurseries just could not stock them all. Experience has shown that 'Living Fire' is one of the best of them, and this is beginning to be recognised. It is more than aptly named as the blooms, which come in small and medium-sized trusses, are orange-scarlet with touches of yellow. They are quite large, fully double and on the globular side. Rain resistance is good, as is recurrence. Dark-green, glossy foliage which is exceptionally healthy completes the picture of this medium to tall, upright grower. It was awarded an RNRS Certificate of Merit.

'Lovers Meeting'. Gandy, 1980. Seedling × 'Egyptian Treasure'. Unlike 'Living Fire', this rose caught on quickly. Why one did and not the other is one of those questions to which there is no answer, for there is not a vast difference between the two. The blooms of 'Lovers Meeting' are also orange-scarlet, but they do not have the yellow tints. The clusters are large, as are the individual double blooms. Growth is upright and fairly tall. A very sound rose for a large bed. It has an RNRS Certificate of Merit.

'Margaret Merril'. Harkness, 1978. ('Rudolph Timm' × 'Dedication') × 'Pascali'. A lot has been written and said about this rose being the replacement for 'Iceberg', but as I said earlier, a replacement is not needed and in any case there are so many differences that I do not think that the comparison is a valid one. True, they are both cluster-flowered and both have white flowers, but 'Margaret Merril' is a much more conventional rose in its way of growth, with sturdy upright canes carrying at the top small to medium-sized trusses of large white flowers with a touch of pearly-pink in the centre, shapely at first and then opening very wide to something like 4 in (10 cm) across and showing pink stamens. Add to this the fact that they are very sweetly scented and we certainly have the best white cluster-flowered variety since 'Iceberg', but one that complements it rather than replaces it. The bushy plant, which will reach medium height, has dark-green, glossy leaves. Black spot should be watched for. It gained at the time of introduction an RNRS Certificate of Merit, Gold Medals in Geneva and Rome, and, with incredible rapidity for a rose in a colour that nobody will confess to liking, the acclaim of the public.

'Marlena'. Kordes, 1964. 'Gertrud Westphal' × 'Lilli Marlene'. A bushy very short grower which, as it has a good covering of glossy, dark coppery-green leaves, makes it a sound choice for weed smothering, as an edging rose, or for patio planting. The plentiful double flowers are a bright crimson and are borne with the greatest freedom and a quick repeat. No scent, but a good health record. It won a Gold Medal in Belfast.

'Matangi'. McGredy, 1974. Seedling × 'Picasso'. I would say that without doubt this is the best so far of McGredy's hand-painted roses. With this variety, the orange-vermilion of the petals 'feathers' rather than merges into the silvery central eye, and the petal reverse is silvery, too. As with all this family of roses, the markings on the petals may vary considerably throughout the summer, but it is not primarily the colours, striking as they are, that to my mind make this the pick of the bunch. Its fine, dark-green, glossy leaves are relatively resistant to black spot, which is more than can be said for the others, and its only serious weakness, if indeed it can be called that for it does not affect its garden performance, is that it does not seem to take up water when cut for the house. The stems will droop within half an hour or so, but for bedding you cannot beat it, robust, bushy and of medium height and with large clusters of its striking blooms coming with excellent continuity. It has won RNRS, Belfast and Rome Gold Medals.

'Memento'. Dickson, 1978. 'Bangor' × 'Korbell'. This is one of the most prolific cluster-flowered roses of recent years, its light salmon-red blooms – or salmon-vermilion according to some – appearing in their well-spaced trusses in a non-stop stream throughout the summer months, making it an ideal rose for bedding and one with a colour that is cheerful but never garish. The plants are bushy and of medium height or a little less, well covered with mid-green, glossy leaves that are above-average in disease resistance. It did not get an award higher than an RNRS Trial Ground Certificate (though even this means that a rose has considerable merit as very few of the roses in the St Albans Trial Grounds get anything at all), but is proving in garden use, which is the ultimate test, that it might well have expected better. Some roses, like some people, develop their talents more slowly than others.

'Mountbatten'. Harkness, 1982. 'Peer Gynt' × [('Anne Cocker' × 'Arthur Bell') × 'Southampton']. Even the raiser seems a little uncertain as to whether this is a cluster-flowered variety or a shrub rose. The Harkness nursery catalogue says 'cluster-flowered', but Jack Harkness, who actually raised it, refers to it as a shrub in the RNRS *Rose Directory*. It was the British Rose Growers Association Rose of the Year in 1982, an RNRS Certificate of Merit winner, and also Rose of the Year in France, in each case classified as a cluster-flowered variety, so let us settle for that, especially as it is not particularly tall. It is a very fine rose with small clusters of very large and very double mimosa-yellow blooms which have some fragrance. They are borne on a strong-growing, bushy plant which has large, glossy leaves of outstanding health, a quality which, to my way of thinking, puts any rose – or almost any – right at the top.

'News'. Le Grice, 1968. 'Lilac Charm' × 'Tuscany Superb'. The late Edward Le Grice gained a Gold Medal from the RNRS for this rose, a reward for having had the imagination to take one of the best of the old gallica roses, 'Tuscany Superb', and to cross it with his own 'Lilac Charm'. The result was a unique colour for a modern rose, described by him as betroot-purple, which is probably as near as you can get but does not sound nearly as

114

attractive as it actually is. The flowers are large and only slightly more than semi-double, and they open flat to show golden stamens, lasting over a long period and being slightly fragrant. The leaves are matt and medium-green and about average for health, although this is a rose that can be affected by rust. It grows strongly to a little less than average height.

'Old Master'. McGredy, 1974. 'Maxi' × ['Evelyn Fison' × ('Orange Sweetheart' × 'Frühlingsmorgen')]. When McGredy's 'Priscilla Burton' came out to a tremendous fanfair, shedding Gold Medals like autumn leaves, it left the quite similar but much better 'Old Master' waiting in the wings, from which it has never really escaped. A great pity, for it is a low-growing, bushy variety with fine, dark-green, glossy leaves that have the health that those of 'Priscilla Burton' most certainly did not. The blooms, in large clusters, are themselves large and open flat, deep-carmine with a white eye and a silvery-white reverse to the petals. It is most striking.

'Pink Parfait'. Swim, 1960. 'First Love' × 'Pinocchio'. In habit of growth, this fine American variety has a lot in common with 'Iceberg', having strong though slender and almost thornless canes which branch well and carry flowers at many levels. If lightly pruned, it will reach 4 ft (1.2 m) or so and make a hedging rose or a specimen. It can, however, be easily kept to a more suitable height for bedding, and as flower production is prolific it has long been a favourite for this, at least among those who do not always demand bright colours. The blooms are shapely in the bud but open informally in the most attractive blends of pink and cream, and it is only a pity that the sweet scent that would go so well with it is completely lacking. The petals do not mind rain, however, and the medium-green, glossy leaves have a good health record, which helped this variety to an RNRS Gold Medal, an RHS Award of Merit and an All-American Rose Selection.

'Playboy'. Cocker, 1976. 'City of London' × seedling. Large clusters of very striking cupped, semi-double blooms in blends of bright-red and yellow which are very quick to repeat make this a showy rose for bedding, although it might not appeal to those who like 'Pink Parfait'. The growth is bushy, height medium and the dark-green, glossy leaves are healthy on the whole. It puts on a fine autumn display and does not seem to mind rain at any time of the year.

'Queen Elizabeth'. Lammerts, 1955. 'Charlotte Armstrong' ×
'Floradora'. Although 'Queen Elizabeth', as one of the world's
greatest roses, ended up with an RNRS Gold Medal and a Gold
Medal and a Golden Rose award at The Hague, together with
an All-American Rose Selection award, it almost missed out on
the latter. It was classed originally as a hybrid tea, but was
marked right down in the judging points as it was considered far
too tall and ungainly for the class. Fortunately, however, it was
also realised that here was a really outstanding rose that was
going to end up without the recognition that was clearly its due,
so a special class was created into which it could fit. It was thus
the first of the grandifloras and it was as one of these that it was
re-entered in the All-American trials – to come out a winner, if
a little late.

Fine as it is, 'Queen Elizabeth' can still be an awkward
customer in the garden and can easily be planted in the wrong
spot. Very tall and upright, it can top 8 ft (2.4 m), with its
flowers mainly very high up. From its growth habit, it might
well be a cross between a rose and a Lombardy poplar, but it
can be restrained to some extent and made to bush out more by
what one might call differential pruning. Some shoots can be
pruned really quite hard each year, some quite lightly, and the
rest in between the two, but even with this treatment you will
never produce a bedding rose. There are plenty of those
already, however, and 'Queen Elizabeth' is for the back of the
border, or for use as a tall hedging variety, when staggered
planting in two lines about 3 ft 6 in (105 cm) apart is advised as
it will not spread sideways much more than about 3 ft (90 cm) or
so. There will be quite a good coverage from its outstandingly
healthy, deep-green leaves low down, but as has been said, the
large, cupped, china-pink flowers will be mainly towards the
top. They stand wet weather exceptionally well and are borne
on long, thornless stems, sometimes singly but more often in
quite large clusters. The long stems make them very good for
cutting and they last a long time in water. Scarcely any scent,
though.

'Rob Roy'. Cocker, 1971. 'Evelyn Fison' × 'Wendy Cussons'.
With one of the best large-flowered and one of the best cluster-
flowered roses as parents it is not too surprising – though in rose
breeding you cannot ever be sure – that a very good rose has
resulted. What is surprising is that comparatively few people
have ever grown it and you will not find it on too many nursery
lists. Maybe this is because it is on the tall side for bedding and
it might be said that the flowers are rather widely spread in the

1. Alpine Sunset

2. Charles de Mills

3. Grandpa Dickson

4. Ulrich Brunner

5. Buff Beauty

6. Korresia

7. Just Joey

8. City of Leeds

9. Rose Gaujard

10. *R* x *harisonii* (Harison's Yellow)

11. Playboy

12. Fragrant Delight

trusses, but it will do very well for a large bed and makes a fine hedging rose or one for growing in a clump of three or four in a mixed border. Although the blooms may be a little widely spaced, there are always plenty of them in evidence, immaculately shaped and pretty well weather-proof and in the purest bright-crimson. The dark-green, glossy leaves set them off well and are above-average in health. There are few thorns on the strong, branching canes. It has an RNRS Trial Ground Certificate.

'Scented Air'. Dickson, 1963. 'Spartan' seedling × 'Queen Elizabeth'. This rose has been included largely on the strength of its strong fruity fragrance, for otherwise it is a good if not outstanding variety (although it won an RNRS Certificate of Merit) with prolific deep salmon-pink flowers, shapely early on but opening informally. There are dark-green, glossy leaves on a bushy plant of average height and of average resistance to disease.

'Southampton' ('Susan Ann'). Harkness, 1972. ('Ann Elizabeth' × 'Allgold') × 'Yellow Cushion'. This is a rose that could be said to have set a standard at which others should aim – a robust and upright grower, branching well, quite exceptionally healthy dark-green, semi-glossy leaves, and flowers carried in a mixture of small and quite large trusses that open more or less continuously one after the other right through the summer. The blooms themselves are an eyecatching apricot-orange, flushed scarlet, are double, and have attractively waved petals. Height is a bit above average, making 'Southampton' a rose for a big bed or for hedging. Faults? One. Only moderate scent. It has an RNRS Trial Ground Certificate.

'Stargazer'. Harkness, 1977. 'Marlena' × 'Kim'. Few people like single roses, although why this should be, goodness knows. Here is one, however, that does seem to be overcoming the prejudice to some extent, a real little charmer that will make a cushion of growth not more than 18 in (45 cm) tall, studded with clusters of blooms in orange-scarlet with a yellow eye. They seem to be looking at you, even after the scarlet changes to carmine after a few days. An ideal rose for a trough or tub or for the front of a shrub border. The mid-green foliage is matt and has a good health record on the whole. It has won an RNRS Certificate of Merit.

117

'Stephen Langdon'. Sanday, 1969. 'Karl Herbst' × 'Sarabande'. An absolutely first-rate rose but a strangely neglected one. It gained an RNRS Certificate of Merit and deserved it as it is a robust and vigorous grower with large, dark-green leaves which are very resistant to disease. The flowers appear a little later than most (at about the same time as those of 'Peace') and are of a very pure and glowing deep-scarlet. They are large with big petals, so that the fact that there are seldom more than five or six to a truss is scarcely noticed. Shapely at first, they later open wide with attractively waved petals. Growth is upright to medium height.

'Sue Lawley' ('Kobold'). McGredy, 1980. [('Little Darling' × 'Goldilocks') × {('Evelyn Fison' × ('Coryana' × 'Tantau's Triumph')) × ('John Church' × 'Elizabeth of Glamis')}] × ['Evelyn Fison' × ('Orange Sweetheart' × 'Frühlingsmorgen')]. It would be more than disappointing if something with that sort of pedigree was not rather special, and with this, another of his 'hand-painted' roses, Sam McGredy does seem to have lived up to our expectations. The large double blooms, which open wide, have been aptly described in the RNRS *Rose Directory* as having a dramatic pattern in soft carmine-pink (which pales a little in the sun) and blush-white. They are certainly most striking and pleasing and, with the exception of the same raiser's 'Regensburg', a much more dwarf grower, are perhaps the most refined so far in this line of development. They will make a most attractive bed and will blend with anything. Growth is satisfactorily bushy, height medium, scent only slight, and the health of the mid-green leaves up to average, although do not discount the possibility of black spot. It has an RNRS Certificate of Merit.

'Sunsilk'. Fryer, 1974. 'Pink Parfait' × 'Redgold' seedling. If you cannot find this rose in a nursery catalogue under cluster-flowered (floribunda) roses, look under large-flowered (hybrid teas) as this is one of those in-between varieties that make classification so difficult. The flowers are large and of good form early on, at times coming one to a stem, and if these are not attribututes of a large-flowered rose, I do not know what are. On the other hand, more often than not there are small trusses, the blooms in a very pleasing soft yellow. The plants are seldom out of flower throughout the summer and the autumn performance is outstanding. The bush is well branched and will reach medium height. Health should not be much of a problem except in areas where rose rust is prevalent. It has an RNRS Trial

Ground Certificate and a Belfast Gold Medal.

'Topsi'. Tantau, 1972. 'Fragrant Cloud' × 'Fire Signal'. Startling is perhaps the most apt, if not the most original, word for the colour of 'Topsi', a rose in the brightest orange-scarlet. A very low grower, it comes in the category of roses for patios, and was one of the first of the current trend for dwarfs, which makes it suitable for tub and trough cultivation and for lining paths and drives. Or for that matter, for a small bed, because its continuity makes it a fine bedding rose. The blooms are semi-double and carried in medium-sized trusses on the short main shoots. The leaves are medium-green and semi-glossy and despite the fact that 'Topsi' won an RNRS Gold Medal, black spot can be a problem on them, as can die-back in any but the mildest winter.

'Trumpeter'. McGredy, 1978. 'Satchmo' × seedling. Like 'Topsi', a compact, low-growing rose, the rather globular double flowers of which have been variously described as orange-red or bright-vermilion, at which point it might be worth remarking that when I give, as I have done already several times, two or even three different descriptions of a flower's colour, this is solely because so many of them are impossible to define precisely, and not because I cannot see them in my mind's eye. With 'Trumpeter' you could toss a coin to decide between the two colours I have given – and might end up with a third variation – but whatever their precise colour, the flowers come in very large trusses for so small a plant and even the short and apparently sturdy main canes may be bowed down by the weight of wet blooms after rain. However, that seems to be 'Trumpeter's' one weakness and a not too serious one. Otherwise, it is a sound low-growing variety, its dark-green glossy leaves rating well in the disease-resistance tables. Not much scent, but it has an RNRS Trial Ground Certificate.

'Warrior'. Le Grice, 1978. 'City of Belfast' × 'Ronde Endia-blée'. If you cannot get 'Trumpeter', try 'Warrior', and, of course, the reverse applies unless you want both. They were introduced in the same year and in many ways are rather similar. However, 'Warrior's' flower trusses are smaller and the leaves distinctive, a much lighter green and semi-glossy. Perhaps the red of the double blooms is purer, too, and has less orange in it, but the height of the plant and hence its uses is the same. So, too, is the good health. This is also an RNRS Trial Ground Certificate rose.

CHAPTER 15

Modern Shrub Roses

I have used the heading 'Modern Shrub Roses' for this chapter, and it will be recalled from discussions of the new classification that all of them have been introduced since the last part of the nineteenth century. Not that a period of time common to them all helps in the least if one is looking for a factor that will fit them into a nice, homogeneous group. They do not fit and never will, for they are as diverse as they possibly could be. While in the previous chapters it was possible to make some valid generalisations that would apply to all the varieties in one or other of the groups, here it cannot be done.

Some of the shrub roses are simply extra-large cluster-flowered (floribunda) varieties. 'Chinatown', 'Dorothy Wheatcroft' and 'Fred Loads' are examples of this. Some like 'Frühlingsgold' and 'Frühlingsmorgen', or 'Scarlet Fire' or 'Golden Wings' resemble wild roses very closely and are often only one or two generations removed from them. Others like 'Constance Spry' have an old garden rose in their parentage and take after the old rather than the new. And the term 'modern shrub roses' now embraces all the members of one group and virtually all of another that were traditionally (if not entirely logically) always grouped with the old roses. I am referring to the hybrid musks and the rugosas. The latter must now quite certainly have two classifications. *R. rugosa* itself, the original wild or species rose from China and Japan, goes back into the mists of time, but it makes a gaunt and unsatisfactory garden plant and is only used as an understock for standard roses. It must clearly be included with the other wild roses, but from it have been produced some quite wonderful garden hybrids. Since all of them, 'Roseraie de l'Hay', 'Blanc Double de Coubert', 'Pink Grootendorst', 'Fru Dagmar Hastrup' and the rest, were raised just before and just after the turn of the century, they are modern shrub roses and not old garden ones. Also fitting into the category of modern shrub roses are the

equally popular roses like 'Frühlingsgold' as a modern hybrid of
R. pimpinellifolia (*R. spinosissima*) and 'Fritz Nobis' as a
modern hybrid of *R. rubiginosa* (*R. eglanteria*).

There has never been any sensible reason for treating the
hybrid musks as being anything other than quite modern. The
only possible explanation for their grouping with older families
would seem to be that to many people, all shrub roses are old.
Actually the hybrid musks are a group created by a clergyman-
cum-rose breeder, the Rev. Joseph Pemberton, early in this
century, and they range from 'Danae' and 'Moonlight' of 1913
up to 'Felicia' of 1928, discounting the few roses such as
'Ballerina' put out from Pemberton's nursery after his death,
the parentage of which is always said to be unknown. Having
recently seen Peter Lambert's 'Mozart' of the same date, and
knowing that it was Lambert's 'Trier' that Pemberton used to
launch his breeding programme, I would be prepared to bet
that 'Ballerina' is a sport from it. I had heard of the likeness
before, but never actually seen 'Mozart' until I made a recent
trip to Germany.

However, that is rather by the way, and the relationship of
Pemberton's musk roses to the true musk rose is very tenuous,
making use of a link many generations back with the noisettes,
which derived from a musk–China cross. There have been
attempts to add other roses to them since Pemberton's time –
crimson-scarlet 'Hamburg', crimson 'Wilhelm' and its sport
'Will Scarlet', and cherry-red 'Bonn' among others, but despite
having the odd common ancestor, these are so completely
different in habit, flower form and colour, and not least in their
lack of scent, that they really do not seem to belong at all. They
are much closer to large cluster-flowered varieties in the way
they grow, but, on the other hand, a rose like 'Buff Beauty',
which seems to have been created by immaculate conception as
recently as 1939, very definitely does belong and might well
have been a Pemberton variety. It could have been one that he
discarded but which someone else recognised as having possibilities and took over. Nobody knows.

The uses to which all these various shrub roses can be put will
mostly be covered when we come to the variety descriptions if a
simple statement of the habit of growth does not make it self-
evident. As far as pruning is concerned, they should be dealt
with in the same way as the type of rose they most resemble.
Those resembling wild roses should be left alone except for the
removal of dead wood; those resembling large cluster-flowered
types should be pruned as if they were normal sized ones;
hybrid musks need controlling more than pruning as they can be

very irregular in growth and can become badly out of balance if left too long.

The rugosas, luckily in view of their fiendish thorns and prickles, need little regular attention, but if they should get leggy after a time, and the less dense growers such as 'Blanc Double de Coubert' and 'Pink Grootendorst' may well do so, hard cutting back or even the complete removal of one or two main canes each year over a three or four year period will rejuvenate them completely and encourage growth low down. With rugosas used to make a hedge, clipping over with shears in winter to neaten them up will do no harm, as long as the natural outline is followed closely and no attempt is made to square them off like a box or beech hedge. Apart from drastically reducing their flowering, they would be robbed of their informal charm, which is what most people grow them for in the first place.

So now for the descriptions of some of the best of the modern shrub roses. All are recurrent unless stated otherwise.

'Angelina'. Cocker, 1975. ('Super Star' × 'Carina') × ('Cläre Grammerstorf' × 'Frülingsmorgen'). I do not know anyone who has seen this rose who is not enchanted with it, and yet it is only stocked so far by a very limited number of nurseries. It is the ideal shrub rose for the small garden (which does not, of course, mean that it is not equally suitable for a large one) in that it makes a dense, rounded bush not more than 4 ft (1.2 m) high with healthy light-green leaves and a profusion of quite large semi-double flowers in light carmine-pink with a white eye and golden stamens that open, and remain, cupped. Perhaps, as I may have had occasion to remark before, it is its brazenness in showing its stamens that offends the more delicately nurtured customers – I was about to say nurserymen until I thought of some of them I knew – for people just do not like seeing them. To me it is a charmer with first-rate continuity.

'Blanc Double de Coubert'. Cochet-Cochet, 1892. Parentage given as *R. rugosa* × 'Sombreuil' or possibly as a sport from *R. rugosa alba*. Pure-white, semi-double, sweetly scented flowers appearing in a nearly endless stream throughout the summer (all rugosas are recurrent, most outstandingly so) have kept this rose popular for almost a century, but in many ways it could not be said to be among the best of the group. The delicate, paper-thin petals simply react like tissue to rain, although against this is the fact that there always seem to be more flowers ready to take the place of those that are spoiled. The bush, which will

122

reach 5–6 ft (1.5–1.8 m), can become rather bare at the base, as I mentioned a little earlier, which means that it is not one of the best rugosas for hedging. The bright-green leaves, typically wrinkled – or rugose – are, as is usual with the family, pretty well disease-proof, but in the case of this particular variety there could, perhaps, be rather more of them.

'Buff Beauty'. As has been said already, the origin of this rose is wrapped in mystery, but the resemblance to the Pemberton hybrid musks is so strong that it is classed as one. Like them, it carries large clusters of fragrant double blooms – in this case coloured a buff-orange – which are shapely early on but open loosely. Often I have seen 'Buff Beauty' recommended for hedges, along with all the other hybrid musks. Well, this is one which, for whatever purposes it is used, must be given something to lean on. It is a real sprawler, not because the shoots are especially thin or lax, but because they seem to grow out sideways as often as they do upwards. In full flush they can be weighed down by the sheer mass of flowers, so for a hedge this rose really must be properly trained on wires. Mildew in late summer is a distinct possibility on the dark-green foliage, which has an attractive reddish-purple tinge when young.

'Cerise Bouquet'. Kordes, 1958. *R. multibracteata* × 'Crimson Glory'. The fine scent of this rose is a fitting tribute to the memory of 'Crimson Glory' which must now, except perhaps as a climber, be regarded as a rose of the past. The sheer rampant vigour of 'Cerise Bouquet' does, however, come from the other side of the family and it will easily top 6 ft (1.8 m) in height, its long, rambling, arching canes reaching out even further than this all round. All along them, although only for a number of weeks at midsummer, there will be a profusion of quite large, loosely-formed, cherry-red double blooms. The leaves are on the small side, grey-green and not very susceptible to black spot or mildew, and leafy bracts surround the flowers. This is a rose that can be used as a short climber on a pillar or low wall as well as grown as a shrub, but you may, regrettably, have to scour a number of nursery lists before you find one that stocks it. Persevere; you will not be sorry.

'Chinatown' ('Ville de Chine'). Poulsen, 1963. 'Columbine' × 'Cläre Grammerstorf'. Shrub roses do not often win Gold Medals from the RNRS or from anyone else, a reflection, I suppose, of their comparative lack of popularity among the discerning, which means that up to the present time not too many of them have been in contention in trials. 'Chinatown' did win an RNRS Gold, and there are probably those who will say that it did so because it is really only a very tall cluster-flowered variety and not a shrub. But that would be doing both 'Chinatown' and the trials judges a gross injustice, for it is a first-rate rose in whatever category you choose to put it. Very robust and upstanding to about 4 ft (1.2 m), it has the most handsome light-green glossy leaves that I have always found to be healthy, although black spot has been reported by others. The long strong canes are crowned with medium-sized clusters of six or seven very large and seemingly rain-proof double yellow blooms, not unlike smaller but more strongly-coloured versions of the flowers of 'Peace'. The latter is practically scentless, whereas 'Chinatown' has the sweetest fragrance. It is a very fine hedging rose as it has a good leaf coverage all the way down. You should be prepared for a brief pause between flushes of bloom with this one.

'Constance Spry'. Austin, 1961. 'Belle Isis' × 'Dainty Maid'. 'Belle Isis' as the seed parent of this rose makes it a modern gallica hybrid, but one would not think so to look at it. About the only thing it has in common with the older group is that it is only in bloom at midsummer, but if it had been descended from the very vigorous bourbon roses, one would have been less surprised. For it makes a lusty if rather lax shrub up to 6 ft (1.8 m) tall and probably rather more across. The flowers are about 5 in (13 cm) in diameter, which is pretty large, with big petals which give them a resemblance to paeonies. They are rose-pink and I have frequently seen them described as very fragrant. My own description of the scent would have been 'slight' and while I am prepared to be convinced – in fact, I would be delighted to be – it has not happened yet. In any case, scent or not, 'Constance Spry' gained an Award of Merit from the RHS and richly deserves it, for apart from just being beautiful, it is one of those versatile roses which will make a very good short climber as well as an informal shrub. Dark, healthy leaves.

'Cornelia'. Pemberton, 1925. This is the first of the hybrid musks in our list that can be reliably credited to Pemberton, and it is one of his best. It carries, over a very long season, large trusses of quite small, double, almost pompon-style flowers in strawberry-pink with perhaps a touch of apricot. They are fragrant and appear against dark-green leaves on a wide-spreading bush that will probably reach 5 ft (1.5 m) or so in height. The autumn show of colour will be particularly fine if

13. Baby Masquerade

14. Margaret Merril

15. Golden Wings

16. Sue Lawley

17. Swan Lake

18. Silver Jubilee

19. Peace

20. Complicata

some dead-heading is carried out, although there is a chance that the late flowers may be accompanied by mildew, so you should spray them, too. A good rose for a hedge provided that you can cope with its width – which I have not given as it will vary so much. However, you would certainly have to allow for 5 ft (1.5 m).

'Dorothy Wheatcroft'. Tantau, 1960. As so often with this raiser the percentage is not given. It should be said that this is a rose that would not fit every garden. This is not because of its overall size but because it is inclined to be gaunt in habit, with long, strong and almost leafless stems which need to be hidden by something else and because it is a startling orange-red with a touch of scarlet which may be difficult to blend with other colours. That said, it is a tough, vigorous rose with qualities than won it an RNRS Gold Medal, and if its legs are camouflaged, it does make the most impressive display, with huge trusses of closely-packed, not quite fully double blooms, which hold their colour and resist rain well. These will be 4–5 ft (1.2–1.5 m) above the ground and have little scent. The leaves are mid-green and may need watching for black spot. As already indicated, they come mostly quite high up the plant. This is a rose much favoured by exhibitors because of its huge and shapely clusters.

'Fountain' ('Fontaine'). Tantau, 1970. Parents not given. A tall, upright grower to 5 ft (1.5 m) or so, with long, strong canes that are well clothed in handsome dark-green leaves, which when young are red-tinted and which are healthy at all times. The flowers are a bright, velvety crimson of great purity and have a pleasing though not particularly strong scent. They are large and shapely in the bud, coming sometimes singly and some-times in fairly large clusters, but since they do not have too many petals they open quite loosely. This is yet another outstanding shrub that deserves to be better known and it has been awarded an RNRS Gold Medal.

'Fred Loads'. Holmes, 1967. 'Orange Sensation' × 'Dorothy Wheatcroft'. An RNRS Gold Medal for this one, one of the very best of modern shrub roses and one raised by an amateur – the man who more recently was responsible for 'Sally Holmes' (which see) as well. 'Fred Loads' is a very tall grower, difficult to keep below 6 ft (1.8 m), its long, strong canes going quite a way beyond this if allowed to. However, they are reasonably well branched and there are plenty of the semi-glossy, bright-green leaves lower down, which resist mildew and black spot better than most. The trusses of quite large, semi-double flowers are truly enormous: they are 18 in (45 cm) or more across and I cannot think of any other rose that will produce bigger ones. They can even make the bushes look a little top heavy at times. The colour is a soft orange-vermilion and there is a good fragrance.

'Fred Loads' may need (and can take) some pretty hard pruning to keep it to a manageable size in a small garden. It is a great favourite with exhibitors, not only because of the size and attractive colours of the trusses, but because of their excellent keeping qualities when cut. Rain will not spoil them either.

'Fritz Nobis'. Kordes, 1940. 'Joanna Hill' × 'Magnifica'. The second parent here is closely related to the Penzance briers and hence to the sweet brier, *R. rubiginosa*, so despite the fact that 'Joanna Hill' is a large-flowered (HT) variety, there is much more of the wild rose about this one, particularly in the way its arching canes range far and wide and in the fact that it is not recurrent. But though it is wide-spreading it makes a reasonably dense and bushy shrub, 4 ft (1.2 m) high and a good deal more across. The semi-glossy leaves are plentiful and a lightish green and I have never experienced health problems with them. The flowers, which appear over five to six weeks, come in medium-sized and small clusters, very shapely at first like small HT blooms and then opening out with waved petals. The colour is a light salmon-pink, and the whole effect of this rose is one of great elegance.

'Frühlingsgold' ('Spring Gold'). Kordes, 1937. 'Joanna Hill' × *R. pimpinellifolia hispida*. This is one of the modern hybrids I cited earlier as closely resembling a wild rose or species, but a hybrid of what? 'Of *R. spinosissima hispida*' one would have said with great confidence until very recently, but one of those maddening botanical conjuring tricks has happened and things are no longer what they seemed. See the latest edition of Bean, *Trees and Shrubs Hardy in the British Isles*, if you want to know how the trick was done; it takes 37 lines of small print to explain it, but 'Frühlingsgold' is now a hybrid of *R. pimpinellifolia hispida*. That's life, I suppose, and we gardeners are nothing if not philosophers, but meanwhile 'Frühlingsgold' has carried on quite unperturbed as if nothing had happened, continuing to be a perfectly wonderful (though only spring-flowering) and very large shrub rose. It will send up long, arching shoots to fully 2 ft (2.1 m), each one laden in early summer along its whole length and on numerous side shoots with very large, semi-double, fragrant, soft primrose-yellow blooms which open from long, pointed yellow buds. The light-green leaves are fairly long and pointed, too, and, being reasonably healthy, keep the shrub attractive after the flowers have gone. It has gained an RHS Award of Merit, Award of Garden Merit and First Class Certificate.

'Frühlingsmorgen' ('Spring Morning'). Kordes, 1941. ('E.G. Hill' × 'Cathrine Kordes') × *R. pimpinellifolia altaica*. Another experiment by Wilhelm Kordes in making a cross between one of the Scotch roses and a large-flowered variety. This time he produced a rather smaller and more bushy plant than 'Frühlingsgold', and one that has quite different leaves, small, rather rounded and a dark grey-green. It is the scented single flowers that are its particular glory, however, for the pink at the outside of the petals melts gradually and enchantingly towards the flower centre into a pale primrose-yellow, set off by a boss of maroon stamens. I have in the past said that this is the most beautiful flower of all, but as always with a statement like that a small voice somewhere whispers: 'What about so and so?' and usually one has to retract. It is a pretty silly exercise trying to name the most beautiful, anyway, and I have given it up. 'Frühlingsmorgen' does usually produce some late blooms, but you cannot always put your money on it happening. It has gained an RHS Award of Merit.

'Golden Wings'. Shepherd, 1956. 'Soeur Thérèse' × (*R. pimpinellifolia altaica* × 'Ormiston Roy'). And here is a rose that might well have been the 'so and so' referred to above, another Scotch rose derivative with what might be termed a double Scotch on one side of the family. It is one that carries on flowering right through the summer and on into the autumn, producing cluster after cluster of large, single, light-yellow flowers with amber stamens and a sweet fragrance. Weather (bad weather, that is) does not worry them. The bush is a 5 ft by 5 ft (1.5 m by 1.5 m) one and never too rampant for a small garden. Hips form quite freely, but as they never become decorative it is probably as well to remove them to help continuity of bloom. The leaves, which I have never had to spray, are a matt light-green and semi-glossy. It has gained an RHS Award of Merit.

'Kathleen Ferrier'. Buisman, 1955. 'Gartenstolz' × 'Shot Silk'. A rose of the larger-than-life cluster-flowered type, sometimes

127

likened to less vigorous, salmon-pink 'Fred Loads' (which see). While not going all the way with that comparison, I agree that there are some resemblances, notably the large trusses of semi-double 2½ in (7 cm) flowers that open out flat and have a delicate fragrance. Growth is upright but with a reasonable spread, and the leaves are dark-green and glossy. Plant this one in groups of three for maximum effect. It has an RNRS Trial Ground Certificate.

'Lavender Lassie'. Kordes, 1959. 'Hamburg' × 'Mme Norbert Levasseur'. Several times recently I have seen this catalogued as a hybrid musk, and I wish to submit with due respect that it is nothing of the kind, even though 'Eva', a hybrid musk, was in the parentage of 'Hamburg'. It bears not the slightest resemblance to any other members of that group and has not even got much scent. And as to being a cluster-flowered rose, which I have also seen it described as, I would say that it is its own very individual self and nothing else. Each of the long, strong canes bears a huge cluster of large, many-petalled, pompon-style flowers up to a height of about 4 ft (1.2 m), but such is the weight of these blooms, that strong as the shoots are, they do need something to help them to keep upright. Considering how many petals the flowers have, they are surprisingly good in the rain. They are a soft-pink with, as far as I can see, not a trace of lavender in it. In hot sun they fade quite markedly to a much paler but still pleasing pink. The leaves are a light bright-green and very glossy. Disease resistance is good.

'Marguerite Hilling' ('Pink Nevada'). Hilling, 1959. A sport from 'Nevada' (which see). A very large, bushy, arching shrub, probably 6 ft by 7–8 ft (1.8 m by 2.1–2.4 m) eventually, which at its peak in early summer will vanish beneath the mass of pink flowers that bedeck and actually overlap on each shoot along its entire length. Each bloom is semi-double with scalloped petals, the pink paling towards the flower centre, where it becomes yellow-tinted behind the golden stamens. There will be a second show of bloom later but this is rather unpredictable and will never be as incredibly profuse as the first. The scent is sweet but not strong, and the leaves small with the leaflets noticeably rounded, a matt-green, and not proof against black spot. Mildew will seldom be troublesome.

'Moonlight'. Pemberton, 1913. 'Trier' × 'Sulphurea'. This rose gained an RNRS Gold Medal as long ago as 1913 and has been going strong in a retiring sort of way with discerning growers ever since, although it must be said that it has never been among the most popular of the hybrid musks. Its small, creamy-white fragrant blooms open flat to show their golden stamens (which may be why it is not particularly popular) and come in enormous trusses on a tall, branching bush of rather unpredictable habit. It will, if it feels so inclined, even make a good climber of modest height, but it is more often grown as a wayward shrub which has the most beautiful dark-green, bronze-tinted glossy leaves as well as lovely flowers.

'Nevada'. Dot, 1927. Possibly the offspring of a hybrid tea called 'La Giralda' and *R. moyesii fargesii*, but nobody knows for certain. Whatever the parents were, however, they have produced what must in anybody's book be counted as one of the finest shrub roses ever. Just about all I have said about 'Marguerite Hilling' applies to 'Nevada', except that 'Nevada's' flowers are a creamy-white with sometimes, after a prolonged hot spell, quite marked pink flushes. It has been awarded an RHS Award of Merit and First Class Certificate.

'Pearl Drift'. Le Grice, 1980. 'Mermaid' × 'New Dawn'. This RNRS Certificate of Merit rose is a newcomer which has yet to establish itself. Any new shrub rose is always up against the built-in-belief of so many people that it will automatically be too big for any garden they are likely to own. It is a fact that many nurserymen would rather call a new rose anything other than a shrub rose, but this one really could not have been described as anything else. It is of particular interest because its seed parent, the climber 'Mermaid', was always supposed to be sterile. Clearly it is not, although it may be nearly so, and this rare offspring turns out to be a short-growing but very wide-spreading bushy shrub which bears large clusters of medium-sized double, blush-pink, scented flowers. The light-green, glossy leaves have so far proved to be very healthy. Some people, although not me, would call this one of the new ground-cover roses. It is not by any stretch of the imagination dense enough for that, but it will cover a lot of ground and so is economic to use.

'Penelope'. Pemberton, 1924. Probably a cross of 'Ophelia' with an unknown seedling or with 'Trier', this was the second rose to gain an RNRS Gold Medal for Joseph Pemberton, in 1925, and it has remained his most popular variety ever since. The first flowering in early summer is truly spectacular, the whole of the 6 ft by 7 ft (1.8 by 2.1 m) bush being hidden under a fragrant mass of semi-double blooms in blends of peach-pink and cream. Provided that a certain amount of dead-heading is carried out, there will be spasmodic blooming throughout the rest of the summer and a second, lesser flush in autumn. It is then that you may be startled by the size of one or two enormous flower trusses that may appear, each bearing up to 100 blooms.

This is a good hedging rose and can be kept to manageable proportions by training it as described in Chapter 1 (under 'Hedges') along horizontal wires. Watch the leaves of 'Penelope' for mildew late in the season. They are an attractive semi-glossy dark-green with, early on, a narrow deep-red edging.

'Pink Grootendorst'. Grootendorst, 1923. A sport from 'F.J. Grootendorst' which is very similar except that its flowers are bright-red. With this one, on the other hand, they are a bright-pink, small, but carried in large clusters, each individual bloom like a miniature carnation because of the fringed edges to the petals. Despite the fact that this is a rugosa hybrid, they have no scent, but there is the group's customary wrinkled foliage, in this instance perhaps marginally less healthy than usual. It makes a tall, spreading, very spiny bush, 6 ft (1.8 m) tall by about as much across. It is likely in time to get a little leggy and is by no means as dense a grower as, for instance, 'Roseraie de l'Hay'. Occasional hard pruning of some of the main shoots will encourage it to bush out.

'Prosperity'. Pemberton, 1919. 'Marie Jeanne' × 'Perle des Jardins'. It has fragrant creamy-white (fading to white), many-petalled, pompon-style flowers in substantial trusses and perhaps the strongest scent of all the hybrid musks. Probably the most reliably recurrent, too, a statement that may puzzle those brought up in the largely erroneous belief that all hybrid musks are submerged under a sea of blossom from late spring to autumn. They are good, but not that good. 'Prosperity' will make a fine flowering hedge about 5 ft (1.5 m) tall, but watch for mildew in the autumn.

'Raubritter'. Kordes, 1936. 'Daisy Hill' × 'Solarium'. One of the small band of roses cited over the years as being suitable for ground-cover, which has meant in effect that it is a variety that keeps to about 3 ft (90 cm) in height but which will send out long, flexible canes until it covers perhaps 6 ft (1.8 m) of ground. Whether the leaf coverage will be dense enough to smother weeds will be largely a matter of luck, but it is the ideal rose to have cascading over a low wall, one perhaps that

130

surrounds a sunken garden, or to allow to ramble at will down a bank. At midsummer – but not afterwards – it will be covered with small, goblet-shaped, semi-double pink flowers, which have a long period when they are at their peak. The main drawback to this otherwise most attractive variety is that it will almost certainly need protection against mildew on its dark, leathery leaves.

'Robusta'. Kordes, 1974. *R. rugosa* × a seedling. An RNRS Certificate of Merit was awarded to this fine new rose in 1980, and although its breeder puts it squarely among the rugosas, nothing less like a typical rugosa hybrid can be imagined. It is usually the rugosa leaves that give things away – if nothing else does – but here they are dark-green and smooth and glossy and without the usual rugosa immunity to black spot – which is not to say that they are unduly likely to be affected by it, either. It is a shrub that will grow to only medium height, which means 4 ft (1.2 m) or so, but it will send up plenty of new growth from the base each year. The flowers are large and single and of a scarlet that really glows. They come in quite large trusses and continuity is good. If there is a slight drawback, it is that a number of the flowers tend to be hidden by the foliage. And there is little scent.

'Roseraie de l'Hay'. Cochet-Cochet, 1902. A *R. rugosa rosea* sport – it is thought, although it seems a little unlikely. But anyway, I would place this as the finest of all the rugosas which, apart from the flowers which we will come to, has the most marvellous bright-green leaves that cover it right to the ground (it is about 6 ft (1.8 m) tall) and which have never even heard of black spot or mildew. Even the greenfly appear to keep clear of the young shoots.

For a hedge, and this is a rose that is ideal for one, a width of 4 ft (1.2 m) will have to be allowed – so do allow it. Then you will be rewarded with a non-stop show of large, sweetly fragrant, wine-red double flowers, which when open show creamy stamens. They are borne in small clusters and there are two main flushes and plenty of blooms in between. No hips follow as these only form on the rugosas with single or semi-double flowers. Apart from the fact that the shoots are quite villainously spikey and so best kept well away from, do not bother with cutting flowers for the house as they will scarcely last more than an hour or two. This is not untypical of the rugosas, except perhaps for 'Sarah Van Fleet' and the Grootendorst hybrids.

'Sally Holmes'. Holmes, 1976. 'Ivory Fashion' × 'Ballerina'. It is probably unprecedented for any selection of about 30 of the finest roses in any one class to contain two varieties raised by an amateur, but that they should both have been produced by the same amateur really is something. Neither 'Fred Loads' nor 'Sally Holmes' could sensibly be omitted from such a list. This rose is certainly easier to accommodate than 'Fred Loads' as it does not grow so tall: it makes a wide, bushy shrub of perhaps 5 ft (1.5 m) with singularly beautiful dark-green leaves. Against these, the clusters of $3^1\!2$ in (9 cm) single, delicately scented, soft-pink flowers show up particularly well. They fade almost to white after a while but are still pleasing, and the recurrence is first-rate.

'Sarah Van Fleet'. Van Fleet, 1926. A rugosa hybrid without doubt, but its exact parentage is uncertain. It is one of the earliest roses of all into flower, its large, double blooms in wild-rose pink opening cupped and having a fine fragrance and a good repeat. The leaves are typical rugosa, wrinkled and healthy, and like those of the other rugosas, they turn yellow in the autumn before they fall. The shrub will reach 6 ft (1.8 m), keeping reasonably upright but spreading to 4 ft (1.2 m) or so. A very good rose for a hedge.

'Scabrosa' (*R. rugosa* 'Scabrosa'). Introduced by the Harkness nursery firm in 1939 but, except for the fact that it was clearly a rugosa, they were as mystified as to its origin then as we are today. The flowers, which come in clusters of five or six, are single and fully 5 in (13 cm) across, mauve-pink with prominent light-yellow stamens. Continuity is outstanding and the blooms are followed by the most enormous round, bright-red hips. The bush will reach 6 ft (1.8 m) and is likely to spread out as far. It has typical and very plentiful rugosa-type leaves.

'Scarlet Fire' ('Scharlachglut'). Kordes, 1952. 'Poinsettia' × *R. gallica* 'Grandiflora'. A rose with enormously long, rambling canes that it can be used as a climber as well as a lax, informal shrub of considerable dimensions sideways but only about 5 ft (1.5 m) tall. The flowers are single and crimson-scarlet, very eye-catching as they can be as much as 5 in (13 cm) across even if they are usually rather smaller. No discernable scent, but the blooms are followed by showy red hips in late summer, for this rose flowers only once a year. The leaves are matt mid-green. Black spot is not unknown.

'Vanity'. Pemberton, 1920. 'Château de Clos Vougeot' ×
seedling. A hybrid musk with a difference, for the flowers are
large, single, rose-pink and very fragrant and carried in
enormous trusses. It makes a more open, spreading rambling
shrub than most of the family and will reach perhaps 8 ft (2.4 m)
in height. The leaves are leathery and a fine rich green.

'Wilhelm' ('Skyrocket'). Kordes, 1934. 'Robin Hood' × 'J.C.
Thornton'. I suppose that this must be counted as a hybrid
musk since the seed parent 'Robin Hood' was a Pemberton
variety, but it is one of the roses which I mentioned earlier as
being completely different from the traditional line. It is much
more like a robustious cluster-flowered rose in which the trusses
of bloom are carried at the ends of the main shoots. In this case,
they can consist of up to 50 crimson, semi-double, slightly
fragrant blooms. The leaves are large, leathery and glossy, and
black spot is more than likely. Upright and vigorous, the bush
may reach 4 ft (1.2 m).

CHAPTER 16

Climbing Roses

There is no very clear line of development here and climbers are an amalgam of many kinds of roses. Undoubtedly there is influence – as there always is – from China through the very rampant *R. gigantea* from the south-eastern part of that country, which will go up to 50 ft (15 m) and has large, creamy-white flowers 4–5 in (10–13 cm) across, and the Banksian roses came from China, too, although they followed an independent line and did not influence others. Then there were the noisette roses derived from the musk rose, the small group of Boursault climbers such as 'Mme Sancy de Parabére', and a lot of the pernetianas were climbers. But no thread linked them all. They were individuals.

Climbers as opposed to ramblers have comparatively small clusters of large flowers and are often – and in the case of the newer varieties, usually – recurrent. They form a permanent framework of strong and not always very flexible canes, and these need only their laterals or side shoots trimmed back by about two-thirds at pruning time.

There was a long period between the wars when very few new climbers were introduced. It is difficult to pin down a reason, although it used to be said that it was because few climbers were sold in relation to the sales of bush roses. But people had bigger gardens then and more room for pergolas and arches, and in view of the numbers of new climbers that are produced – and sell – today, that argument does not really stand up. At any rate, nurseries then seemed to concentrate on a few old stalwarts like 'Mme Gregoire Staechelin' and 'Mme Alfred Carrière' and for the rest relied on climbing versions or sports of bush varieties. These often did not flower anything like as well as the originals even in the first flush and a large number of them were not recurrent. Their energy went into growth rather than the production of late flowers, although there were a few honourable exceptions. If you see the word 'Climbing' either before or after a variety name in a nursery catalogue, that means that the rose is a climbing sport of that variety.

Since the Second World War, two breeders in particular have changed the climbing rose scene with their new introductions, which tend to be less vigorous, not to say overwhelming, than many of the old types and are more suitable for the gardens of today; their names are Wilhelm Kordes and Sam McGredy. A number of their varieties will appear in the descriptions that follow, together with many of others that have followed in their footsteps.

'Aloha'. Boerner, 1949. 'Mercedes Gallart' × 'New Dawn'. I never tire of extolling the virtues of this rose, which only now, after just over 30 years more or less on the sidelines, is beginning to be recognised as one of the best climbers of moderate vigour that there is, even if it takes a little time to get going. In the 20 odd years during which I have had it covering part of the front of my house, it has never once needed spraying against either black spot or mildew, its bright-green, glossy leaves remaining immaculate throughout the season.

The flower buds when they first start to open look a little strange, stumpy and almost as if they had been cut across with a knife, but this is only a brief phase, for they open into very large, very double pompon-style flowers in a rich rose-pink that has a touch of orange-pink in the heart at the early stages. Scent is very strong and, despite the many petals, rain hardly affects them at all. There will be a pause after the first really spectacular flush in early summer and then a good repeat performance, if not on quite the same scale. If there is one drawback, it is that the clusters of flowers come on rather long stems for a climber and they will need a certain amount of tying in, particularly in wet weather, but these same almost thornless stems mean that the rose is a fine one for cutting and it does last very well in water. 'Aloha' makes an excellent medium-sized shrub as well as a climber.

'Altissimo'. Delbard-Chabert, 1966. 'Tenor' × unknown rose. Another very healthy climber although a shorter one than 'Aloha'. This means that 7–8 ft (2.1–2.4 m) will be its maximum and that consequently it makes a fine pillar rose. It is, too, one of the very few climbers that can truly be said to be constantly in bloom. In catalogues, many are described as perpetual that are nothing of the sort, but 'Altissimo' does not follow the usual pattern of climbers by putting on a spectacular main flush with a secondary one later and little if anything in between. Instead it keeps going with a steady but certainly not overwhelming stream of small clusters of large, single, velvety, deep-red, slightly fragrant flowers, each one with a boss of golden stamens and of singular beauty. They and its all-round excellence gained it an RNRS Certificate of Merit.

'Autumn Sunlight'. Gregory, 1965. 'Danse du Feu' × 'Goldilocks'. A very free-growing and vigorous climber with clusters of rather globular, double, fragrant, orange-vermilion flowers of medium size and carried with great freedom in two main flushes with the odd bloom or two in between. The leaves are a bright shiny green, glossy, and reasonably free from disease. It will reach 10–12 ft (3–3.7 m).

The enormously popular 'Danse du Feu' was one parent of 'Autumn Sunlight' and it may be wondered why, as you read on, this does not have an entry to itself. The reason is quite simple: I do not feel that I can recommend it with any enthusiasm, for within hours of opening, the glowing orange-scarlet of the blooms has turned to a dull and rather dirty red, and the petals do not fall cleanly, particularly if they get wet. This for a climber is almost the ultimate crime in my eyes, as there is likely to be very little you can do about it if the flowers are more than 6–7 ft (1.8–2.1 m) up. The petals of 'Danse du Feu' turn brown when wet.

As I have diverted already and am on the subject of omissions, this may be the place for getting one more out of the way; I am referring to the climber called 'Schoolgirl', which is constantly in demand but really ought not to be. I think it is popular because it is the only climber in its particular soft orange colouring, which is a colour that everybody has been attracted by in recent years in bedding roses as well as in climbers. But 'Schoolgirl' is a gaunt, leggy grower with about half the number of leaves and half the number of blooms – beautiful as they are individually – that it should have. So I do not include it, except in this negative sort of way.

'Banksian Yellow' (*R. banksiae lutea*, **'Lady Banks' Rose'**). Introduced by Parks from China in 1824. There are actually four different Banksian roses all of a very similar habit: a white with single flowers, a double white, a single yellow and the double yellow which is described here and is, perhaps, the most attractive of the quartet. It is enormously vigorous and will easily reach 30 ft (9 m) or even more on the warm wall it needs for its protection as it is not completely hardy in a climate such as that of the United Kingdom. In late spring, for it is a very early starter, it will literally be covered with clusters of 1-in (2.5-cm), goblet-shaped, soft-yellow blooms, which are slightly fragrant and it will be a sight you will not easily forget. The foliage is almost evergreen if the rose is growing in a place where it has some protection. Care is needed in pruning the almost thornless shoots as the flowers come on the old wood, which they cannot do, of course, if it is cut away. In other words, prune only as is needed to keep the rose in bounds.

'Bantry Bay'. McGredy, 1967. 'New Dawn' × 'Korona'. It has gained an RNRS Certificate of Merit. Big clusters of quite large, slightly fragrant blooms in a pale rose-pink. They are loosely double and open to show their golden stamens. A vigorous grower to about 8–9 ft (2.4–2.7 m), making it a good pillar rose or one for a fence. The plentiful mid-green, semi-glossy leaves are reasonably healthy with me, although I have heard reports of black spot from others. A good second crop of blooms follows the first.

'Cécile Brunner, Climbing' ('The Sweetheart Rose'). Hosp, 1894. The 2 ft 6 in (75 cm) bush form of this rose was described in the chapter on China roses. Here we have its climbing sport, which is a very different cup of tea, for it will send out enormously long, plum-red shoots each season and eventually reach 20 by 20 ft (6 by 6 m) with ease if grown against a wall of sufficient size. Or it will go rambling up a tree, for which purpose it is ideally suited.

The flowers are the same as those on the bush form, light-pink and thimble-sized, opening loosely from exquisite little buds. They are carried in small, medium-sized or occasionally very large trusses in early summer; later there is usually only a scattering of bloom. The leaves are larger than those on the bush rose, long and tapering, very dark green at first but becoming lighter, and they are exceptionally healthy, as one would expect with a China rose. The scent can best be called fleeting.

'Compassion' ('Belle de Londres'). Harkness, 1973. 'White Cockade' × 'Prima Ballerina'. Blends of pink and apricot make this an obvious choice if you want a good rose to take the place of the less than admirable 'Schoolgirl'. The colour is not identical, but it is pretty close. The flowers are quite large, double and shapely, and they have the sweetest scent imaginable. Continuity is very good, with the first flush especially profuse. This is not a rampant grower, but makes a fine pillar rose or one for a house wall, well covered with healthy, dark-green leaves. It is strongly recommended.

'Dortmund'. Kordes, 1955. Seedling × *R. kordesii*. The whole of this chapter could well consist of descriptions of excellent recurrent climbers from the German breeder of this one, most of them of extreme hardiness. They have largely been developed from *R. kordesii*, a new species that arose by chance in the Kordes breeding establishment as the result of spontaneous chromosome doubling in an *R. rugosa* × *R. wichuraiana* hybrid. Those that are not excessively rampant, and this includes the majority, make excellent lax shrubs as well as good pillar roses, and 'Dortmund' is one of them. It bears clusters of very large and single blooms, a pure bright-scarlet with a white eye, and with attractively waved petals but little if any scent. The leaves are dark-green and leathery.

'Dublin Bay'. McGredy, 1976. 'Bantry Bay' × 'Altissimo'. One of those moderately vigorous climbers which, like 'Dortmund' one might consider growing as a shrub. The trouble is that with this variety it is sometimes the rose itself which decides which it wants to be and refuses to climb when you may want it to. When it does behave, however, you can see why so many people decide to take a chance with it – if they know that they are taking a chance, that is, for nurseries are not always as frank as they might be about certain roses' peculiarities. It has beautifully formed bright-crimson blooms in small clusters and in great profusion, less numerous, however, in the second flush. Scent is only slight, but the leaves are handsome, dark-green and usually healthy.

'Gloire de Dijon'. Jacotot, 1953. Possibly a tea rose × 'Souvenir de la Malmaison', or else a tea rose × a noisette climber. One of the few older climbers that I have included in this selection because they have something special about them, something that has probably been responsible for their longevity. In the case of 'Gloire de Dijon', the special virtue is that it is one of the earliest into flower and possibly more continuously in bloom thereafter than any other climber before or since. It is generally classed as a noisette rose, a group long since absorbed into others but originating in America when, as I mentioned earlier, a China rose and a musk rose were crossed, although development of them took place in France under the guiding hand of Philippe Noisette. 'Gloire de Dijon' was one of the first roses with tea-style blooms ever raised in a reasonably strong yellow colour, although perhaps it should more properly be described as buff-yellow – the colour of shammy leather. The scented blooms are large and have many petals which generally get themselves into a fine old muddle. No high centre and symmetrical reflexing here, but they are very fragrant. Watch for mildew on the mid-green leaves, and make sure you buy plants from a nursery that can be relied upon to provide the best. Certain stock of this rose has deteriorated over the years and there are some poor plants about.

'Golden Showers'. Lammerts, 1957. 'Charlotte Armstrong' × 'Captain Thomas'. One of the best roses ever to come out of America and deservedly one of the most popular everywhere. The bright-yellow blooms, in clusters on long, practically thornless stems, are shapely for a short while but do not have too many petals and open loosely. They fade fairly quickly to a paler yellow, but more keep coming with great enthusiasm over a long season – early summer to late autumn. Not very much fragrance. At about 8 ft (2.4 m) maximum, this is a climber for a pillar or the wall of a small house or bungalow. Naturally an upright grower, it seems to need horizontal training less than most climbers for it to stay in flower fairly low down, which is a great advantage if your wall space is split up by windows with not too much room for normal training in between. I have seen it used, free-standing, to make a most colourful hedge, which was a mass of bloom at all levels. The dark-green, glossy leaves are exceptionally healthy.

'Guinée'. Mallerin, 1938. 'Souvenir de Claudius Denoyel' × 'Aimi Quinard'. Perhaps the darkest of all the dusky deep-red roses with what seem to be blackish shadings, plus the kind of strong sweet scent we associate (not always correctly) with varieties in this colour range. The blooms are double and quite large, opening out flat. The first flush in early summer leaves nothing to be desired, but later the performance is unreliable. The leaves are a leathery medium-green and may need watching for mildew. It grows to about 10 ft (3 m).

'Handel'. McGredy, 1965. 'Columbine' × 'Heidelberg'. This is a rose that well deserves its great popularity except, to my way of thinking, for one weakness. When first they open, the cupped, not quite fully double flowers are enchanting, the creamy-white of the petals being edged a rosy-pink. Gradually, however, the pink suffuses the whole flower and they lose both their novelty and a good deal of their attractiveness. Rain does not seem to worry them, however. This is a vigorous rose that will go up 15 ft (4.5 m) or so, and it has dark-green leaves with a bronze tint to them, which are not immune to either mildew or black spot. It has been awarded an RNRS Trial Ground Certificate.

'Leverkusen'. Kordes, 1955. *R. kordesii* × 'Golden Glow'. Like 'Dortmund', this Kordes hybrid is a tough one that will stand up to a really harsh climate, and like it, too, it is comparatively short and so is suitable for a pillar. The semi-double flowers are a pleasing pale-yellow, come in large clusters, and there is an exceptionally good repeat performance in early autumn and some mini-flushes in between. Good health is another plus for this rose and the semi-glossy, mid-green leaves are plentiful. It makes a good shrub.

'Maigold'. Kordes, 1953. 'Poulsen's Pink' × 'Frühlingstag'. A Kordes climber that has *R. pimpinellifolia* rather than *R. kordesii* in its parentage, which perhaps accounts for its fierce thorns, even if they are not exactly on a par with the spines of the Scotch roses. This one comes into flower in late spring and has a season of extreme beauty lasting perhaps five to six weeks, but there will not be a second show. Those weeks will, however, be memorable for the profusion of the large, bronze-yellow, semi-double, very fragrant blooms, which cover the plant from head to toe. It will reach 10–12 ft (3.1–3.7 m) on a tall pillar or arch, or once again this is one that will be very effective as a free-standing shrub. The leaves are an added attraction, healthy and a fine glossy mid-green. It has an RNRS Trial Ground Certificate.

'Mermaid'. Paul, 1918. *R. bracteata* × a tea. A favourite pretty well since its introduction by William Paul's nursery, and a very remarkable and distinctive rose in many ways, not least in that it casts its spell on those who usually turn up their noses at single roses. And certainly the fragrant blooms, which come in small clusters and first appear considerably later than those of most other climbers, are of singular beauty individually. They can be up to 5 in (13 cm) across and the pale-yellow of the petals is well set off by a ring of deep orange stamens, which persists for a long while after the petals fall. There will be a main flush and then spasmodic blooming throughout the rest of the summer and well into the autumn. The fine, healthy, shiny leaves remain on the plant unless the winter is particularly severe, a characteristic inherited from *R. bracteata*, which is practically evergreen.

Generally 'Mermaid' is bought as an apparently puny little plant in a pot, which is because it is not a rose that transplants easily. It will take a year or two to settle down and then, provided it is given a reasonably sheltered site, which it needs in a climate such as that of the UK, it will romp away and there will be no stopping it. It does not take kindly to routine pruning such as most climbers seem to thrive on. This is, in a way, a blessing as each of 'Mermaid's' thorns is a stiletto. It has more of them than any rose has a right to. It won an RNRS Gold Medal in 1917.

'Mme Gregoire Staechelin' ('Spanish Beauty'). Dot, 1927. 'Frau Karl Druschki' × 'Château de Clos Vougeot'. The sight of this old Spanish rose spreading 15 ft (4.5 m) or so in all directions and smothering the wall of a house in very early summer with its huge and sumptuous scented pink blooms is breathtaking. Each flower has attractively waved petals and although basically rose-pink, there can be some deeper shadings – almost crimson – and some crimson splashes on an occasional petal. The mid-green foliage is large and plentiful, but by no means mildew-proof. Following the flowers very large hips are formed and it is a pity that they remain green and not particularly conspicuous. There are no further flowers after the first breathtaking flush.

'New Dawn'. Somerset, 1930. A sport from 'Dr W. Van Fleet'. A recurrent climber that sported from a once-flowering rambler and turned out to be one of the best and most popular moderately vigorous climbing roses there has ever been, not only with the general public but also with breeders of new varieties. It has appeared in the family tree as either seed or pollen parent of countless good roses since it was introduced. The flowers are of medium size and are carried in medium-sized clusters, covering the plants in tremendous profusion early in the summer and continuity thereafter is good. The colour is a soft, pearly pink, fading a little after a while, and there is a pleasing fragrance. The mid-green glossy leaves are not proof against mildew, but will not be the first in the garden to welcome it.

'Parade'. Boerner, 1953. 'New Dawn' seedling × 'World's Fair'. 'New Dawn' has here passed on a lot of its good qualities to produce a climber of moderate vigour – it will reach 10 ft (3 m) – this time with blooms in bright crimson-red. They come in good-sized clusters, only slightly fragrant, and there is a good repeat performance after the first flush. It has handsome foliage and above-average health.

'Parkdirektor Riggers'. Kordes, 1957. *R. kordesii* × 'Our Princess'. This rose has been lucky that its name, so unattractive-sounding outside its native Germany, has not killed it stone dead, as has happened to other good roses in the past. It is, too, perhaps the least healthy of the Kordes climbers, but despite these two drawbacks it is a tremendous performer, the clusters of semi-double, bright scarlet-crimson blooms coming with remarkable freedom and a good repeat later. As far as health is concerned, both mildew and black spot can be a problem, so be warned. Spraying climbers, even those that will not go much above 10 ft (3 m), is not the easiest occupation. Most of the time, however, the leaves are an attractive dark-green.

'Pink Perpetue'. Gregory, 1965. 'Danse du Feu' × 'New Dawn'. Another 'New Dawn' offspring, which must be among the most free-flowering of all climbing roses and one of the few which puts on a show in the autumn that could truly be said to match that of the early summer flush. To achieve this, the raiser does, however, recommend some cutting back of laterals after the first flowering. The blooms, in large clusters, are not particularly big, but they have plenty of petals, rose-pink with a carmine reverse, an attractive combination. Not a great deal of scent. A first-rate rose for a pillar, fence or low wall. It has gained an RNRS Certificate of Merit.

'Swan Lake' (Schwanensee'). McGredy, 1968. 'Memoriam' × 'Heidelberg'. There are not many good white climbers, which is a pity as they are some of the best roses of all to grow against red brick or the golden honey of the stonework one finds in many country districts. 'White Cockade' and 'Climbing Iceberg' are two good alternatives to this one, but neither has the large, high-centred double flower of classic form that is found in 'Swan Lake'. The blooms, even though they may at a distance give the impression of being so, are not quite pure-white, for there is the palest of pink flushes, intensifying in the heart of the flower. For a rose with so many petals and especially a white rose, rain resistance is good, but there is disappointingly only a slight fragrance. However, 'Swan Lake' is fully recurrent and the glossy leaves are reasonably resistant to disease, even if a watch for black spot late in the season would be advisable. Quite a strong grower that will cover a large wall or could be used on a pergola.

'Zéphirine Drouhin'. Bizot, 1868. Some bourbons which are normally grown as shrubs can be used as short climbers, but here is one that is a true climber which will reach 10–12 ft (3–3.7 m) in a situation that suits it. The blooms come in clusters of five or six, fairly large and deep-pink with a white base to each petal and a fine fragrance. The freely branching shoots are practically without thorns which, following through with re-morseless logic, has led to 'Zéphirine Drouhin' being known as 'The Thornless Rose'. They bear the rather loosely formed flowers over a long season as the rose is recurrent, but unless the light-green leaves are thoroughly sprayed against mildew, the later blooming does tend to be marred.

CHAPTER 17

The Ramblers

It is difficult to tell the difference between some wild climbing roses and ramblers, and even rambler hybrids are much closer as a rule to their wild rose forbears than the climbers most of us grow in our gardens. A typical rambler has large trusses of small flowers, by which is meant blooms of anything from $1^1{}_2$ in (4 cm) downwards, with up to 150 blooms in the trusses of a few of them. They have only one flowering period and this begins rather later than the first one of the climbers, a few weeks after midsummer as a rule. A rambler's canes will usually be fairly thin and flexible, making them easy to train. On the other hand, they can be the very devil to prune if one really has the patience and energy to do it properly, untangling them from their supports and cutting out the old so that new growth can be tied in in its place. Even if few people actually carried this out in the past, perhaps it was the nagging thought that they ought to be doing so, and not simply the fact that ramblers only flower once each season, that led to their decline. For decline they have and nurseries nowadays carry only a small selection of the most popular. This is a very great pity, for during their relatively short period of glory each summer they do put on a really remarkable display, probably unmatched by any other climbing plant. And they are, of course, the ideal roses for growing up trees and for weeping standards.

Most of the ramblers we still grow are descended from *R. wichuraiana*, some from *R. arvensis* making up the Ayrshire group, and a number have *R. sempervirens*, *R. multiflora* and a few other species in their family tree. A very close relative of *R. wichuraiana*, *R. luciae*, appears to have been used to produce a small group, of which 'Albéric Barbier' and 'Albertine' are the most familiar, and which can best be described as coming half-way between ramblers and climbers. They flower earlier than the other ramblers, their flowers are bigger and in smaller clusters, their canes are stiffer, and they do not just produce new growth from ground level, which means their pruning has to be different. Yet by ancestry they are ramblers, and they are not recurrent.

The French firm of Barbier was instrumental in breeding many of the best ramblers round about the turn of the century, and they rapidly became enormously popular. In America the name Walsh is associated with many fine varieties. Some of the best from all sources, all of which can still be bought today, though not from every nursery, are:

'Aimée Vibert' (Bouquet de la Mariée', 'Nivea'). 'Champney's Pink Cluster' × a *R. sempervirens* hybrid. With this parentage, this is, I suppose, strictly speaking a noisette climber, but it is so like a rambler in appearance and habit that it is usually included among them. It has clusters of small, double white flowers with a sweet perfume, and is of moderate vigour, ideal for a pillar. The leaves are very dark and attractively glossy.

'Albéric Barbier'. Barbier, 1900. *R. luciae* × 'Shirley Hibberd'. One of the healthiest of all ramblers, which have a reputation for mildew, especially when grown on walls where the air circulation is likely to be poor. The leaves of 'Albéric Barbier' are particularly good, a dark, bronzy green and glossy, and they stay on the plant long after those of most others have dropped. This extremely vigorous rose easily reaches 15 ft (4.5 m) or so and is suitable for fences, pergolas, trellises or for hiding an unsightly old shed, unsightly new garage or an old tree stump. The flowers have orange-yellow buds at the early stages and these open to creamy-white flowers, high-centred at first but opening with rather muddled petals. They have a good scent and come in small clusters in tremendous profusion early in the summer with possibly the odd bloom later on.

'Albertine'. Barbier, 1921. *R. luciae* × 'Mrs Arthur Robert Waddell'. In the United Kingdom I would guess that 'Albertine' is grown in at least as many gardens as 'Peace', and when one sees it in full bloom and strolls past it in the cool of the evening when its sweet fragrance fills the air, one can understand why. The flowers, which come in clusters, are coppery-pink in the bud and open light-pink, but they are only shapely in the early stages. They are borne in tremendous profusion in the early months of summer on a plant of quite remarkable vigour, which is why in most situations it will need ruthless cutting back after flowering to keep it in bounds. The new canes are plum-red and carry dark-green, semi-glossy leaves that will almost certainly need spraying against mildew.

This is 'Albertine's' main weakness, but it must also be said that after prolonged rain it can look a sorry sight. Normally the petals of the spent flowers fall reasonably cleanly, but not when they are wet. Then they stick together and turn brown, like small, sodden paper bags. Not very beautiful, but I still grow it and so do thousands of other people, although not, I hope, as a weeping standard, in which form it is frequently sold. Its canes are far too stiff for this purpose and it will never weep satisfactorily.

'Dorothy Perkins'. Miller, 1901. *R. wichuraiana* × 'Mme Gabriel Luizet'. I have talked about 'Albertine' and mildew, and cannot help wondering if I should now be recommending another rose, this one over 80 years old, which everybody who has ever grown ramblers will know is also a welcoming host – or hostess – to mildew spores. Probably not, but in my garden, provided that it is sprayed with a suitable fungicide, it makes such a superb display as a weeping standard that I feel it cannot be left out. The canes are long and flexible and hang down in exactly the prescribed way, each one laden a week or two after midsummer with huge clusters of small, rose-pink, double blooms. If you wish to grow it on an arch or pillar, it will reach 15 ft (4.5 m) and the foliage, if you can keep it disease-free, is a singularly bright and attractive green and very glossy.

'Dr W. Van Fleet'. Van Fleet, 1910. (*R. wichuraiana* × 'Safrano') × 'Souvenir du Président Carnot'. A popular and very reliable rambler and still a useful one if what you are looking for is what is virtually a more vigorous version of 'New Dawn' and are not concerned that it will only have one flowering season a year. The large clusters of pearl-pink double blooms are very fragrant and carried with great freedom over a long period. After a while they fade almost to white, and as much of the flowering is on the old wood, pruning should really be confined to keeping the rose under control. Try growing it up a tree, when pruning will be impossible anyway. The leaves are dark and glossy.

'Excelsa' ('Red Dorothy Perkins'). Walsh, 1909. All that I have said about 'Dorothy Perkins' will equally apply to this rose, except that its blooms are rosy-crimson. It gained an American Rose Society Medal in 1914.

'Félicité et Perpétue. Jaques, 1827. A *R. sempervirens* sport. A really old rambler which has survived on sheer merit. It comes into flower just after midsummer, when the shoots and leaves will be pretty well hidden beneath the massed clusters of small, many-petalled, pompon blooms. These are white, although there is sometimes a pink staining on a few of the outer petals. It is a pity that they are practically scentless, but that is really only a minor drawback with a rose that has so many other good qualities. In addition to its spectacular period of flowering, the leaves, dark-green and glossy, and the plum-red new canes, play a very important part. The leaves stay on the shoots through most of the winter and for a rambler they are singularly healthy. Growth is vigorous to something like 15 ft (4.5 m), and as mildew is unlikely to be much of a problem this is a rose to try on walls as well as for arches and pergolas. It may be too vigorous for a pillar, for it sends up such a multitude of new shoots each summer just before and after flowering that few pillars could cope. There is some controversy at the moment about the correct name for this rose, one school of thought holding that the 'et' should not be there and the other that it should, one that it comes from the names of two saints, one that it doesn't. Since it is unlikely that we will ever know the answer, I am not taking sides.

'Goldfinch'. Paul, 1907, 'Hélène' × an unknown rose. This has very large clusters of small, semi-double blooms, deep-yellow in the bud, opening a much paler yellow and eventually fading to cream. At all stages they are very fragrant but after the flowering at midsummer there is no repeat. It is not one of the very strong growers and will not go much over 10 ft (3 m), but that does not mean that it lacks vigour within those parameters as there is always new growth forming. Planted on its own without support it will make a most pleasing shrub. Light pruning gives the best results.

'Kiftsgate'. (*R. filipes* 'Kiftsgate'). Introduced by Murrell's nursery in 1954 and named after the Gloucestershire garden, Kiftsgate Court, from which this particularly good and incredibly vigorous form of *R. filipes* came, this is actually one of the climbing wild roses that I referred to at the beginning of this chapter. It flowers only once, a few weeks after midsummer just as many ramblers do and, like many of the so-called musk ramblers, has immense heads of tiny, single, creamy-white flowers. Each cluster may have up to 100 blooms and they will scent the air for yards around, for this is one of what are known as the synstylae roses. They are distinguished by the fact that the styles are formed into a single column, and it is from this that their fragrance goes out far and wide. With the synstylae one does not have to bend close to smell the flowers as one does with most other kinds.

For all its wonderful qualities, do not be tempted to plant 'Kiftsgate' unless you are quite certain that you have both the space for it and something substantial enough to support it. A space of 20–30 ft (6–9 m) each way could be just a beginning in a place that suits it, and it will scramble through and probably eventually smother other shrubs that are planted near it. It conquers all, but what rewards there are when it does so. A benevolent tyrant.

R. longicuspis (*R. lucens*). A climbing wild rose that came from western China in 1915 and is for those who want a rose that is not quite so dauntingly, not to say flauntingly, invasive as 'Kiftsgate'. It is very similar to it, both in its flowers and in its growth style, but it is a good deal more restrained. Not that it is a midget, for it will go to 15–20 ft (4.5–6 m), and it is an excellent variety for a pergola or for growing up a tree of medium size. The large heads of small, white single flowers are followed by equally small-scale orange-red hips. It is sometimes said to be a little tender, but I have seen it apparently quite happy in the most exposed positions so it is worth trying anywhere.

'Sanders's White Rambler'. Sanders, 1912. We are now back among the *R. wichuraiana* hybrids and with one of the best of them. Mildew seldom seems to attack its bright-green, glossy leaves, and its very full, rosette-shaped blooms in snowy-white are very fragrant. They appear in great profusion a few weeks after midsummer. A sturdy but not rampant grower, it is ideal for a pillar or for a weeping standard.

'Seagull'. Pritchard, 1907. The parentage is unknown but there are indications that this may be of the *R. multiflora* family. An ideal arch or pergola rose, and I have seen it used to cover a low wall, draping itself over the top of it and actually covering both sides most effectively. The flowers are white and single to semi-double, have prominent golden stamens, and are large for this type of rose, which only means that they may be something over 1 in (3 cm) across. They are carried in large trusses with great freedom and although there is some fragrance, it is not particularly strong.

'Temple Bells'. Morey, 1973. An interesting and comparatively modern American *R. wichuraiana* hybrid which is often recommended as a ground-cover rose and you probably realise by now that I am not altogether convinced by any of these claims. I have already described *R. wichuraiana* itself and its other hybrid 'Max Graf' in Chapter 1. 'Temple Bells' has a similar habit, and even if it never really becomes dense enough to leave weeds gasping for air beneath it, it still makes an attractive change to see a rose growing low across the ground. The flowers of 'Temple Bells' come in clusters and are very dainty, small and white. It has masses of equally small and very glossy leaves.

'Veilchenblau'. Schmidt, 1909. 'Crimson Rambler' × 'Souvenir de Brod'. The second parent of this very unusual rambler has just been unearthed by that great authority Jack Harkness, and most books (including my own earlier ones) still give it as an unknown rose. Its colour at times verges on purple so that it must have contributed to no small degree to 'Veilchenblau's' deep lilac-blue, which lightens almost to pure-white towards the centre of each of the small flowers. They are carried in very big clusters at midsummer, and their unusual colour holds its intensity if the plant is given a little shade during the hottest part of the day. Very good, bright-green, glossy foliage that stays healthy in most seasons. The shoots, which remain the same bright-green as the leaves, will take this rose up to about 10 ft (3 m) on a pillar or arch.

CHAPTER 18

Miniature Roses

Many of the characteristics of the earliest miniatures are so close to those of the China roses that the first one was actually given the specific name of *R. chinensis minima* and it seems certain that they came to us from the Far East. Possibly the earliest was a dwarf sport from a China rose, but nobody really knows exactly how and when the miniatures came to the West. They seem at some time to have reached the island of Mauritius in the Indian Ocean (the second time, you will notice, that an island in those remote seas figures in the story of the rose) and from there progressed first to England and then to France and elsewhere. It was a good many years, however, before they were regarded as anything more than a novelty and became really popular. This occurred early in the nineteenth century but even then the vogue did not last and they practically vanished from sight for a number of years. Then in 1918 a pink miniature was discovered by a Major Roulet growing in a pot on a window-sill of a house in Switzerland, who passed it on to a nurseryman acquaintance, a M. Correvon. The latter named the rose *R. rouletii*, although it is not, of course, a wild rose, and there is a school of thought that holds that it is identical to 'Pom Pom de Paris', which was a well-known conservatory rose in Paris in the eighteenth century. Whatever the truth of the matter, *R. rouletii* is now regarded as the type plant of the miniatures from which all the modern varieties have sprung. The Dutchman Jan de Vink, the Spanish breeder Pedro Dot and a few others from France and Germany, but above all Ralph Moore in the United States have been responsible for the enormous strides that have been made, but as far as I am concerned it is a great pity that, in an effort to increase the colour range of these little roses, more and more of the large, cluster-flowered types have been introduced into the miniature strain. All the colours one could desire are there now, but many of the roses are so large, either overall or perhaps in their flowers or leaves, that they hardly qualify as true miniatures any more.

That does not, of course, mean that they have no uses in the garden, for they make fine patio roses and are ideal for lining paths and drives, but in my eyes real miniatures should not grow more than 8–9 in (20–23 cm) and have the flowers and leaves in perfect proportion.

Miniature roses, with a few exceptions, are perfectly hardy and should be grown out of doors – or in a cool greenhouse if they are in pots. They will not thrive in the average house, in which the atmosphere is likely to be much too dry (making the leaves yellow and drop off) and the light insufficient. It is possible, by the use of pebble tray irrigation and fluorescent strip lighting, to create the right conditions, but it is really better, and certainly easier, to bring the roses indoors when the buds are just begining to show colour and to take them out again as soon as flowering is over.

Miniatures take readily from cuttings and will not grow as big if on their own roots.

Some of the best miniatures are:

'Angela Rippon' ('Ocarina', 'Ocaru'). De Ruiter, 1978. One of the larger miniatures, growing to about 12 in (30 cm) and with double, coral-pink, fragrant flowers. Bushy and compact, and one that is used a great deal by exhibitors.

'Baby Gold Star' ('Estrellita de Oro'). Dot, 1940. 'Eduardo Toda' × *R. rouletii*. A rather unpredictable rose that can be bushy or rather open in growth, and that can be very healthy or a martyr to black spot. Nevertheless it has remained extremely popular since its introduction, if not with the purists, for it can reach 18 in (45 cm) in height and has large double flowers in the golden yellow that its name suggests.

'Baby Masquerade'. Tantau, 1956. 'Peon' × 'Masquerade'. The flowers have most of the attributes of the full-sized 'Masquerade' and change colour in the same way from yellow through pink to deeper red, all colours being on the bush at the same time. However, in this case the final red is not the unattractive rather dirty-looking tone of the parent rose. This is an outstanding variety for edging, showing and even for bedding, since it will usually be between 18 in and 2 ft (45 cm and 60 cm) tall, as much, in other words, as a shortish cluster-flowered (floribunda) variety. This is not, however, an in-between rose in any other way in that both the flowers and leaves are of true miniature proportions. It makes a fine, bushy grower and on the whole a very healthy one.

'Bambino'. Dot, 1953. A sport of 'Perla de Alcanada'. A sound all-round pink variety with plenty of double, slightly fragrant blooms and a good bushy habit. Lasts well when cut and is a good rose for showing.

'Cinderella'. De Vink, 1952. 'Cécile Brunner' × 'Peon'. Raised by a Dutchman responsible for a number of good miniatures, this to my mind approaches the ideal. It will keep to 9–10 in (23–25 cm), upright and bushy, with a dense covering of minute, pointed, glossy leaves and quite delightful, blush-pink flowers with an incredible number of petals so that it looks for all the world like the smallest of large-flowered (HT) roses. The flowers come in small clusters but there is not much scent. Health is good.

'Coralin'. (**'Carolin'**, **'Carolyn'**, **'Karolyn'**, **'Perla Corail'**). Dot, 1955. 'Méphisto' × 'Perla de Alcanada'. The rather large double blooms of this one are variable in colour but perhaps best described as coral-pink. It is a tall, upright grower, too, probably reaching 15 in (38 cm). The attractive leaves are bronze-tinted.

'Darling Flame' (**'Minuetto'**). Meilland, 1971. ('Rimosa' × 'Rosina') × 'Zambra'. This makes a fairly large bush of something over 12 in (30 cm) and must be counted as one of the outstanding introductions of comparatively recent years. The flowers are carried with exceptional freedom, in good trusses, double and a bright orange-vermilion with a yellow reverse to the petals. Good, glossy leaves, but an eye must be kept open for possible black spot.

'Easter Morning'. Moore, 1960. 'Golden Glow' × 'Zee'. A strong, spreading grower and one of the taller miniatures at about 15 in (38 cm). The blooms are of the fully double, large-flowered (HT) rose type, shapely and of a pure ivory-white. The glossy leaves have an exceptionally good health record.

'Fire Princess'. Moore, 1969. 'Baccara' × 'Eleanor'. Medium-sized, scarlet, double blooms on a rather tall and upright plant. A good one when cut and hence for the show bench, but it makes a fine garden variety too.

'Gypsy Jewel'. Moore, 1975. 'Little Darling' × 'Little Bucka-roo'. It is an attractive rose-pink. The double blooms and the clusters in which they grow are quite large and the bush itself is on the tall side at 15 in (38 cm). However, growth is satisfactorily bushy and although the long shoots spread quite widely they are well branched.

'Judy Fischer'. Moore, 1968. 'Little Darling' × 'Magic Wand'. A small, neat variety which is unlikely to top 10 in (25 cm) and that has moderately full, deep-pink blooms which hold their colour exceptionally well but are only slightly scented. It is free-flowering and sturdy, with healthy bronze-tinted leaves.

'Lavender Jewel'. Moore, 1978. 'Little Chef' × 'Angel Face'. The blooms are large and very double but have little fragrance. However, they are carried with great freedom and are an attractive pink with just a touch of the lavender that gives this variety its name. The growth is bushy but this is a more lax and spreading miniature than most. It is a popular show variety.

'Little Flirt'. Moore, 1961. (*R. wichuraiana* × 'Floradora') × ('Golden Glow' × 'Zee'). The curiously named variety 'Zee' appears in the parentage of a number of miniatures raised by Ralph Moore, especially his climbers. It is itself a pale-pink climbing miniature, though not in commerce, and it is difficult to see its influence in the breeding of 'Little Flirt', which has colouring akin to the large-flowered (HT) variety 'Piccadilly' – orange-red with a yellow petal reverse, fading quite quickly. The blooms have up to 50 petals and are quite large. Growth is upright and on the tall side.

'Magic Carrousel'. Moore, 1972. 'Little Darling' × 'Westmont'. One of the most popular of all the newer miniatures and an outstanding rose for the show bench. Those who have grown the older and rather less hardy 'Toy Clown' will find that this could be described as a much improved version, the white, moderately full blooms having the same pink edges to the petals. There is some fragrance as a bonus. Growth is strong and upright to 10 in (25 cm).

'New Penny'. Moore, 1962. (*R. wichuraiana* × 'Floradora') × seedling. Not one of the very tall miniatures, rarely exceeding 10 in (25 cm) and making an upright, bushy plant with medium-sized, moderately full, light-coppery to coral-pink blooms, which have a slight scent.

'Perla de Alcanada' ('Baby Crimson', 'Pearl of Canada', 'Titania', 'Wheatcroft's Baby Crimson'). Dot, 1944. 'Perle des

Rouges' × *R. rouletii*. As can be seen from the date, this one has been going a long time, but it is still among the best in its colour, which is actually a rosy-red and not crimson. The clustered blooms are rather more than semi-double and the base of the petals is white, although this is not usually visible. The dark, glossy leaves cover well a quite wide-spreading bush that will reach 10 in (25 cm).

'Rise 'n' Shine' ('Golden Sunblaze'). Moore, 1977. 'Little Darling' × 'Yellow Magic'. Despite some susceptibility to black spot, this is rapidly establishing itself as one of the best yellow miniatures for all purposes, for the garden, as a cut flower – the blooms are quite large – and as a show variety. The double flowers are a bright-yellow that fades a little, but have no scent that I can discern. The height of the bush is medium to tall, which means 10–15 in (25–38 cm) but it is a well-branched and bushy grower.

'Sheri Anne'. Moore, 1973. 'Little Darling' × 'New Penny'. A very good orange-red rose that is much favoured by exhibitors and here it may be worth remarking that, unlike a good many other exhibition roses, particularly among the large-flowered (HT) varieties, a miniature that is good for showing is also usually good in the garden as well. This one is, with plenty of sprays of the large, full flowers, which, for a change, have a fine fragrance. An upright grower, a little on the tall side.

'Snow Carpet'. McGredy, 1980. 'New Penny' × 'Temple Bells'. Completely different from all the miniatures described so far in its habit of growth, this is, to my mind, the first true ground-cover rose. It really does creep across the ground and has a good coverage of glossy, dark-green leaves, which will smother weeds over a diameter of 2–3 ft (60–90 cm). Throughout the summer and autumn it will be covered with fairly large, very double, white, slightly fragrant blooms.

'Starina'. Meilland, 1965. ('Dany Robin' × 'Fire King') × 'Perla de Montserrat'. Double, bright orange-vermilion flowers in enormous profusion and of considerable size for a miniature on a bushy plant that will reach 18 in (45 cm) with little difficulty. Whether it can truly be called a miniature or not, it is an outstanding rose and the blooms are among the most long-lasting when cut.

'Sweet Fairy'. De Vink, 1946. 'Peon' × seedling. A real

miniature to finish on, which will keep to a maximum of 8 in (20 cm), has apple-blossom-pink blooms of some 60 petals each with a sweet fragrance, and a full coverage of dark-green leaves.

CHAPTER 19

Choosing and Buying Roses

Although for one reason or another it may not always be practical, there is really only one way of making sure that you have just the roses that you want and that is to see them growing, preferably properly looked after, as plants at least three years old in someone else's garden. This someone else does not have to be a friend or neighbour, because unless you are very lucky and live near to a real rose enthusiast, the range of varieties grown and from which you would have to make your choice would be likely to be quite small – even assuming that your friend or neighbour knew what they were in the first place. There are, however, many parks and public gardens where a wide range of roses is grown and where they are properly labelled; the gardens of many National Trust properties and other stately homes, such as Castle Howard in Yorkshire, Wisley Gardens of the RHS in Surrey, Queen Mary's Rose Garden in Regent's Park, London, and above all the gardens of The Royal National Rose Society near St Albans in Hertfordshire are examples. And one can, of course, see the rose fields where nurseries grow the plants they are going to sell, but it must be remembered that these will be by no means fully grown and it will be quite impossible, especially with the larger shrub roses, to assess the size to which they will ultimately grow. It is all very well to read in a book that a certain rose will reach perhaps 6 ft by 4 ft (1.8 m by 1.2 m), but it takes quite a bit of experience to be able to visualise just what this means in reality because roses do not all grow in the same way. A dense mound of interlacing branches at 6 ft by 4 ft (1.8 m by 1.2 m) would give a very different effect from that of an open-growing species rose like, for example, *R. rubrifolia*, even though the basic dimensions were exactly the same. Some nurseries do have display gardens where the varieties they sell (or most of them) are growing permanently and these are a much better guide, but wherever it is that you inspect them, try if possible to do it more than once, the ideal being at least three or four times over one summer. This does, of course, mean exercising some patience, but it really is the only way of assessing the true colour of a variety, the lasting qualities of the blooms, general health, weather resistance and, as has already been said, the habit of growth. And, of course, if you do take the trouble to visit some of the outstanding rose collections, you may easily discover roses in them which you have not previously heard of and of a beauty you have only dreamed of.

I mentioned above the assessment of the true colour of a rose, which can rarely be done from nursery lists. The variations and blendings of colours in rose petals are really much too subtle to be captured properly on the page of a catalogue, even with the great strides there have been in colour printing in the last 30 years. Things can, in fact, start going wrong with the colours even before the printer becomes involved, because capturing certain flower tints on film, particularly some of the reds, seems next to impossible. By the time these and some other colours, already photographically inaccurate, have gone through the many processes involved in reproducing them in a sales catalogue, it is not to be wondered at that they are often adrift by the time they reach the page. And you cannot really – although nurserymen and rose writers continue to try – describe even halfway to adequately, let alone effectively, the colour of a rose in words.

Again when ordering roses from a catalogue there will usually be very little information in it about how prone the varieties offered are to the various rose diseases. There are certain roses that are particularly susceptible to black spot or mildew or whatever it may be, and the better rose nurseries will generally sound a discreet warning. But you cannot really blame nurserymen in general for maintaining a fairly universal silence about disease because its incidence will vary enormously from year to year and from one part of the country to another. A nursery is, after all, in business to sell roses and would be foolish to scare a customer on the north-east coast of England away from a particular variety that gets black spot badly only in the south-east.

However, if it is possible for you to visit a good rose nursery, you will be able to obtain at first hand much more information than it is possible for them to put in their catalogues. Nurserymen as a race seem to enjoy being helpful and respond with enthusiasm to keenness on the part of a customer. And do not be afraid of asking for some of the old roses because you do not know how to pronounce their names. As likely as not the nurseryman will not know either!

Rose growers' catalogues often mention in their descriptions of various roses whether they have won an award from one of the many international trials. This can be a valuable pointer to the rose's worth if one knows a little about where the trials were held. An award gained in the climate of the south of France, for instance, has not a great deal of relevance to growing a rose in the United Kingdom, and the reverse of course applies as well.

The trials carried out and the awards subsequently made by the Royal National Rose Society, by the All-American Rose Selection organisation and the British Association of Rose Breeders and the Belfast trials in Northern Ireland are among the best and are based on careful observation of new varieties grown over a number of years and given ratings for such things as health, habit of growth, continuity, flower form, purity of colour, scent, novelty and so on. It is, however, a fact that many roses that do well in the United States do not cross the Atlantic too happily and, of course, vice versa, so provided there is a sensible trials system in one's own country, the wise thing is to be guided by that one first of all. The Royal National Rose Society's trials are conducted over a three-year period and during that time a panel of experts operates a rota system so that the roses are seen every single week during the growing season from June to October each year. At the end of the three years a rose may be awarded a Gold Medal for something really outstanding, a Certificate of Merit for a rose just below Gold Medal standard, or a Trial Ground Certificate for a rose that can be expected to put up a good all-round performance in the average garden. There is a special award for the most fragrant rose as well (although fragrance is taken into account in the overall judging) and one for the best new variety raised by an amateur. The All-American Rose Selection is (like the British Association of Rose Breeders award) organised by the rose trade and in America is the result of careful assessments of the same variety growing in many different parts of the country, which is especially necessary given the widely differing climates and growing conditions the roses may expect to encounter if they are distributed nationally.

Having dealt at some length with choosing the varieties to buy, the second and certainly equally important thing to make sure of is that you are getting top-quality plants. As with anything else, you get what you pay for, and tempting as they may sound it is well to go cautiously if you are likely to be beguiled by the many cheap offers one sees in the newspapers. If these do not specify that the plants are first-grade – and to be described as such they must conform to certain standards which

I will come to in a moment – they are most unlikely to be so, and could well be those rejected by nurseries that only sell the best. The cheaper roses offered prepacked in stores and supermarkets may well be in the same category and although the packing of these has shown signs of improvement in recent years, it is still far from ideal. The rose is an incredibly tough plant and will stand all sorts of ill-treatment when it is dormant, but the trouble with store-bought roses is that one rarely, if ever, knows under what conditions they have been stored and for how long, and there is a limit to what even a rose will put up with. One can get good plants in this way, but one really must know what to look for. The shoots should be green and firm and unwrinkled, and there should be no signs of disease or pre-emerging shoots which look like little white worms and which have been forced into growth by excessive humidity (the polythene packing acting like a miniature greenhouse) and, judging by their colour – or lack of it – in a steamy darkness. Roses can be and are stored after lifting in vast quantities by wholesale growers but only at the right temperature and the right humidity, which a local store can hardly be expected to match.

A rose you buy should be just as good underground as above, which means that it should have a good, fibrous root system, but short of unpacking the roses, which would require more than average resolution on the part of a buyer in the middle of a crowded store, it is difficult to tell what sort of roots you are getting. Maybe they are all right, maybe they are not.

In order to conform to the British Standard Specification of a First Grade plant, a rose should conform to certain given dimensions, but since it is unlikely that most people will actually measure a plant they are buying and it is easy enough to tell by eye if the plant is near enough to the ideal, it is more sensible, I think, to say that a bush rose should have at least two firm canes no thinner than a pencil, that there should be a good fibrous root system, and that the neck (between the roots and the budding union) should be of thumb thickness. Standard roses should be double-budded, which means a bud inserted one each side of the stem, and climbers should have at least two firm canes at least 30 in (75 cm) long.

In fact, the roses one gets from the better nurseries as often as not exceed these minimum requirements and in America a No. 1 Grade large-flowered rose is required to have at least three strong canes with two of them at least 18 in (45 cm) long, and much the same for the cluster-flowered varieties. Climbers, too, must have three canes, in this case at least 2 ft (60 cm) long.

159

Whereas in the UK there is only First Grade and then the rest, in the USA there are two other grades, No. $1\frac{1}{2}$ and No. 2, that set progressively lower standards. The lowest standard in either country is Dead.

In fairly recent years there has been a gradual revolution in the way in which roses, and indeed shrubs in general, are sold. It is not so many years since the selling was almost all by mail order, and while this is still carried on to some extent, particularly by the bigger specialist nurseries, container-grown roses have taken over a large slice of the market, sold not only through the nurseries themselves but also through the garden centres which not so long ago scarcely existed.

The greatest advantage in buying container-grown roses is that they can be planted at virtually any time, even when in flower, although you would probably be wise to keep them in their containers, and to keep the containers watered, if you buy in the middle of a prolonged drought. The fact that you can actually buy a rose bush that is in flower can, however, lead the unwary into trouble. I remember once buying, out of a collection of container-grown roses at a nursery, the only one that happened to be in bloom that day. The nurseryman said to me: 'I had a bet on that that would be the first to go.' He was perfectly right, of course: it did catch the eye, but luckily I knew enough about roses to make sure that the plant underneath the flowers was up to scratch. Even a weak and spindly plant can put on what seems an impressive show in a container but will be much less impressive when fighting for attention among others in a bed.

Always make sure when buying, by asking if necessary, that container-grown roses really are container-grown. It is by no means unknown for roses unsold by Christmas time (which quite probably means the least vigorous specimens) to have their roots ruthlessly chopped off so that they will fit into a standard sized container and then to be sold as container-grown in spring. They may well take a very long time to recover, but, apart from asking, one can generally tell if a rose has been in its container for some time. If it has, there may well be green, mossy growth on the soil surface and a few more venturesome roots are likely to be pushing through the drainage holes in the base of the container. There should be no difference in the requirements for a First Grade rose between those that are container-grown and those that are sold as bare-root plants, but it is nevertheless true that the extra-large and extra-vigorous plants – those far exceeding the minimum for the top grade –

rarely find their way into containers: they are too large. In such a labour-intensive job as container-growing there has to be some standardisation of container size to make it an economic proposition.

Every year there are new rose varieties put on the market – far too many of them, in fact – and many are launched with considerable ballyhoo. Is it wise to buy these in their first year? They will almost certainly be a good deal more expensive than the more established roses and are they really worth it?

This is a question that nobody can really answer sensibly. It is a choice that each person must make for himself. Some people get a considerable kick out of always having the latest novelty, and if a rose has been through one of the recognised trials with credit, buying it is a fair enough gamble. But valuable as trials are, experience has shown that only after being grown in gardens over a good many years and in widely differing situations will a rose show its true worth. A beginner might be well advised to give novelties a miss.

There is a final thought on buying roses and one that cannot be reiterated too often. Whether you are going to pick up the roses yourself at a nursery or are writing away for them, put in your order early. It helps the nursery no end, but if you feel that this should not be your concern, it also means from your point of view that you will get what you want. As Bernard Shaw put it: 'Get what you like, or you will learn to like what you get.' You will only get what you like if your order arrives before stocks run out.

At the back of this book there is a List of Suppliers providing names and addresses of some of the best rose nurseries with a note of any type of rose in which they specialise. Wherever you may happen to be reading this book, a number of the nurseries listed will be in another country. It is possible to buy roses from abroad, although you would probably have to be after something very special to make it worthwhile, for there are many regulations that have to be conformed with and special procedures to go through. And forms to fill in. To import into the UK, it is necessary to contact the Ministry of Agriculture, Fisheries and Food, Plant Health Administrative Unit, Room 145, 1st Floor, Great Westminster House, Horseferry Road, London SW1P 2AE or your local Ministry of Agriculture office. In the USA you should contact the Permit Unit, U.S.D.A., PPQ, Federal Buildings, Room 638, Hyattsville, Maryland 20782. It should, however, be mentioned that not all nurseries are prepared to export. One cannot blame them; there is a lot of extra work involved for a comparatively small return, although possibly attitudes might change for an order, say, of 20,000 bushes.

CHAPTER 20

Cultivation

Provided that they are in a place where they will have full sun for a large part of the day, roses will grow and thrive practically anywhere, although there are some kinds of soil in which they will do better than others. With a few exceptions, such as the rugosas and the pimpinellifolia group, roses are not over-fond of hot, dry, sandy soils and chalky soils are not ideal either, but there is a great deal the gardener can do to make both types more suitable, not only for roses but for many other things as well. Then there is that most persistent of myths that roses prefer to grow in clay. They are, it is true, perfectly happy in a clay soil that drains well, but will hardly survive in one that does not. They do not like their roots half submerged in water and in the unlikely event of the late Mr Stapleton in 'The Hound of the Baskervilles' having tried to grow roses in the Great Grimpen Mire, he would not have succeeded. Roses do, of course, like moisture and plenty of it, but not if it hangs about, and a well-drained, medium loam is every bit as suitable for them as any kind of clay. The particles that go to make up a clay soil are so small as to become what is virtually a solid mass when they are compressed by, for instance, someone walking on a wet rose bed. Then when it dries out – concrete.

I have said that roses need a site in full sun, yet nurseries often recommend certain climbers as being suitable for north walls. Except possibly on the equator, where few of us live, roses in such a position would not get any direct sunlight at all and while it is true that some of the tougher varieties will put up a show of sorts in this kind of position, they would be a great deal better on a south-facing wall. Then Dickens's description of Chesney Wold in *Bleak House* can become a reality: 'The house, with gable and chimney, and tower, and turret, and dark doorway, and broad terrace walk, twining among the ballus-trades of which, and lying heaped upon the vases, there was one great flush of roses, seeming scarcely real in its light solidity, and in the serene and peaceful hush that rested all around it.'

Cultivation

Try to avoid planting roses under trees, even if a fair amount of sun can reach them there. They will tend to lean out towards the light and are likely to become leggy in reaching for it, quite apart from the fact that they will be in direct competititon with the tree roots for moisture and plant foods. The only exception to this advice is when you are planting a rambler or climber which will eventually grow up the tree, but even then it should be planted as far as possible from the tree's trunk as is consistent with training it towards the tree along a stake or cane. Such vigorous roses will find their own way to the light of the sun by scrambling upwards through the branches of the tree.

In a hilltop garden or other windy site, roses will probably need the protection of a windbreak, not because the rose plants cannot stand up to a good deal of buffeting – even if they would be much better without it – but because the flowers would be likely to be damaged. And the salt-laden winds of the seaside can be countered to some extent by growing roses of the rugosa family, which not only stand up to them remarkably well themselves, but will form substantial windbreaks behind which other roses can find some shelter. No rose, however, will thrive in the kind of draughty situation that one can find in the gap between two houses.

The Soil and its Preparation

Roses are remarkably tolerant of the kind of soil in which they grow but do prefer one that is slightly acid or about 6.5 on the pH scale. So let us first of all assume that we are dealing with a good loam with about the right pH reading. Is there something that should be done before the roses are planted?

The answer to this becomes obvious if one considers that the roses are going to be in their new home for a great many years, during which time they will give us endless pleasure. It makes sense, then, to be sure that that home is prepared for them in the best possible way, so even with soil that is apparently suitable, something more should be done. If the soil drains well, there is no need to double-dig, which means going right down to the subsoil to break it up and adding ashes, peat or something else to lighten it and open it up. You can simply add compost or leaf-mould to the upper layer, making sure that it is well broken up and mixed in. Do this at the end of the summer if you are going to plant the roses in the autumn, as the soil will then have plenty of time to settle down and consolidate and the humus-forming materials will have begun their work by the time the roses go in.

A clay subsoil can be improved in texture by the addition of calcium sulphate at 3 lb sq. yd ($1^1{}_2$ kg m^2). Nitro-chalk will reduce the acidity of soil and is safer to use than lime. Perhaps because of the comparative cheapness of the latter it is all too easy to overdo the application and getting rid of lime once it is there is like getting treacle out of a bag of sawdust. Peat will help to increase acidity and so will leaf-mould.

If your garden is on chalk with only a shallow layer of top soil, roses will not be the easiest plants to grow – except possibly a number of the old hybrid perpetuals that do not seem to mind it too much. To succeed with the others it will be necessary to dig out a hole for each plant, preferably about 2 ft by 2 ft (60 cm by 60 cm), and fill them with a planting mixture of soil and peat in the proportions of 1:1, with plenty of bonemeal added.

Before finishing with soil preparation, a word of warning. So far it has been assumed that we have been dealing with a new rose bed where roses have not grown before. It may be, however, that a bed contains roses that are clearly approaching the end of their useful lives and you wish to replace them. Unfortunately, this is not as straightforward as it sounds, and unless the soil is completely changed to a depth of 18 in–2 ft (45 cm–60 cm), the new roses will never do well. Simply adding manure and other fertilisers will not get rid of the problem, for the soil will have become what is known as rose-sick. The reasons for this do not seem to be fully understood – if they were, there would hardly be so many conflicting explanations given for it – but one can add that it is not a problem confined to roses and affects conifers and fruit trees among others, when it is known as a transplant problem. If a rose in an established bed dies and you want to replace it, dig out as much soil as you can without disturbing neighbouring plants but making a hole certainly not less than 18 in by 18 in (45 cm by 45 cm) and fill it in with soil from another part of the garden. Rose-sick soil will not affect other plants if dumped elsewhere.

Planting

If you have ordered your roses in plenty of time, which means not later than the second half of the summer, they should reach you from the nursery in late autumn, which is the best time to plant them. The soil will not really have cooled down yet so that the roses' roots can start into active growth right away and help to establish the plants before the frosts of winter bring dormancy.

It may be that when the roses arrive you are in the middle of a frosty spell, which will be more likely if you are planting just after the turn of the year, or the ground may be waterlogged. Both these conditions make the soil unsuitable. Again, previous commitments may make putting the roses in immediately impossible, but they can be stored, unpacked, in a cool but frost-proof shed for a week to ten days with complete safety. Should the delay be longer than this, the roses should be heeled in.

Heeling in consists of unpacking the roses and then burying them almost completely in a shallow trench with at least 6 in (16 cm) of soil over the roots. You can actually bury the plants entirely if you wish, as long as you remember just where you have put them, and they can be left heeled in for five or six weeks if such a delay is unavoidable. Do, however, plant them properly as soon as you can.

Either before heeling in or before final planting, inspect the newly unpacked roses. If you have bought them from a good nursery, there should be few damaged or diseased canes, but if you come across any, cut them back to a healthy bud below the damage. Trim back long thick roots by about two-thirds and snip off any remaining leaves. There should be no sucker growth on the roots but it is worthwhile checking that there is none. Should you find a sucker, give it a sharp tug to pull it away. If the roses look at all dried-up put them in a bucket of water for an hour or more to soak.

It will get the roses off to a much better start if, while they are soaking, you prepare a planting mixture. This should consist of about half a bucketful per rose of equal parts of granulated peat and soil, well mixed together after a handful per plant of bonemeal has been added. It can be taken to the new rose bed in a wheelbarrow ready for use when the actual planting begins.

How close roses should be planted must depend on the habit of the variety. A narrow upright grower such as 'Grandpa Dickson' will need much less space around it than a sprawler like 'Josephine Bruce'. Too close planting restricts air circulation which not only encourages the spread of disease but at the same time makes spraying against it more difficult. On the other hand, if the roses are too far apart and a lot of soil shows between them, the whole bed can look rather bare unless other plants are used to fill the gaps, so all in all it comes back once more to knowing your roses. If you have seen them growing elsewhere, you will have noted just how much space they will take up and can plan your planting accordingly, but if this is not possible for some reason, a good average distance between bushes, both large- and cluster-flowered, is about 18 in (45 cm).

The planting holes should be dug large enough for the rose roots to be well spread out and deep enough so that the budding union (the point from which the rose shoots are sprouting) is just below soil level. This can be checked when the rose is in place by placing a cane across the hole at soil level.

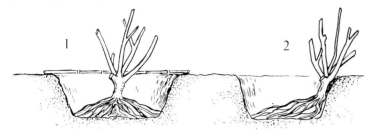

Figure 20.1
Planting a bedding rose.

1. Shows a rose placed centrally in the planting hole with the roots spread out evenly all round. Notice the cane placed across the top of the hole to enable the level of the budding union to be checked.

2. Shows the way to plant a rose that has all its roots pointing in one direction.

When the first bush is in its hole, the level has been checked and the roots are spread out, hold it upright with one hand and tip in some planting mixture from a bucket or shovel. Work this well between the roots and tread it down lightly. Pull in soil from the surrounding bed on top of this until the hole is filled and once more tread firmly but not too heavily. Top up with more soil and water well. Tread round the roses again after frosty spells during the winter as they may have become loosened in the soil.

Due to modern mechanised methods of planting the root-stocks on to which rose varieties are grafted, many roses have their roots growing all in one direction and if these are strong, it may be quite impossible to spread them out in the ideal way without straining them to the point of breaking. So if you have roses like this, do not try. Put them in to one side of your planting hole and spread the roots out fanwise over as much of the hole as possible. The important thing in either kind of planting is that the roots should not all be bunched together so that they rob each other of nourishment.

Climbing roses against walls where the soil is likely to be hot and dry should always be planted not less than 18 in (45 cm) from the wall and the rose positioned so that its shoots are leaning in towards the wall and its roots are fanned outwards towards moister earth, particularly if it is a house wall where eaves may keep rain away.

167

Figure 20.2
Planting a
climbing rose.

Planted so that its roots grow outwards away
from the wall up which it will be trained and so
penetrate into damper soil.

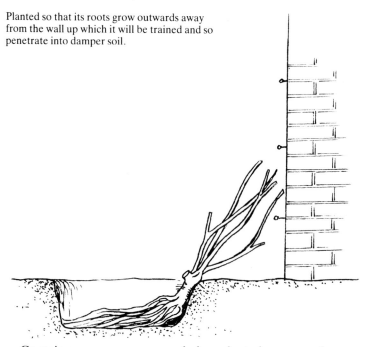

Container-grown roses are being planted more and more
nowadays but it is not enough, particularly in heavy soils,
simply to dig a hole the size of the container (which is, of
course, the size of the rootball when the rose is taken out of it)
and pop the rose into it. Unless the soil is very well drained, you
may simply have dug a sump in which water collects and this
will do the rose no good at all. Make your planting hole every
bit as big as you would for a bare-root rose and use the same
planting mixture. Loosen the soil a little at the bottom of the
rootball before planting. Then make firm and water well. It is as
well to soak the rose in the container before planting it as
container-grown plants can dry out all too easily and it is not
always immediately obvious that they have done so.

With standard roses, the roots and the stem on to the top of
which your variety is budded are usually of a rugosa stock. This,
particularly if planted deeply, is inclined to sucker, so plant
your standards no deeper than the soil marks – these should be
easy to see on the bottom of the stems when they arrive from
the nursery. Standard roses need a strong stake and this should
always be driven in before the rose is planted to avoid possible
root damage that might occur if it were done later. The top of
the stake should just reach into the head of the rose to give it
some support and should certainly not protrude above it. There
are many kinds of tie on the market to hold the rose to the

168

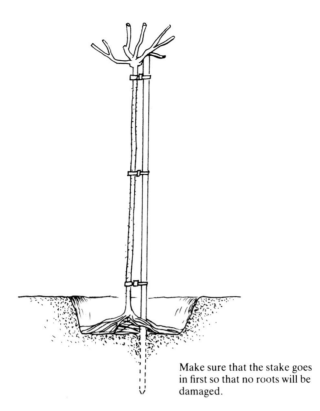

Figure 20.3
Planting a standard
rose.

Make sure that the stake goes
in first so that no roots will be
damaged.

stake, but whatever kind is chosen it should have a buffer to
hold the rose and the stake an inch or two (2.5–5 cm) apart to
avoid rubbing. Make sure the ties are good strong ones. There
are a number of plastic designs on the market which are much
too flimsy and do not last more than one season without
splitting. Leave the ties quite loose for a few weeks after
planting the rose to allow both it and the soil to settle down, but
when tightening them up eventually, remember to allow room
for the standard stem to grow. We neither want the rose left
hanging after soil subsidence, nor strangled at a later date.

Training

Primarily, training is confined to climbers and ramblers as these
are the roses which, if left to themselves, would get quite out of
control. Their long shoots need some sort of guidance and
restraint, but there is a second reason for training them. If the
shoots of a climber are allowed to go straight up, a chemical
inhibitor within the plant will tend to prevent most of the side
buds from breaking into life and forming flowering shoots. The
flowers will only come at the ends of the main shoots, which

means in practice at about the level of the bedroom windows if the climber is on the wall of a house. This is only acceptable if you spend your days lolling in bed, which not all of us are able to do, so the answer is to fan the shoots outwards and train them as near to the horizontal as possible along galvanised iron wires. These should be strung about 18 in (45 cm) apart from vine eyes driven into the wall so that the wires are 3–4 in (7.5–10 cm) away from its surface. Tie the shoots to the *outside* of the wires with plastic-covered garden wire. If the shoots were tucked behind the horizontal wires, you would have trouble disentangling them at pruning time, but you will find that many grow that way in any case without any encouragement.

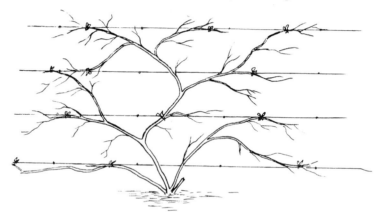

Figure 20.4
Training a climbing rose on a wall or fence.

The shoots are fanned out sideways and tied in to horizontal wires to encourage flowering side shoots.

You can also use the galvanised iron wires on a close-boarded fence or simply string them between uprights of rustic poles to form a rose hedge, but the important thing is to keep the shoots growing out sideways so that the bud growth inhibitor will cease to be effective and you will get flowers at all levels. The rose will climb upwards in time and cover the wall or fence as the upper side shoots are bent over and tied in in their turn. On anything other than a trellis, through which the wind can blow, the shoots are kept well away from the surface by the wires so that at least some air can circulate round and lessen the chances of fungus spores getting a hold. Ramblers, being naturally rather prone to mildew, are best kept away from walls altogether.

If you wish to grow a climber or rambler on a pillar, arch or over a pergola, you clearly cannot train the shoots horizontally, or at least not until they have reached the top of the vertical uprights with the latter two. There is an answer though, which is

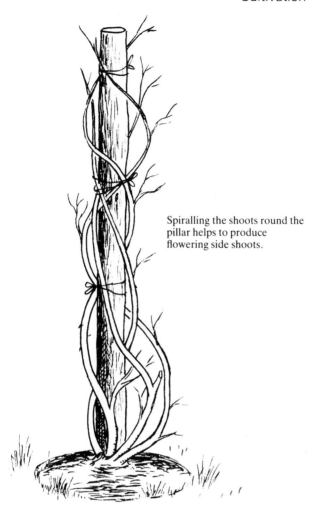

Figure 20.5
Training a climber
or rambler on a
pillar.

Spiralling the shoots round the
pillar helps to produce
flowering side shoots.

to wind them in a spiral round the posts, although this can be difficult with some climbers which have very stiff and unbending growth. The answer is to begin training as soon as growth starts and while the shoots are still quite soft, but it must be done very gently at that early stage as they can easily be damaged or snapped off altogether.

There are three other aspects of rose training, both of which were more often practised in the past than they are nowadays. Weeping standards are not too often seen, which is a great pity as they can give the added dimension to a rose bedding scheme which can best be seen in many of the great continental rose gardens where they are still popular. Although some climber varieties are sold for this purpose, the only roses that will really 'weep' properly, which means that the canes should hang down

171

all round almost to ground level (making them look less like a lollipop than other standards), are the ramblers with their thin, lax shoots. To get the full effect, the stem of a weeping rambler is much longer than that of other kinds. It can be as much as 6 ft (1.8 m) and the supporting stake must be proportionately thicker and stronger. An evenly balanced head is much easier to achieve if a special galvanised wire 'umbrella' is fixed to the top of the stake and the rose shoots tied in to this in the initial stages, but these frames are becoming progressively more difficult to obtain, in the United Kingdom at least.

Figure 20.6

A climber that is to grow up a tree should be planted well away from the tree trunk so that it does not have to compete with the tree roots for water and nutrients. The rose shoots can then be trained in towards the trunk along wooden stakes.

If you wish to grow a rose – again preferably a rambler – up a tree, a little initial training is helpful, after which it can generally be counted on to look after itself. You can and should plant the rose at least 3–4 ft (90 cm–1.2 m) away from the tree trunk so that competition from the tree roots for water and soil nutrients is at least a little reduced though certainly not eliminated, and the shoots can then be trained inwards along sloping canes. After a while they may need some tying in to the trunk itself until they have begun to hook their thorns over the lower branches, after which they will go hand over hand upwards, questing for the light. When they reach it they will arch over naturally and hang down laden with festoons of blossom, a sight which once seen will not be forgotten.

It may be of some help to plant one of these ramblers on the side of a tree from which the prevailing wind comes as this will blow the first young growths into the branches rather than away from them. Do, however, bear in mind that you want to see the rose yourself and you are not planting it solely for the benefit of your neighbours, so the position of planting must be governed by this as well. The shoots of the rose will always head at top speed for the most sunny side of the tree, so this kind of planting, except for philanthropists, is not for the southern side of your garden.

One final kind of training can be mentioned fairly briefly as it has already been covered fairly fully in Chapter 10 (Hybrid Perpetuals). This is pegging down, widely practised in the second half of the last century and the early days of this one when the hybrid perpetuals and bourbons were the popular garden rose. With the hybrid perpetuals particularly, the pattern was one of long, strong shoots sent up in late summer, in some varieties as much as 5–6 ft (1.5–1.8 m) long, and the question gardeners had to ask themselves was: 'What do I do with them?' Pruning them all away seemed such a waste of the rose's energies, but if they were left flowers would come only at their tips, holding on for dear life when the wind blew and altogether looking most ungainly. The answer, the Victorian gardeners found, was to remove the soft tips of the shoots in autumn and bend the rest of the shoots gently but firmly over until the ends could be tied to short wooden pegs driven into the ground. A variant, in a large bed with many roses, was to cover the earth with a criss-cross of wires strung between pegs and to tie the rose shoots to the wires. In both cases the effect achieved was exactly that of training climbing roses along horizontal wires and the side buds would be activated and produce flowering spurs. Pegging down need not, of course, be confined to bourbons or hybrid perpetuals. It can be used to increase the flowering of any tall and lanky rose, provided the shoots are reasonably flexible, and can be carried out with great effect with a number of the not-too-vigorous modern climbers if you decide to try them as free-standing shrubs.

Roses are not really greenhouse plants and will, if they are to thrive, spend more time out of it than in. The greenhouse is used solely to bring the roses into flower a few months early, and if it is heated you will have blooms in early spring. Even in an unheated one, flowering should commence by late spring, so that your rose season is extended quite considerably. And such cosseted blooms, which do not have to contend with the eccentricities of wind and weather, will be of a quality and, if

Roses in the Greenhouse

some disbudding is carried out, of a size that you might not always match in the garden later. Many-petalled varieties especially, those that tend to 'ball' in wet weather and seldom open properly, can reveal their true beauty unfailingly under glass.

Having said which, it is not suggested that a rose such as 'Royal Highness', which hates rain but is a very tall upright grower, is ideal pot-rose material. Lanky varieties look ungainly under glass and it is much better to pick reasonably bushy and compact growers. Some possibilities, among, of course, a great many more, are 'Alec's Red', 'Allgold', 'Ernest H. Morse', 'National Trust', 'Grandpa Dickson', 'Fragrant Gold', 'Korp', 'Korresia' and 'Mullard Jubilee'.

Most roses, except perhaps the most vigorous, can be kept in 8 in (20 cm) pots for the first two years or so after which 10 in (25 cm) pots are preferable. John Innes potting composts, either No 2 or No 3 or their equivalent, are suitable growing mediums, removing a little from the soil surface each year and replacing it with fresh and carrying out complete repotting every three to four years.

The cycle for roses under glass begins in October, using varieties bought in especially and potted up or moderately sized bushes lifted from the garden. Since the roses should not be forced in their first year after potting, one can take a short cut by buying container-grown varieties which will be already established, but as one does not know how well these may have been grown and looked after, this is taking something of a risk. With other roses, thick stubborn roots that will not fit easily into the pots must be cut back as necessary. Water them well after planting and stand them in a reasonably sheltered but sunny spot out of doors. Make sure the surface on which they stand allows free drainage from the pots.

The roses will remain where they are until the following autumn, being sprayed regularly against pests and diseases and kept well watered through the summer. The roses should be brought into the greenhouse early in the winter and pruned much more drastically than they would be if grown out of doors. This means leaving the shoots only about 3–4 in (7.5–10 cm) in length. Add about 1 oz (25 g) of a proprietary rose fertiliser to each pot and fork it lightly into the surface, watering well afterwards.

If your greenhouse is heated and you want the very earliest roses, keep the night temperature above about 41°F (5°C) and by day if the weather is mild make sure that there is adequate ventilation, which will help to keep away mildew. Top ventilation is to be preferred to that from the side.

Greenfly may appear but can easily be controlled by one or other of the many modern sprays, and caterpillars can be picked off by hand unless you are growing your roses in truly vast quantities. Black spot will not, so early in the year, be a problem you have to deal with.

When, from early spring onwards, new shoots are developing rapidly and flower buds beginning to form, a weak liquid feed may be given once a week. It may – indeed it will – be tempting once the flowers begin to open to take the pots into the house, but this really should be resisted as the atmosphere will be much too dry for them. It is far better to use the roses as cut flowers.

By midsummer the pot roses will have finished flowering and the pots should be taken out of the greenhouse and returned to their sheltered, sunny spot until the following autumn.

CHAPTER 21

Routine Maintenance

Fertilisers and Mulches

Both of these would have fitted equally well into the last chapter, but as the application of both fertilisers and mulches is an operation repeated at regular intervals, perhaps it is better to keep information about them under the routines of the rose garden.

As has been said already, roses are extremely tolerant and will grow in a wide range of soils, although some are better for them than others. However, they do like to live well and a rose that is well nourished will be much more likely to remain healthy than one that is not. Light soils are generally to some extent deficient in many of the chemical salts roses need and those that are there are either fairly rapidly used up or washed away by rain. But even the best of soils can usually do with some additional fertiliser when growing roses, and this can either take the form of a mulch of well-rotted farmyard manure or well-rotted garden compost, applied about 3–4 in (7.5–10 cm) thick to the rose bed in late spring when the soil has warmed up a little, or else an artificially composed fertiliser – organic or inorganic. The manure or compost, in addition to providing food for the roses as it is broken down by the soil bacteria, will also improve the soil structure by making humus.

A balanced rose fertiliser needs nitrogen for strong growth, phosphates to help build the roots and flowers and potash for ripening and resistance to drought and disease. A balanced rose fertiliser should contain:

sulphate of ammonia	$2\frac{1}{2}$ parts
sulphate of iron	1 part
sulphate of magnesium	1 part
sulphate of potash	5 parts
superphosphate of lime	8 parts

but this will lack the minute quantities of boron, iron, manganese, magnesium, molybdenum and a few other minerals collectively known as trace elements that the rose does need but which would be practically impossible to add in the right proportions. The majority of soils will probably supply them, so there is no great need to worry, and in any case mixing your own fertiliser is only really worthwhile if you grow a great many roses or have a liking for experiment by varying the quantities according to your (or someone else's) analysis of your soil. For most people one of the proprietary rose fertilisers, of which there are many on the market, which incorporate the necessary trace elements, or a general garden fertiliser such as Growmore will be satisfactory and much less trouble, as you do not have to make it up. The rate of application is one small handful sprinkled round each bush and lightly hoed in. This should be done at a minimum of twice a year, once at pruning time in spring and again in about a month after midsummer, although no later or autumn shoots will be encouraged and these will not have time to ripen so that the frosts of winter will kill them off. Sulphate of potash on its own at the rate of 2 oz per sq. yd (50 g per m^2) will help in the ripening of late summer canes.

Always use gloves – preferably rubber ones – when handling fertilisers or for that matter any gardening chemical. Those of us who have been trying to put over this common sense point at every opportunity for years find it not a little frustrating that pretty well every single television gardener uses his bare hands for bonemeal, fertiliser and everything else.

Some people, particularly those who wish to exhibit, will use more than two applications of fertiliser and will probably supplement it with foliar feeding. This means that a liquid fertiliser is sprayed on to the leaves so that it is absorbed straight away into the plant's system and bypasses the roots altogether. For the average gardener, however, foliar feeding is an unnecessary chore, although it can be used with advantage if yellowing or other leaf discoloration indicates that a rose is having difficulty in taking up some particular chemical from the soil. A shortage of iron is the most common deficiency and is likely to occur in alkaline soils.

Mulches

A mulch of farmyard manure or compost has already been mentioned and these two are the most important ones for adding nutrients to the soil. However, a mulch does have a number of other beneficial functions, helping to prevent the evaporation of moisture being one of the main ones, so that it should never be put on when the soil is dry. You cannot help to conserve what is not there in the first place.

A mulch will also help to prevent a wide variation in the temperature of the soil, which is advantageous. This means that it should not be put on too early in the year when the soil is still icy-cold from winter frosts as the mulch will hold back the natural warming up as the year advances. Mid to late spring is the time to apply it, which will be just about the time when the main crop of weed seedlings is emerging. These will be most effectively smothered, which is another important function of a mulch, but it would be as well to make sure that the very strong-growing and persistent perennial weeds like couch grass and creeping buttercup are removed from the rose bed first or dealt with by a weedkiller. Even the most ruthless mulch would hardly conquer some of them.

Manure is progressively more hard to come by and there are few gardens that produce compost sufficient for their needs. Where this is so, peat can be used as a mulch and looks neat, but it is an expensive item to buy, and the contents of what appears to be an enormous bale seems to shrink to about one-quarter of their volume when spread out on the beds. It protects the soil only and provides no nourishment, and when dry it can blow about. On balance the comparatively recently introduced pulverised forest bark seems a better bet and, so far, until, of course, it reaches the stage where everybody wants it, it is cheaper than peat. Some concern was expressed when it first came on the market that the gradual process of its decomposition on the soil surface would rob the soil (and hence the roses) of nitrogen, but in practice this does not seem to be a serious problem. The same objection is raised to the idea of using fallen leaves as a mulch without letting them rot down first, but once again experience has shown that there seems to be enough nitrogen about for all. Fallen leaves can, however, really only be used in amongst reasonably closely planted shrub roses where they stand a chance of being held in place when the wind blows. Otherwise, your garden will soon look a mess, especially if the leaf coverage extends to the edges of the beds, from which blackbirds will scatter them over surrounding lawns like a medieval lord distributing money to the poor.

Pruning

Whether or not they are pruning or have pruned their roses correctly worries more people than any aspect of rose growing, except perhaps what to do about black spot. They approach their bushes at pruning time as though they were wired up to the mains.

There are two particular reasons for this, the first coming

about because most gardeners try to learn their pruning from a book or magazine and it is a very difficult operation to put over in words, even if they are supplemented by diagrams. No two rose bushes are the same and a drawing of one may bear little resemblance to what a would-be pruner actually sees in front of him or her in a rose bed. Even though it may be made clear in the text that the diagrams are only intended to indicate the principles to be followed, the nervous beginner, faced with reality, will find this of little help if the diagram and his rose bush differ to a great degree. And if described in words alone, pruning, in reality a simple operation based purely on common sense, sounds impossibly complicated.

The second reason why there can be worry and doubt in many people's minds over pruning is that even the experts disagree over certain aspects of it. One will advocate late-autumn pruning, another late-spring; one will go for really hard pruning, another for light or medium – and so it goes on.

With such widely differing opinions among those who should know, it should be clear that it does not matter very much whose advice you follow. One theory is as good as another, so pick the one that suits you best. Time and experience will show you whether it also suits your roses and the climate you live in, for it must be added that the severity of winters likely to be experienced in a particular part of a country (and even the severity of frost pockets in an individual garden) may decide for you without any question whether you should prune in autumn or spring. Frost damage to autumn-pruned canes may mean in a very hard winter a second going over in spring and much harder cutting back overall than one would wish. In other words, while following certain basic principles, one must be prepared to adapt to special circumstances.

This may, of course, sound even more terrifying than trying to follow a book of rules, but this really is not so. The one and only secret to successful pruning is to understand why you are doing it at all – what you are trying to achieve. Once this is mastered, how and when you go about it becomes, as I said earlier, largely a matter of common sense.

Since it is unlikely that a Sydney Carton is going to come along and do your pruning for you and it is something that you will have to face up to yourself sooner or later, let me see if I can prove, as far as is possible in words and pictures alone, that what I have just said is true. It would be easier if I were out in the garden demonstrating, but there it is. I am not.

So, why is it that we prune? There are four main reasons.

(1) To get rid of dead or diseased shoots and those that are

so spindly and weak (those that are much less than pencil thickness) that they are unlikely to bear any worthwhile flowers in the summer to come.

(2) To replace the old shoots with strong new ones. With bedding roses the best flowers are borne on these new shoots, which should grow from at or near the base or crown of the plant each year. Pruning the old main shoots back to dormant buds not too far above ground level will encourage these to grow away and form the shoots we need.

Since there may sometimes be difficulty in recognising a dormant bud, this might be the place to expand a little on buds in general. Roses (and other plants) have two kinds of buds: those that open into flowers at the tips of main or side shoots and those that form in the angle where a leaf joins a shoot so that they are called leaf-axil buds. The latter kind are the ones that produce new shoots and so are the ones we are concerned with in pruning. When a leaf falls, and most of them will have done so by the time spring pruning comes around, the dormant leaf-axil buds can still be seen as raised half-circles on the rose stems, although many will have actually started to swell and be easily recognised.

(3) To remove surplus shoots in order to open out the centre of a bush that has become congested. Air circulation will be improved and the chance of disease lessened, a statement that is probably true though a difficult one to prove when disease comes anyway. At least, however, shoots that are crossing and rubbing together, or are likely to do so if they continue to grow in the same direction, should be removed before they can really damage each other. A wound in the bark of a shoot, however it is caused, opens the door to disease spores.

(4) The final reason for pruning is purely an aesthetic one. A balanced rose bush looks much better than a lopsided one. 'I have also learnt from cottage gardens,' Gertrude Jekyll wrote in *Wood and Garden*, 'how pretty are some of the old roses grown as standards . . . I have taken the hint, and now have some big, round-headed standards, the heads yards through, of the lovely Celeste and of Madame Plantier that are worth looking at, though one of them is rather badly shaped this year, for my handsome Jack (a donkey) ate one side of it while he was waiting outside the studio door while his cartload of logs was being unloaded.'

With standards balance is probably of even more importance than it is with bushes (except those grown as specimens) because the roses are more likely to be seen from all sides. In bedding, the odd peg-leg is less likely to be noticed, but, in general, evenness of growth is a thing to be desired. Not all roses are particularly keen to co-operate, of course, and are very stubborn about sending out shoots just where you want them, but quite a lot can be done by cutting to a bud facing in the right direction.

Having now, I hope, established the reasons for pruning, the next stage is to learn a few basic techniques that apply to the pruning of virtually all roses. Differences will emerge when we deal with each group individually, but these differences are merely variations on the principles already outlined.

Pruning is most easily done with secateurs, which should always be kept sharp and, in an ideal world where time is limitless, be cleaned with methylated spirit after every use to prevent the passing from one rose to another of disease spores. A good pair of secateurs will not be cheap, but they will last a lifetime and will not distort or bruise the rose shoots when cutting them. Bruising can, like other surface damage, lead to die-back and other troubles. Pruning cuts should be made about $\frac{1}{4}$ in (6 mm) above a bud and sloping downwards away from it at an angle of about 45°. Cutting to an outward-facing bud will encourage a compact, upright rose to spread itself, but a sprawler will benefit from cutting to an inward-facing bud so that it will gain some height. Do not worry if you cannot find a bud where you want to cut. Later, I will be suggesting that large-flowered (hybrid tea) roses should be cut finally to 8–10 in (20–25 cm), but this must be taken as a guide only. It would be better to cut the shoot to 6 in (15 cm) if there is a good bud at that point and none between the 8–10 in (20–25 cm). It may be, however, and this applies more especially to the cluster-flowered roses, that you cannot find a bud at all. In such cases cut where you think is suitable and it is amazing how often a formerly invisible bud will spring into life from nowhere after a week or so. The stump above the bud, which would have died back anyway, can then be trimmed away.

And talking about stumps, make sure that all dead ones from previous prunings are removed. It may be necessary with very thick and tough ones near the base of the plant to use a fine-toothed pruning saw, after which rough or torn edges should be pared smooth with a sharp knife. Should you cut into shoots that look healthy from the outside but find that the centre of one or more is brown and discoloured, this means that die-back is spreading down the shoot. Try cutting to the next bud, and continue downwards from bud to bud until clean white wood is reached – even if it means going right to ground level.

The traditional time for pruning is quite early in the spring when the buds on the roses are just beginning to break, but it is quite in order to prune at any time when the roses are dormant or nearly so. One must, as in so much of gardening, be guided to a large extent by the weather and by one's own growing conditions. One should never prune in the middle of a frosty spell, which can be one of the major causes of die-back. If pruning is done in the autumn and a mild winter follows you will be perfectly all right. If there should be prolonged and heavy frosts, however, it will, as I mentioned earlier, almost certainly be necessary to go over the bushes in spring to cut away damage caused by the cold. It will not, of course, be a complete repruning, but it will be an extra job which few of us want.

If you plant roses in the autumn, they should be pruned in the spring at the same time as those you already have, with the exception of climbers and ramblers which should be left just as they were received from the nursery. The shoots of all other roses that are newly planted should be reduced to no more than 3–4 in (7.5–10 cm) long. This will take some courage, as carrying out what appears to be butchery on something which you have just spent money on requires a resolute hand. But it

Figure 21.1
Before and after
pruning a large-
flowered (hybrid
tea) rose.

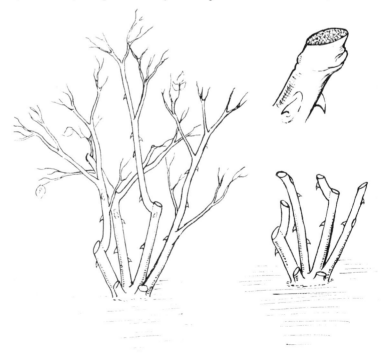

The top drawing on the right shows the correct pruning cut just above a dormant bud. It should slope at an angle of about 45°.

182

does pay in the long run and the rose, developing more slowly than it would otherwise do, has time to build up a sound root system and a really strong initial framework of shoots. If you plant roses in the spring, prune them at the same time.

So much for general principles. Now to specifics.

Large-flowered Roses (hybrid teas). Aim to leave only those shoots that are of pencil thickness or more, cutting away any that are diseased or spindly. Remove stumps left from previous prunings from which no new growth has sprouted. Thin out the centre of the bush if needed and finally cut the main shoots, leaving them (to the nearest bud) 8–10 in (20–25 cm) long. For garden display this is just about the right length. Harder pruning, which you would certainly give if you were exhibiting seriously – or even half-seriously – will produce bigger blooms but probably fewer of them. With lighter pruning you get more and smaller flowers and, much as it goes against the grain to say so, with no pruning at all you will still get quite a display, but only for a time. The shoots you have left untouched will deteriorate over a few years and the health of the plant gradually decline.

Very tall and strong-growing large-flowered roses such as 'Peace' and 'Alexander' should not be pruned too hard and can be left at 2–3 ft (60–90 cm) or even more if you want them to develop into substantial shrubs.

Figure 21.2

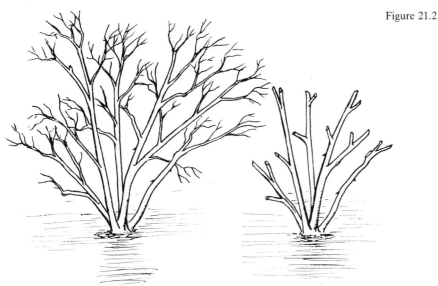

Before and after pruning a cluster-flowered (floribunda) rose. The shoots are left longer than those of a large-flowered variety.

Cluster-flowered Roses (floribundas). Follow the instructions for the large-flowered types but leave the main shoots at 12–14 in (30–35 cm) in length and cut back strong side shoots by about two-thirds. With these roses one is after quantity of flower rather than the highest quality in each individual bloom, so they do not need to be cut back so hard. The equivalents here of 'Peace' and 'Alexander' are 'Queen Elizabeth' and 'Fred Loads'. As mentioned under its detailed description in Chapter 14, the former can be made to bush out more than it would otherwise by pruning its shoots to various lengths.

Climbing Roses. These, with their permanent framework of main canes, need only to have the side shoots or laterals cut back to two or three eyes (buds). If the rose becomes bare at the base after some years, cut back a main shoot hard and with luck you should get new growth coming low down. If not, and some roses such as 'Paul's Lemon Pillar' are extremely reluctant to exert themselves in this way and take amputation philosophically, you will just have to plant a low bush of another kind in front of it.

Figure 21.3

When pruning a climbing rose it is only necessary to trim back side shoots or laterals by about two-thirds and to remove small, twiggy growth. The main shoots should not be pruned except to keep them in bounds.

Ramblers. With the wichuraianas and other small-flowered groups such as the multifloras, after blooming cut all canes that have carried flowers down to the ground and tie in newly-formed shoots in their place. If these are scarce, retain some of the old ones and trim back their laterals. They will produce some flowers. With the ramblers allied to 'Albertine', cut out old growth that has flowered just above the point from which a new shoot has sprouted.

Standard Roses. We have already dealt with the importance of a balanced head with these. Most standard roses, or at least most of those easily obtainable, utilise large- or cluster-flowered varieties, or if they are weeping standards, a rambler. Follow the pruning pattern for these three types exactly, just as if the tops of the standards were at ground level and no long stem intervened between the roots and the shoots.

Miniature Roses. Although not everyone agrees with me on this, I have found that miniature roses get along very nicely with the absolute minimun of pruning. All that is needed is trimming back, more to keep them neat and tidy than anything else, and also possible thinning out of those varieties that develop into a thick tangle of twigs. Dead wood should, of course, be removed, too.

Old Garden and Shrub Roses. These vary so enormously in their type and habit of growth that one can only generalise to the extent of saying that dead wood should always be removed when seen, and that if one of them grows like a cluster-flowered rose for instance, prune it like one. Most old garden roses and modern ones like the hybrid musks respond with more flowers if their laterals are shortened by about two-thirds in winter. The more twiggy gallicas are almost certain to need thinning out, and if grown in hedges, can be lightly clipped over at pruning time to keep them neat. Rugosas will stand some clipping, too, but wild or species roses should not be touched at all except for the removal of dead wood. The only possible time that they may need a little attention is in their very early years if they start to grow lopsided. A wayward shoot may have to be removed then.

Insect Pests and Diseases

There is a large number of different kinds of insects and a much smaller number of fungus diseases that can trouble roses, but very few of the insects at least need be of concern to gardeners. Table 21.1 on pages 187-9 is reasonably comprehensive, but from among the pests listed, only greenfly (aphids) and in some years and some areas caterpillars and the leaf-rolling sawfly (which does seem to be on the increase) are likely to be present in such numbers that steps against them have to be taken. Of the diseases, black spot and, in certain localities and

185

on certain varieties, rose rust, are the ones to cause serious problems. Mildew, though a nuisance in that it makes the bushes very unsightly if it gets a hold, is less lethal and more easily controlled.

Figure 21.4
The effects of four
of the commonest
insect pests.

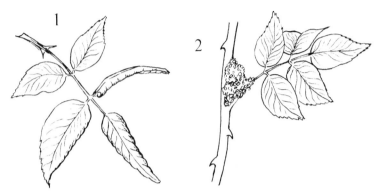

1. Leaf-rolling sawfly.   2. Froghopper (cuckoo spit).

4. Tortrix moth caterpillar.   3. Greenfly (aphids).

Chemical sprays are the easiest and quickest way of dealing with both insects and fungi. Systemic liquid sprays enter the plant's system, making the sap toxic, and since they cannot be washed off by rain, they will keep active for several weeks. However, it should be remembered that there are several types of systemics, those that can be taken up by a plant's roots, those that have to be sprayed on foliage and stems and are then carried in the sap stream throughout the whole plant, and finally those that, sprayed on the top of a leaf, will penetrate to the other side but no further. One can see that rather different spraying techniques are needed for each, but with none of them

Table 21.1: Insect Pests and Diseases
INSECT PESTS

Pest	Description and symptoms	Control	Remarks
Caterpillars	Mainly those of moths, eating irregular holes in leaves. The lackey moth caterpillar spins a white, silken tent; that of the winter moth hides between two leaves stuck together.	Remove by hand and destroy. For a severe infestation, spray with trichlorphon, fenitrothion, gamma BHC (HCH) or permethrin.	A winter-wash in early spring may destroy over-wintering eggs of winter moths.
Chafers	Medium-sized to large beetles, the cockchafer or May-bug, the rose chafer and the garden chafer, which nibble rose petals and anthers.	Spray with trichlorphon, fenitrothion or gamma BHC (HCH).	All lay eggs in the ground, and the white grubs may eat rose roots. BHC dust may help to destroy these.
Froghopper	Small, greenish-yellow insects which suck rose sap and protect themselves in easily seen blobs of froth (cuckoo spit), usually in the junction of two shoots.	Pick off and destroy, or use one of the sprays recommended for greenfly, but not pirimicarb. Derris is also effective.	Only the nymphal stages produce cuckoo spit, and damage ends at midsummer as insects reach the adult stage.
Greenfly (Aphids)	Small green or pink insects, some winged, which cluster on bud and flower stems, new shoots and leaves, generally on the underside. They multiply with incredible rapidity.	Spraying with a systemic insecticide will last several weeks. Effective are: dimethoate, heptenophos or ethiofencarb. Suitable contact insecticides include malathion, fenitrothion, pirimiphos-methyl and pirimicarb.	Burning prunings will destroy over-wintering eggs, as will the use of a winter wash.
Leaf-cutting bee	A small bee which cuts regular, circular holes in leaves.	Unlikely to be a serious pest. No control recommended.	In rare cases, when the infestation is severe, swat the bee as it cuts the leaf.
Leafhopper	A small, agile, pale-yellow, winged insect, which sucks sap from the undersides of rose leaves, leaving white mottling. Papery, grey-white, moulted skins under leaves should be looked for.	Use one of the sprays recommended for greenfly, but not pirimicarb. Derris is also effective.	More troublesome on roses grown against a wall or in warm, sheltered positions.

Pest	Description and symptoms	Control	Remarks
Leaf-rolling sawfly	Small, black flying insects that lay eggs in the leaf margins, injecting a toxin that rolls the leaf up lengthwise to protect eggs and larvae.	Pick off and burn affected leaves. Spray in late April or early May with trichlorphon, fenitrothion or pirimiphos-methyl.	More prevalent in wooded, sheltered areas.
Red spider mite	Minute, yellowish-green or red, sap-sucking animals, most troublesome under glass or in hot, dry situations. Difficult to see, but their tiny webs are a tell-tale sign.	Hard to control, but they do not like cold water. A systemic insecticide, e.g. dimethoate, may be of some help.	Biological control, using the predatory mite *Phytoseiulus persimilis* can be used, particularly under glass.
Rose leaf miner	Small moth grubs which bore their way into the leaf tissues. Light-coloured, twisting lines on the leaf surfaces are the signs to look for.	Spray with trichlorphon, fenitrothion or gamma BHC (HCH). Pick off and burn affected leaves.	Not usually a damaging pest.
Rose slug-worm	Small, black sawflies, the greenish slug-like grubs of which eat the leaf surfaces between the veins so that the affected areas turn brown.	Spray with gamma BHC (HCH), malathion, permethrin, fenitrothion, derris or pirimiphos-methyl.	Damage occurs shortly before and shortly after midsummer.
Scale insects	Small, scaly, limpet-like excrescences on rose stems which hide the female insects and eggs.	Spray with dimethoate or malathion. A winter wash helps to eliminate over-wintering larvae.	Dabbing scales with methylated spirit is an old but effective remedy.
Thrips (Thunder flies)	Lovers of hot, sunny spells, these tiny flies suck sap from leaves and also buds and flowers, leaving them ragged-looking.	Use any of the sprays recommended for caterpillars.	
Tortrix moth	The green or greeny-brown caterpillars bore holes in flower buds and eat holes in leaves. They hide in rolled-up leaves held together with silken threads.	Use sprays recommended for caterpillars.	

DISEASES

Disease	Description and symptoms	Control	Remarks
Black Spot	Rounded black spots with fringed edges on the leaves. These increase in size, the leaf yellows and drops off, weakening the plant.	Spray as soon as seen with benomyl, triforine, bupirimate-triforine or thiophanate-methyl. Remove and burn affected leaves. Winter-wash with Bordeaux mixture.	Does not usually appear before midsummer and attacks older, lower leaves first. Early preventative and then regular control sprayings every ten days may be needed in bad areas.
Canker	Disease spores which enter by a wound in a shoot and form brown, sunken and probably cracked areas.	Cut away the affected shoot below the canker. Copper sprays can be effective.	Clean secateurs afterwards with methylated spirit to prevent spread to other bushes.
Mildew	First seen as whitish, powdery-looking spots on leaves and flower stems, spreading out quickly until the whole bush may be covered. Will move onto other bushes by airborne spores.	Spray as soon as seen with benomyl, triforine, bupirimate-triforine, thiophanate-methyl or propiconazole.	Spraying with modern fungicides gives almost complete control.
Rose rust	Orange spots on the undersides of leaves, changing later to black.	Spray at once with oxycarboxin or propiconazole.	Some rose varieties and some districts are more prone than others. Rust can be fatal to roses if neglected.

is it necessary to spray both sides of the rose leaves as it used to be with the older contact sprays. For the increasing number of people who do not like using possibly dangerous chemicals, there are substitutes containing such natural products as pyrethrum, but none of them are systemics and their active life on the plant is likely to be short.

Whatever spray you choose to use, unless you decide to be adventurous and make up one yourself from a recipe in one of the old gardening books from the turn of the century, it will be expensive. Couple with this the fact that, to me and to many other people I know, spraying is one of the few really boring gardening activities and you have a cast-iron case for saying do not spray unless you really have to. This means do it only when you actually see a few greenfly on your roses or the first signs of black spot on the leaves. The only exception to this would be if you live in an area where black spot has always been rife and some form of preventative spraying has to be carried out.

Never spray in hot sunshine or the rose leaves may be scorched. Keep the job for very early in the morning or, better still, for the evening.

On Table 21.1, an application of a winter-wash of Bordeaux mixture is recommended for black spot. Some people would substitute Jeyes' Fluid, suitably diluted for this. Bordeaux mixture has been the recommendation of all the authorities for many years for the elimination – or at least partial elimination – of over-wintering disease spores, but recent trials at Wisley Gardens by the RHS, the results of which were published in *The Garden*, have cast doubt on its effectiveness in the case of black spot. It may help to clear away the eggs of harmful insects, but the findings seem to show that disease spores over-winter on parts of the plant and not on the soil as was previously thought. Those spores on the under sides of fallen leaves (assuming that they have not been removed and burned, as they should have been) will not be reached by the spray, and if the chemical constituents of the spray are strong enough to be effective, plant tissue is likely to be damaged. The prime source of lurking infection is spores in between the sheaths of dormant buds, which are extremely difficult to reach, and all in all it does sound as if we may have been wasting both time and money in hoping that our winter sprays would deal black spot a mortal blow. Time will tell, I suppose, but as the incidence of disease varies so much from year to year it is going to be extremely difficult to assess results oneself. It will be like trying to decide whether the pain would have gone away of its own accord if you had not taken the tablet.

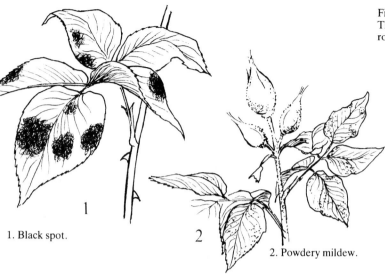

Figure 21.5
The two commonest
rose fungus diseases.

1. Black spot.

2

2. Powdery mildew.

When using the chart, one or two things should be borne in mind. Sprays that deal with both insect pests and diseases can be bought ready to use. With others, two sprays will have to be mixed, but always make sure that it is safe to do so. Incompatible chemicals mixed together might scorch the leaves of your roses. A number of manufacturers put out leaflets showing what will safely mix with what, but they naturally tend to cover only their own products.

There are some sprays that will kill only harmful insects and these should be used when possible. The labels on the packets or bottles containing the spray ingredients or the ready-mixed spray itself will always tell you the active ingredient used, what a particular spray will deal with, and exactly how it should be used. Always follow the directions to the letter.

Dead-heading

With the rose, as with any other flower, there is a natural growth cycle. Flowers form, are pollinated and the petals drop. Hips form in their place and these contain the seeds which, if allowed to, will germinate in the soil and make new plants. Dead-heading halts this cycle mid-way through by the removal of the hips before they start to swell, with the result that the roses will try again and produce more flowers. Do not, however, simply pull off the flowers as soon as they are spent. You will only be left with unsightly flower stalks which will gradually die back and you will not get new flowering shoots very quickly and when they do come they will be spindly. For

191

dead-heading use secateurs and cut the shoot about 4–5 in (10–13 cm) down, just above, perhaps, the third or fourth bud below the old bloom. You are carrying out, in actual fact, a mild form of pruning, but do not, in a moment of absent-mindedness, dead-head a rose that you are growing at least in part for its autumn hips. Generally speaking, non-recurrent roses need not be dead-headed.

Figure 21.6
Dead-heading.

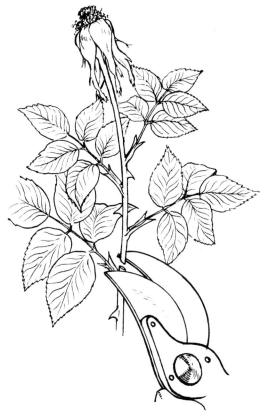

Do not just pull off the spent flower. Use secateurs and cut some way down the stem as shown.

Disbudding

This is something that you can do or not as you wish, although if you hope to exhibit your roses successfully, it is pretty well essential. It consists with large-flowered varieties of pinching out a number or perhaps all of the side flower buds on each shoot as soon as they are big enough for you to do so. This diverts the maximum amount of growing energy into the production of a limited number of much bigger blooms, one or perhaps two to a stem.

192

Figure 21.7
Disbudding or the
removal of side buds
to increase the size
of the main central
flower.

It may have been noticed that the truss of a cluster-flowered rose is made up of a number of smaller clusters on side shoots, each one containing a central bloom that is always the first to open. Disbudding consists of removing these central flowers while still in the early bud stage. Those surrounding them will then open a little earlier and all at the same time. For showing, it is important that as many flowers as possible on a truss should be open simultaneously.

Very nearly all the roses that you buy are budded on to rootstocks. This means that they are grown on the roots of a wild rose or at least a selected and specially developed form of one. It gives the cultivated variety added vigour and, by the choice of the right rootstock, the ability to grow well in heavy or

Suckers

193

light soils, plus other desirable qualities such as winter-hardiness and longevity.

Figure 21.8

Earth has been scraped away from around the base of this rose in order to find the source of a suspected sucker. The sucker can be seen growing out from one of the roots.

There are times, however, when these rootstocks like to take on a life of their own and they send out shoots from below the budding union, which is the point on the neck of the stock into which the bud was inserted. These are the dreaded suckers, but there is a gleam of light on the horizon for some of us as there should be less of them in the future. Careful selection of rootstock roses has produced some roses like the now very popular 'Laxa' which are much less likely to send up suckers than most others. 'Laxa', however, does not grow as well on heavy soils as the stocks which are variants of *R. canina*, and these do sucker, so one cannot say that the end of the tunnel has been reached. We progress, however, even though the millions of roses already planted all over the world will continue to plague us with their suckers for years to come.

How do you tell a sucker from a shoot that should be there? Very easily if you know how, and once the knowledge clicks into place you will wonder what all the puzzlement was about. In general a sucker will be a lighter green, the thorns will be of a different shape and colour, as will the leaves, which may have seven leaflets. If there is any doubt, scrape away some soil where the suspect sucker emerges and trace it back to its source. If it is growing from below the budding union, it is a sucker. Do not cut it as all you will be doing is pruning it so that

194

it will grow away more vigorously than ever. Give it a sharp tug and it should come away easily, together with dormant buds clustered about its base, which otherwise would be left to do their worst.

Even in winter you cannot put your rose garden entirely on automatic pilot. In early autumn it is advisable to shorten the shoots of tall-growing bedding roses by about one-third to prevent them from being rocked by the winds of winter and loosened in the soil and possibly damaged. All fallen leaves and weeds should be removed from the beds, but whether or not you decide to use a winter spray must depend on your conclusions after reading the earlier part of this chapter.

In a climate such as that of the greater part of the United Kingdom, no winter protection of your roses should be necessary, but if you do live in an exceptionally cold area, some earthing up of the bushes in autumn will help survival, and straw or bracken woven and tied into the heads of standard roses will protect their most vulnerable part.

CHAPTER 22

Growing Roses from Cuttings

Before anyone decides to try to grow roses from cuttings, they ought to be made fully aware of the pros and the cons because, although I still take cuttings myself because I enjoy experimenting, I think that on the whole there are more cons than pros. However, let us consider the plus factors, and first among these must come the fact that it is certainly the cheapest and (when it works) the easiest way of increasing your stock of roses, although it will only widen your range of varieties if your cuttings come from someone else's collection of roses. It can also, in the case of miniature roses, be said to be the best way of increasing numbers, as miniatures on their own roots are much more likely to stay true miniatures than they would if they were budded on to rootstocks. But this very factor, which is such a plus for the small roses, often becomes a disadvantage with the larger kinds, which, lacking vigour, seldom make such satisfactory plants as those which are budded.

Not all roses take equally well from cuttings – not even all varieties within one group or class – but in general it does seem that the closer a rose is to its original wild ancestor the more ready cuttings from it will be to take root and grow away vigorously. Thus ramblers will usually succeed as they have not come very far down the evolutionary scale from such species as *R. multiflora* (*R. polyantha*), *R. wichuraiana*, and so on. And, of course, many species will succeed, too, although this is not always an advantage as a number of them on their own roots will just become a tangle of thin wispy shoots, suckering madly all over the place and sadly deficient in the strong, graceful arching, flower-laden canes that otherwise would give them such distinction. Budding on to a rootstock concentrates their energy and keeps them disciplined and they should only rarely sucker if the right rootstock has been used. This is just as well as it can be much more difficult to distinguish a rootstock sucker from the legitimate shoot of certain species, as the rootstock will be a species itself, although almost certainly a different one.

Probably the most difficult roses of all to grow successfully from cuttings are the large-flowered (HT) varieties, which is, of course, the most highly bred and developed group of all, but even here there is no hard-and-fast rule as some large-flowered roses will root easily and do quite well. All one can usefully suggest is that anyone interested should experiment and see what happens with a particular variety. Certainly I have had a quite high percentage of success with roses from every group, including all the old ones.

If you want to grow roses from cuttings, you must not be in a hurry. Nurseries propagate roses by budding on to rootstocks not only because these will give the cultivated varieties added vigour and other desirable qualities but because strong, well-developed plants can be produced and put on sale in under two years from the time of budding. Growing roses from cuttings, even supposing the percentage that root satisfactorily could be guaranteed to be something approaching 100 per cent – which it cannot – would take more than twice as long, which would not make sense commercially, even allowing for the fact that for budding the nurseries have to pay for seedling rootstock plants in the first place. As far as I know, only miniature roses, which take very readily, are propagated commercially by at least three British and a number of American nurseries from cuttings and these will reach their full stature as plants fairly quickly. Otherwise one must allow four to five years for the larger roses.

Rose cuttings can be taken at any time between late summer (though not in the middle of a drought or heatwave) and late autumn if the season is a mild one. The place to grow them is a piece of ground in a reasonably open position that gets plenty of light but is shaded from the sun during the hottest part of the day. This is important as the cuttings must not dry out as they might do if they had a thorough baking. Preparation of the ground is minimal. If your soil is heavy, all you need to do is to dig a narrow trench 6 in (15 cm) deep with one vertical side and to scatter some coarse sand along the bottom. If your soil is light and sandy, all that should be necessary is to push in your spade vertically about 6 in (15 cm) and to move the handle backwards and forwards to form a slit. How long the trench or the slit should be will depend on the number of cuttings you intend to take, but these can be put in as close as 2 in (5 cm) apart. A 6-in (15-cm) gap between them would, however, be better if you are likely to be lifting the cuttings individually once they have rooted as neighbouring ones would be less likely to have their growth checked by root disturbance. The new roots, which will be fragile in their early stages, will be delving down well in excess of the initial 6 in (15 cm) so that there will be quite an upheaval of the earth when they are dug out.

Figure 22.1

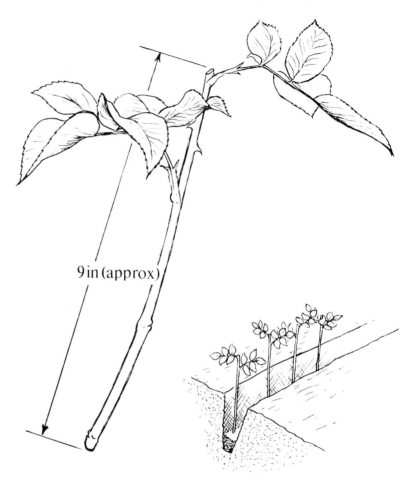

9 in (approx)

The preparation of a rose cutting and four cuttings in a planting trench. Note the small layer of sand along the bottom of the trench which helps the cuttings to root in heavy soils.

As to the cuttings themselves, these should be taken from rose shoots that are what is termed 'half-ripe'. This means long strong firm shoots that formed in the current season, most of which will have borne flowers in the midsummer flush of bloom. The soft tip of a shoot should not be used, but one, two or more 9 in (23 cm) lengths can be cut from the centre section. The cuts, to be made with a sharp knife or secateurs, should be at an angle similar to that used in pruning and be made immediately above a leaf joint and immediately below another one lower down. Remove all leaves except the top pair and snap off the

198

thorns, which should come away easily if the shoot is in the right condition. It may not be necessary, but to make as sure as possible of rooting, the bottom ends of the cuttings can be moistened and dipped into hormone rooting powder. Then each one in turn is placed upright against the vertical side of the trench or pushed into the slit in the earth. Gentle treading on each side of the slit will firm the earth round the cuttings, or if a trench has been used, it should be filled in and once again trodden firm. Since both trench and slit are 6 in (15 cm) deep, about 3 in (7.5 cm) of each cutting (carrying the pair of leaves) will be left above soil level. Water the cuttings in well and that is all that has to be done for a while except to make sure that they do not dry out if there is a long period without rain.

If there are hard frosts during the winter following planting, the cuttings may become loosened in the soil, so following a frosty spell tread along the rows again if this seems to be necessary. During the autumn and winter months a callous should form at the base of each cutting and from this roots will grow in the spring. By then the old leaves will have dropped off, but the leaf axil buds will begin to swell and eventually form new shoots if the cuttings have taken.

Apart from continuing to make sure they have adequate water, bearing in mind that there are often long dry spells in the spring which are less obviously so as they can be accompanied by day after day of grey skies, all that has to be done during the next few months is to remove any flower buds that form. Tempting as it may be to let them develop just to see what they may be like, even if common sense tells you they will be just the same as those on the rose you took the cuttings from, the temptation ought to be resisted. Cuttings should have a stern upbringing with no time for the frivolity of flower production or, to put it another (and more horticultural) way, all the energies of the newly developing plants should go into building up a strong root system before anything else. Do not be downcast if there are failures, even in some cases after healthy growth appears to have started and new shoots and leaves have formed. There is nothing exceptional in this, although the percentage of success, as was discussed earlier, will be higher with some roses than others.

By the autumn following that first summer, it should be safe to transplant the rooted cuttings to their final home, but whether or not you do so must depend on how long you are prepared to wait before they will really make an impact there and how anxious you are to have those spaces filled up quickly. The new roses will still be small and generally I find it more satisfactory to leave them in the cuttings bed for another twelve months, although an alternative, if you need the space for something else, is to pot them up as an interim measure, using John Innes No 2 potting compost.

CHAPTER 23

Hybridising and Budding

Hybridising can best be described as the creation of a completely new rose through a combination of flare, skill, a study of heredity, botanical know-how and a very high percentage of pure luck. How large a part the luck factor can play can be illustrated by the by no means exceptional case of a popular and recent large-flowered variety, 'Elizabeth Harkness' and its parents. This is a very shapely cream-white rose with some buff and pink shading on its petals, and it was bred from a cherry-red cluster-flowered rose called 'Red Dandy' and the yellow and red bicolour 'Piccadilly'. It is to be presumed that factors from earlier generations must have come into play and influenced the result of the breeding, but just the same it should not be inferred from what I have said and from this example that planned hybridising can never be carried out. Quite obviously it can or Sam McGredy could never have created his 'hand-painted' series or other breeders such as Jack Harkness made progress towards healthier varieties, but even so, from the time the rose breeder puts the pollen from one rose on to the stigmas of another, he would do well to keep his fingers crossed. Rose ancestry has been too inextricably mixed over many centuries for there to be any certainty about anything, which is, of course, what gives rose breeding most of its fascination. There is always the chance that you will produce a masterpiece, even if the odds against your doing so are something like 1:26,000. I made that figure up, but whatever they really are they must be enormous. However, hybridising, or at any rate hybridising for fun, which is all we are concerned with here, involves you in very little trouble. The basic technique is as follows.

Choose the two roses with which you wish to make the cross. The one which is to provide the pollen is the pollen parent and always given second when naming a rose's forbears, and the one which will produce the hips and in due course the seeds is the seed parent. Remove the petals of the seed parent just as the

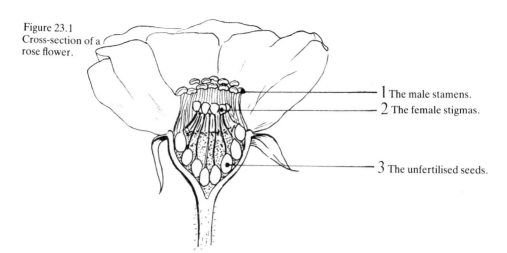

Figure 23.1
Cross-section of a
rose flower.

1 The male stamens.

2 The female stigmas.

3 The unfertilised seeds.

flower is beginning to unfold, but has not opened enough for an insect to have been able to get inside and pollinate it. Snip off the stamens and tie a small plastic bag over it, once again to prevent interference from insects. Cut the flower which is to be the pollen parent and remove the petals. Snip off the anthers into a small, plastic box or similar kind of container, labelling it with the name of the variety. Put this safely away until the following day, by which time the orange pollen grains should have been released and be lying in the bottom of the box. At the same time the stigmas of the seed parent will have begun to exude a sticky substance and be ready to receive the pollen.

Remove the plastic bag from the seed parent and, using a scrupulously clean watercolour brush, transfer pollen to the sticky stigmas, replace the plastic bag and label the cross with the names of the two roses involved, e.g. 'Red Dandy' × 'Piccadilly', 'Red Dandy' being the seed parent and coming first. If you are only carrying out one or two crosses, this labelling may seem superfluous, but I can assure you that it is not. After well over two months during which the hips will have been ripening, it will take a phenomenal feat of memory to remember just what has crossed with what, especially if your hybridisation has been carried out in the garden on bushes dotted here and there. If you have a greenhouse, it is easier to hybridise there, where control of temperature, humidity and insect pests will be that much simpler, and under glass the hips will stand a much better chance of ripening.

If the crosses have taken, the hips will swell and grow in size. If not they will shrivel. After the two months plus mentioned above, the exact period depending naturally on the amount of sunshine, they will, according to the types of roses involved, have turned red, yellow, russet or maroon, and the ripening process will be complete. They are then cut from the bushes (not forgetting to keep the appropriate label with each) and the seeds should be ready for stratification. This is simply a reproduction of the cooling process they would go through in winter in the wild, and germination will not take place without it. There are three methods of stratifying seeds, all of which seem to give equally good results.

In the first method, the hips are cut open and the seeds removed. They are quite large and easy to handle and their viability (whether they are fertile) can be tested by putting them in a shallow dish of water. Those that sink are viable and should be put, together with some damp peat, into small polythene bags, one bag for each cross, with their labels attached. The bags are then put in a refrigerator at a temperature of about 41°F (5°C) for about six weeks, or as an alternative the hips can be put whole into the bags and the viability of the seeds tested later.

The third method of stratification means burying the hips whole in damp sand or peat in flower pots, and leaving them out of doors during the coldest months in a place where mice cannot get at them.

Early in the New Year the seeds can be sown. If you have a greenhouse, use a seed tray at least 3 in (7.5 cm) deep and sow them $2\frac{1}{2}$ in (5 cm) apart and about $\frac{1}{2}$ in (1 cm) deep in a seed compost that has had about one handful of sharp sand per tray added. In a reasonably mild climate the seeds can safely be planted in a seed bed out of doors, but whichever method is used, be prepared for very irregular germination. Some seeds will take two full seasons before showing any signs of coming to life while others, which are apparently identical, will come up in the first year.

If the seeds are grown in a seed tray, transplanting to pots should take place as soon as the first pair of leaves that actually look like rose leaves have formed. They will be very fragile at this stage, so great care is needed.

The seedlings may well flower in their first year, but the blooms are unlikely to bear much resemblance to those the rose will ultimately bear. It can take several years for a seedling to show something of its potential, and how and when each individual makes his or her decison as to whether to persevere with a particular example or to discard it is a matter on which no sensible advice can be given. If it is white with mildew from early spring on, the answer is clear: scrap it, but otherwise each new rose will be different with different qualities that can only be judged by looking at them and with experience that will be reasonably quickly gained. Such experience might show, for instance, certain repeated patterns of development, not necessarily absolutely identical, but which seem to lead each time to similar results which can be noted down for the future, but many of the variations will be so subtle that nobody could put them into words. All one can usefully add as a finale to the description of the actual process of hybridisation, as opposed to the genetic and botanical theory, is that worthwhile seedlings – if there are any, of course – must eventually be budded on to rootstocks if a true comparison is to be made with other cultivated varieties.

Budding

There has been discussion earlier about rootstocks and the fact that some are more suitable for a light or a heavy soil than others and that some are less likely to send up suckers. If you wish to bud your own roses, it will be a question of picking a stock that best fulfils your particular requirements and the person to advise you on this would be the manager of your local rose nursery. Remember, however, that if you are budding your own roses you are not buying them from him, so he will be doing you a favour in giving advice. If you are really on friendly terms he will not mind this and may even be prepared to sell you a few rose stocks. Otherwise there are firms that specialise in growing them which advertise in the gardening press and which, though basically wholesalers, will supply small quantities to the amateur. These stocks are almost always grown from seed and are likely to be much more uniform and reliable in growth than those you might consider raising from cuttings of wild roses.

Plant your rootstocks in late autumn about 1 ft (30 cm) apart and if you have enough to make more than one row, leave $2\frac{1}{2}$ ft (7.5 cm) between them. As the actual insertion of the bud has to be made into the short, straight neck of the stock, this should not be buried too deeply. Better to earth it up after planting, which will keep the bark moist and supple.

Budding should ideally take place in mild, showery weather some time during the two months immediately after the midsummer following planting. The stocks should by then be growing away strongly and have made quite a lot of top-growth. Use a special budding knife or else a very sharp penknife.

Select strong shoots of the rose you wish to bud – shoots that have recently flowered – and snip off the leaves, leaving only the leaf-stalks, which will facilitate your handling of the buds

204

later. From the central portion of a shoot it should be possible to cut four buds at least.

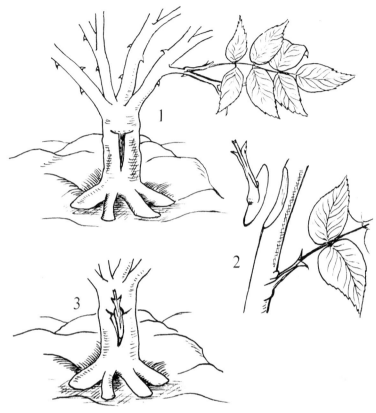

Figure 23.2
The three main
stages of budding.

1. Making the T-shaped cut in the neck of the stock. 2. A bud scooped out from a shoot with the budding knife. 3. The bud inserted under the bark flaps of the T-shaped cut. It is then bound in place with damp raffia or with a rubber budding tie.

Clear the soil away from the neck of the first rootstock and wipe it clean with a damp cloth. With the budding knife, make a T-shaped cut in the bark, just deep enough to penetrate it. The top of the T should be about ¼ in (6 mm) long and the vertical cut about ¾ in (19 mm). Using a scooping action, cut a bud from one of the shoots so that a sliver of wood and bark comes away with the bud. Remove the wood from behind the bark shield by gripping its edge between your finger and thumb and giving it a sudden but not too violent twist. Trim the ends of the bark shield.

Using the budding knife very gently so as not to tear them, lift up the triangular flaps of bark contained within the arms of the T-shaped cut and then slide the newly cut bud down under the flaps. Bind it in place firmly but not too tightly with damp raffia or with one of the special rubber budding ties, which are pinned in place. Either of these will rot naturally and should fall away just about the time the bud, if it has taken successfully, begins to grow.

The budding 'take' may not be 100 per cent, but this is nothing unusual. With those that have taken, however, as evidenced by infant shoots growing from the bud, cut away the top-growth of the stock early in the spring following budding, leaving only a stump about $\frac{1}{2}$ in (13 mm) long. This will prevent the possible downward spread of canker and can be trimmed away a month or two later. At the beginning of their existence support new shoots by tying them to a cane stuck in the ground. Although a union has taken place between bud and stock, it takes quite a while for it to become firm and strong and, without such a support, a gust of wind might easily wrench the bud right out. The insertion of two buds per stock is almost essential with standard roses to achieve a balanced head. With standard roses, the buds are inserted into lateral growths as close to the stem as possible if brier stocks are used, or into the stem itself with rugosa stocks.

CHAPTER 24

Exhibiting

This chapter is not being written for anyone who considers that they have reached the stage where they can consider exhibiting their roses in any of the big national shows. To stand a chance of winning in that company one must make growing and preparing your roses very nearly a full-time occupation, which does not let up to any marked degree even in the winter. One becomes a specialist who has little time for roses grown for enjoyment in the garden, and while I will make some references to what the top exhibitors do, I intend to concentrate in this chapter on those who wish to enter their blooms in a local flower show and then progress perhaps to their town or county horticultural show.

Anyone who grows roses in their own garden, provided that they are prepared to take a little bit of extra trouble, can both show and win prizes at these levels. It is not even essential, although it helps, to grow any special varieties, as most of the usual range of cluster-flowered roses are suitable for exhibition and there are many of the large-flowered varieties that are equally good in the garden and on the show bench. These include 'Pink Favorite', 'Honey Favorite', 'Piccadilly', 'Fred Gibson', 'City of Gloucester', 'Wendy Cussons', 'Fragrant Cloud' and 'Grandpa Dickson', but it is nevertheless true that many of the best show roses, because their blooms will not stand up to rain or because they do not produce more than a very few of them each season, are not the best to grow for garden display. However, many of them will be all right for it if the weather is fine, and in a number of summers you would get more than your money's worth in using them for bedding. It is a decision that each grower who is a potential exhibitor must make for himself or herself as to whether or not some of them could be tried.

If you do wish to progress in your exhibiting beyond the village fête, a selection could be made from 'City of Bath', 'Red Devil', 'Bobby Charlton', 'Royal Highness', 'Oxfam', 'Gary

Player', 'Big Chief', 'Admiral Rodney', 'Champion', 'Hot Pewter', 'Embassy', 'Lakeland', 'Northern Lights', 'Kathleen O'Rourke', 'Gavotte', 'Peter Frankenfeld', 'Red Lion', and 'Sunderland Supreme'. It is possible to buy special bloom protectors for such large-flowered roses as these, one for each individual flower and which, looking like Chinese coolie hats on the ends of garden canes, should be put into place over the roses just as the buds begin to show colour. Protectors are not permitted with the cluster-flowered varieties, but the majority of these are pretty well rain-proof anyway. Reliable varieties that have large trusses of bloom for showing in this category are: 'Fred Loads', 'Anne Harkness', 'Dream Waltz', 'Evelyn Fison', 'Dorothy Wheatcroft', 'Iceberg', 'Tony Jacklin' and, provided that it has not been raining, 'Europeana'.

Provided that you follow the cultural routines outlined in Chapter 21, you should produce quality roses. Regular spraying is just as important as feeding for in the exhibition classes for vases and bowls, clean, healthy foliage counts for a lot. Very keen exhibitors will give extra applications of fertiliser and use foliar feed quite extensively, too, as it appears to add an extra dimension to the leaves. Usually each exhibitor works out his own secret formula for success in feeding, and no two will be the same, at least in part because no two soils will be the same either. Disbudding will be needed with many varieties, both large-flowered and cluster-flowered, and the technique has been fully described in Chapter 21.

More and more rose shows are staging classes for miniature roses, in vases and bowls and also in exhibition boxes for displaying six individual blooms, which to my mind simply make them look grotesque. The future of box classes for large-flowered roses is in the balance at the time of writing, and they have never been popular or much used outside the United Kingdom. To introduce them now for miniatures, in which the overall cluster effect is as important as it is for the full-sized cluster-flowered varieties – which nobody would dream of showing in boxes – seems ludicrous. However, some more about boxes anon. This would seeem to be the place, I think, to reproduce (with grateful permission) an extract from the Royal National Rose Society's show schedule which sets the pattern for the whole exhibiting world. It shows very clearly just what the judges will be looking for in exhibition blooms of all types, and defines, too, the kind or kinds of rose eligible for any one class. Often in a show schedule you will see the worlds 'Judged under RNRS rules' or if the society running the show is affiliated to the Rose Society their rules should be followed – if the show secretary can find competent judges who know them! This by no means always happens, but if you read what follows and conform to it to the letter, you will know that you at least are right.

CLASSIFICATION

For exhibition purposes the roses have been classified in accordance with the new system adopted by the World Federation of Rose Societies and are divided into two major groups – 'Modern Garden Roses' and 'Old Garden Roses'.

MODERN GARDEN ROSES
These are roses of hybrid origin not bearing any strong resemblance to wild roses (species) and not included in classifications in general use before the introduction of Hybrid Tea roses. The group comprises Climbing, Shrub, Bush and Miniature roses. For the purpose of these schedules the Bush roses have been sub-divided into three separate groups and given the following headings.
1. Large-flowered Roses – Specimen Blooms.
2. Large-flowered Roses.
3. Cluster-flowered and Polyantha Roses.

Large-flowered Roses – Specimen Blooms
These will be Hybrid Tea type roses and will include climbers and shrubs of the type.

Large-flowered Roses
These will be Hybrid Tea type roses having flowers of medium to large size which may be double, semi-double or single and will include climbers and shrubs of the type.

Cluster-flowered and Polyantha Roses
The cluster-flowered and Polyantha roses have been merged under one single heading for competition purposes and include those previously described as Floribunda, Floribunda HT-Type, Floribunda Shrub, cluster-flowered Climber and Rambler, Hybrid Polyantha and Polyantha Pompon.

Miniature Roses
These are roses with miniature size flowers, foliage and growth and include climbing miniatures.

OLD GARDEN ROSES
These are roses already well established in classification in common use before the introduction of the Hybrid Teas. Types in this group are described in the RNRS publication *The Rose Directory*.

Exhibiting

Form of an individual bloom

(a) *Large-flowered (Hybrid Tea and Hybrid Tea type)*
    In the 'perfect state', it should be half to three-quarters open with the petals symmetrically arranged giving a circular outline and regularly surrounding an upright and well formed centre.

(b) *All other types*
    In the 'perfect state', the petals should be symmetrically arranged within a circular outline and the stamens, if exposed, should be fresh and of good colour.

(c) *All types in the 'bud stage'*
    They should be showing full colour with one or two petals commencing to uncurl above an opening calyx.

(d) *All types in the 'full bloom stage'*
    They should be fully open with the petals symmetrically arranged within a circular outline; the stamens, if exposed, should be fresh and of good colour.

FORM OF CLUSTER. The inflorescence should be circular in outline with the blooms gracefully arranged and so spaced as to permit their natural development, neither being crushed together nor exposing wide gaps between them. (This standard does not apply to large-flowered (HT type) roses.)

SUBSTANCE. This refers to the petals. These should be firm, smooth and of good texture, neither coarse nor flimsy, and free from blemish.

SIZE OF THE INDIVIDUAL BLOOM. This implies that the bloom should be of a good average size for a well grown plant of the particular variety. Except in classes for 'specimen' blooms, a bloom of above average size should not be regarded as being of special merit.

FRESHNESS OF BLOOM. This implies a sparkling and clean appearance with no suggestion of tiredness, staleness or unnatural preservation.

BRILLIANCE OF COLOUR. The colour should be bright and glowing, not dull or faded.

PURITY OF COLOUR. The bloom should display the full depth of the true seasonal colour of the variety, with no suggestion of deviation, blueing or tarnishing.

STEM. The stem should be straight and gracefully proportionate in thickness and length to the size of the bloom it supports, being neither unduly thin and spindly, nor coarsely thick and clumsy. A stem is defined as an original new growth which has received no check from pinching, stopping or pruning from the time of starting into growth to flowering and which carries terminal blooms, including buds, but not subsequent lateral growths. Disbudding does not constitute an offence under this rule.

FOLIAGE. This should be adequate in quantity and size; undamaged, fresh and clean in appearance and of good colour and substance for the variety. (Stem and Foliage standards are not applied when judging 'Specimen Blooms' in boxes.)

MINIATURE ROSES
In the classes for miniature roses the whole exhibit, flowers, stems, leaves and containers should be staged immaculately and gracefully and characterised by the simple word 'dainty'.

The number of blooms on each stem and their varietal size should be in balance with the rest of the exhibit. Blooms may be in various stages of development on the same stem (from the opening bud to the full open bloom).

It is desirable that the blooms in their dainty formation should be firm in substance, sparkling in freshness, brilliant and pure in colour; they may be single or double, borne singly or in clusters, but not on lateral stems (except when permitted in the schedules).

'Varietal size should be in balance with the rest of the exhibit' implies that a stem of small bloomed 'Cinderella' in the same container as a large bloomed 'Little Flirt' would fall short of being regarded as a top class exhibit.

Stems should be in proportion to the blooms, neither weak nor coarse and preferably with at least two sets of leaves. Particularly it is essential to avoid lateral growth (except if permitted in the schedule).

Notice the importance given again and again in all classes to the freshness and purity of colour of the blooms. Miniature roses that have done well in shows include: 'Starina', 'Darling Flame', 'Sheri Anne', 'My Valentine', 'Rise 'n' Shine', 'Judy Fischer', 'Stacey Sue', 'Magic Carrousel' and 'Fire Princess'.

Timing is of the utmost importance to successful showing, and to get it even approximately right – for you will always be fighting a duel with the weather – you must get to know your roses very well. After a while it will be possible to bank – more or less – on a certain variety or varieties being just right for a show on a certain date because you have learned through experience just how long the time will be between the rose or roses showing colour in the bud and opening out fully. But that is not the end of it as far as timing is concerned. A rose like 'Red Devil' will hold its immaculate shape more or less for ever once it is open, even for the duration of a two-day show in a hot marquee. A variety like 'Piccadilly' on the other hand, with far fewer petals, will 'blow' very rapidly so that it takes a lot of skill to have it just right at the moment of judging, but it is a marvellous feeling when you do manage it. I have often heard visitors at a show express wonder that a sorry-looking bloom should have been a first-prize winner, and from what they are seeing, perhaps late in the afternoon of the show, one cannot blame them. But they are not seeing it at the moment of judging. When most roses start to open the petals never stop moving, but some move much faster than others, a fact which must be constantly to the fore of an exhibitor's mind.

If you do decide to enter a show, send for the schedule of the horticultural classes (or the rose classes if they are separate) and study it carefully. It will probably look something like the one set out below, which is an actual schedule from a recent medium-sized show in South London. A local flower show would probably have fewer classes, four or five perhaps, but this one was chosen because it gives quite a large number of different permutations for exhibits.

SCHEDULE
Open to all amateurs: no entry fees

1st   2nd   3rd

Large-flowered (HT type) roses – Specimen Blooms
Class 1   Box, 12 blooms, 1 or more varieties
Class 2   Box, 6 blooms, 1 or more varieties
Class 3   Vase (8in) 3 blooms, 1 variety

Large-flowered (HT type) roses
Class 4   Bowl (10in) not more than 12 stems,
           1 or more varieties
Class 5   Vase (8in) 5 stems, 1 or more varieties

Cluster-flowered (Floribunda type) roses
Class 6   Bowl (10in) not more than 12 stems,
           1 or more varieties
Class 7   Vase (10in) 5 stems, 1 or more varieties
Class 8   Vase (8in) 3 stems, 1 variety

Miniature roses
Only varieties classified as 'miniature' may be exhibited
Class 9   Bowl, not more than 12 stems,
           1 or more varieties
Class 10   Bowl, not more than 9 stems,
           1 or more varieties

For amateurs who do not grow more than 100
rose trees
Class 11   Vase (8in) 3 stems of HT type roses,
            1 or more varieties
Class 12   Vase (8in) 3 stems of Floribunda roses,
            1 or more varieties

The Royal National Rose Society Bronze Medal will be awarded for
the Best Bloom in the Show.
Staging from 6.00am until 11.00am. Judging at 11.15am. No exhibit to
be removed before 6.00pm.
Vases and bowls will be provided and these only may be used.

Judged under RNRS rules

An amateur is understood to be a person who, not being a nurseryman,
either personally or with unpaid or paid assistance maintains a garden,
or grows plants and/or flowers for pleasure and enjoyment and not for
his livelihood; does not sell rose plants, rose blooms or rose buds for
budding, nor is a resident member of the household of one debarred
under this definition. As an exception to the foregoing, an amateur
may sell new seedlings or sports of his own raising but only to
nurserymen.

All exhibitors and their assistants shall leave the place of exhibition
punctually at the time appointed for judging and any exhibitor or
assistant who remains in the place of exhibition after the time stated in
the schedule for judging shall be liable to have his exhibits disqualified.

Do not enter more classes than you are quite sure that you
can manage comfortably. If you fall down on some of them,
there will be empty spaces on the show benches and nothing
looks worse or is more unfair to the organisers than a show tent
or hall only half filled. Weather problems may cause late
withdrawals, but these are something that cannot be helped,
and even so it is worth remembering that if your blooms look a
little worse for wind or rain, it is likely that other people's will,
too. Withdrawals because of over-ambitious entries are quite
another matter, and it is probably enough to try for a maximum
of three classes until you really know what you are doing. In the
above schedule these could be Class 5 for large-flowered roses,
Classes 7 or 8 for cluster-flowered varieties and Class 10 for
miniatures. That is enough to be going on with, for quite apart
from the fact that you might not have enough roses to fill any
more vases with top-quality blooms, it always seems to take
about twice as long as you have calculated on to carry out your

staging. Greater speed will come with time; it is a very slow business to start with.

Most shows nowadays provide bowls and vases to a standard specification, which means that everyone has the same, which is clearly desirable. You can buy these vases, but if you are only showing once a year at your local fête you may not feel that it is worth it. If you have to use other vases, keep them as plain and simple as possible. It is the roses that are being judged and not a flower arrangement.

It is many years since there was a firm that made exhibition boxes and exhibitors in the box classes have had to make their own to a pattern and size laid down by the Rose Society so that all of them would be identical. At the present time, due to the ever-increasing cost of returning boxes to exhibitors after a show and the general unreliability of rail transport, the organisers of shows have understandably shown a reluctance to continue helping in this way. At national show level, much lighter and less bulky display boards are being tried out, but no official decision about them has yet been made.

It is best to cut your roses on the evening before the show. Remove the lower leaves and thorns and keep them overnight up to their necks in a bucket (or buckets) of water in a cool shed, or at least some place where they will be sheltered from rain and wind. Carrying them to a show without damaging the delicate blooms can be tricky, especially if you have a car journey of any length, when they should, ideally, be kept in water. A number of plastic detergent bottles with their tops cut off and held a few inches apart in a home-made frame will not only keep the roses upright and separated, but if the bottles are only half filled with water they are narrow enough for it not to spill, even when crossing a bumpy field to a show tent.

On arrival at the show, find the show bench where the classes you have entered are to be staged before you unload. There should be a separate staging table nearby. Pick up your class entry cards from the show secretary, recognisable as being the most worried-looking man in the show tent and sitting at a table near the entrance with a mass of cards in front of him.

You can now carry your roses straight to the staging table, under or on which there should be a supply of vases and bowls. Make sure that you pick out ones of the size specified in the schedule, as failure to get this elementary point right could mean disqualification. Blocks of Oasis in the vases make it easy to arrange the roses as you want them. They should be symmetrical, and if there is one rose larger than the others it is a good plan to put it at the front. It is from the front that they will be judged, so it is a waste of time to make an arrangement that looks pleasing from all sides. The blooms should be close together, but not touching, and if the colours blend well this adds to the effect. With cluster-flowered roses it is important to snip off faded blooms with a pair of nail scissors as long as this does not leave obvious gaps. Use a water-colour brush to remove insects or specks of dust from either blooms or foliage.

When you have done all that you can, check the schedule to make quite sure that you have carried out all the requirements. It is all too easy to make a mistake, especially if the final stages of staging are rushed, and if you do do something wrong you will find the dreaded letters NAS on your class card after judging, which stands for Not According to Schedule. It adds interest to an entry if, as well as placing your class card in front of it when you have finished, you also place a second card listing the variety or varieties in your exhibit. The judges will not need to be told what these are if they know their jobs, but the public likes to know, especially if your entry is a winning one.

Finally, before you go off to bite your nails in the car park while the judging is taking place, top up your vases with water.

USDA Hardiness Ratings by Zone

FOR GROUPS OF ROSES DISCUSSED IN THE TEXT

Zone 5 (−10° to −20°)

The Gallicas
The Damasks
The Albas

Zone 6 (0° to −10°)

The Centifolias and Moss Roses
China Roses
The Bourbons and Portland Roses
The Hybrid Perpetuals
Large-flowered Bush Roses (Hybrid Teas)
The Polyanthas
Cluster-flowered or Floribunda Roses
Miniature Roses

Zone 8 (20° to 10°)

Tea Roses

List of Suppliers

America and Canada

Armstrong Nurseries Inc., PO Box 4060, Ontario, CA 91761.

Fred Edmunds, Roses by, 6235 SW Kahle Road, Wilsonville, OR 97070.

Historical Roses, 1657, West Jackson Street, Painesville, OH 44077.

Jackson & Perkins Co., 1, Rose Lane, Medford, OR 97501.

Joseph J. Kern Rose Nursery, Box 33, Mentor, OH 44060.

Lowe's Own Root Rose Nursery, 6, Sheffield Road, Nashua, NH 03062.

McDaniel's Miniature Roses, 7523, Zemco Street, Lemon Grove, CA 92045.

The Miniature Rose Company, 200, Rose Ridge, Greenwood, SC 29647.

Oregon Miniature Roses Inc., 8285, SW 185th Avenue, Beaverton, OR 97007.

Pallek, Carl, & Son, Nurseries, Box 137, Virgil, Ontario LOS 1TO, Canada.

Pickering Nurseries, 670, Kingston Road, Pickering, Ontario L1V 1A6, Canada.

Roses of Yesterday and Today, 802, Brown's Valley Road, Watsonville, CA 5076.

Sequoia Nursery, Moore Miniature Roses, 2519, East Noble Avenue, Visalia, CA 93277.

Springwood Miniature Roses, Box 255, Port Credit PO, Mississauga, Ontario L5G 4L8, Canada.

Thomasville Nurseries Inc., PO Box 7, Thomasville, GA 31792.

Europe

Austin, David, Roses, Bowling Green Lane, Albrighton, Wolverhampton WV7 8EA, England. (Old Rose Specialist)

Beales, Peter, Roses, London Road, Attleborough, Norfolk NR17 1AY, England. (Old Rose Specialist)

Cants of Colchester Ltd, The Old Rose Gardens, London Road, Stanway, Colchester, Essex CO3 5UP, England.

Cocker, James and Son, Whitemyres, Lang Stracht, Aberdeen AB9 2XH, Scotland.

Fryer's Roses, Knutsford, Cheshire, WA16 0SX, England.

Gandy's Roses Ltd, North Chilworth, Lutterworth, Leicestershire, LE17 6HZ

Gregory's Roses, The Rose Gardens, Stapleford, Nottingham, NG9 7JA, England.

R. Harkness & Co. Ltd, The Rose Gardens, Hitchin, Herts, SG4 0JT, England.

Hillier Nurseries (Winchester) Ltd, Ampfield House, Ampfield Romsey, Hants, SO5 9PA, England.

W. Kordes Söhne, Rosenschule, Rosenstrasse 54, 2206 Klein Offenseth-Sparrieshoop, Holstein, West Germany.

Le Grice Roses, Norwich Road, North Walsham, Norfolk, NR28 0DR, England.

Mattock, John, Ltd, Nuneham Courtney, Oxford, OX9 9PY, England.

Notcutts Nurseries Ltd, Woodbridge, Suffolk, IP12 4AF, England.

D.T. Poulsens Planteskole ApS, 60, Kelleriisveg, DK 3490 Kvistgaard, Denmark.

Sanday, John, (Roses) Ltd., Over Lane, Almondsbury, Bristol, BS12 4AD, England.

Scotts Nurseries (Merriott) Ltd, Merriott, Somerset, TA16 5PL, England.

Rosen Tantau, Postfach 1344, 2082 Uetersen bei Hamburg, West Germany.

Timmermans Roses, Lawdham Lane, Woodborough, Nottingham, NG14 6DN, England.

Wheatcroft Roses Ltd, Edwalton, Nottingham, NG12 4DE, England.

Bibliography

Anderson, Frank J. *The Complete Book of Redouté Roses* (Abbeville Press, New York, 1979). Useful to have colour reproductions of 169 of Redouté's paintings, even if a number are very small. Text commentary very suspect.

Bagatelle et ses Jardins, Librarie Horticole, 1910. The famous French château and its gardens.

Bean, W.J. *Trees and Shrubs Hardy in the British Isles*, 4th vol. of 8th edn (Murray, London, 1980). Has an authoritative and comprehensive survey of the genus *Rosa*.

Buist, R. *The Rose Manual* (Lippincott, Grambo, Philadelphia, Pa. 1844). Every aspect of growing roses suitable for the eastern USA in the mid-1800s.

Bunyard, E.A. *Old Garden Roses* (Country Life, London, and Scribner, New York, 1936). For a long time, this book by a Kentish nurseryman was a standard work.

Cochet, P.H.M. and Mottet, S.J. *Les Rosiers* (Paris, 1896). The transitional period between the hybrid perpetual and the hybrid tea.

Darlington, H.R. *Roses* (J.C. & E.C. Jack, London, and Stokes, New York 1911). One of the best guides of the period.

D'Ombrain, Rev. H.H., *Roses for Amateurs, The Bazaar*, 1887. By one of the co-founders of The Royal National Rose Society.

Edland, H. *The Pocket Encyclopedia of Roses* (Blandford, Poole, 1963), updated several times by L.G. Turner. Over 400 varieties described and illustrated in colour.

Ellwanger, H.G. *The Rose* (Dodd-Mead, New York, 1882). Descriptions of 956 old roses and practical comments on many.

Fitch, C.H. *The Complete Book of Miniature Roses* (Hawthorn, New York, 1964). The most comprehensive and best illustrated book on the subject so far published.

Foster-Melliar, Rev. A. *The Book of the Rose* (Macmillan, London, 1894). Much on the hybrid perpetuals and how to show them successfully.

Gault, S.M. and Synge, P.M. *The Dictionary of Roses in Colour* (Ebury Press and Michael Joseph, London, and Grosset and Dunlap, New York, 1971). Large in format with colour pictures and descriptions of over 500 roses.

Gibson, M. *Shrub Roses for Every Garden* (Collins, London, 1973, and Muller, Zürich, 1978). The history and cultivation of the best shrub roses and climbers. 195 varieties illustrated in colour.

—— *The Book of the Rose* (Macdonald, London, 1980). One of the most comprehensive rose books ever published, illustrated with quite exceptional paintings of roses of all periods.

—— *Shrub Roses, Climbers and Ramblers* (Collins, London, 1982). An expansion and updating of the author's *Shrub Roses for Every Garden* (see above). Illustrated with colour photographs.

Gore, C.F. *The Book of Roses, or The Rose Fancier's Manual* (Colburn, London 1838). Descriptions of over 1,400 varieties of roses available in France in the 1830s.

Gravereux, J. *Les Roses*, Edition d'Art et de Literature, 1912. By the Director of the Roseraie de l'Hay.

Harkness, J. *Roses* (Dent, London, 1978). Comprehensive coverage by a leading nurseryman and hybridist who can really write.

Harvey, N.P. *The Rose in Britain* (Souvenir Press, London, 1950 and Van Nostrand, New York, 1951). Despite the title, rose history on a world scale.

Hennessey, R. *On Roses* (West Coast Printing, Portland, Oregon, 1942). An amusing and rather eccentric but highly informative book by an American nurseryman.

Hibberd, S. *The Rose Book* (Groombridge, London, 1864, re-titled *The Amateur's Rose Book*, 1874). First-rate guide to roses and their cultivation in large gardens in the 1800s.

Hillier & Sons, *Manual of Trees and Shrubs* (Hillier, Winchester; hardback, David and Charles, Newton Abbott, 1972). Basically a very fine descriptive catalogue, exceptionally strong on species roses.

Hole, Dean S.R. *A Book About Roses* (Blackwood, Edinburgh, 1874). A rose classic by a co-founder of The Royal National Rose Society who had very strong opinions of his own and was not afraid to express them.

Hollis, L. *Roses* (Collingridge, Feltham, 1969). One of the best reasonably modern guides, better on new than old roses.

Jekyll, G. and Mawley, E. *Roses for English Gardens* (Newnes, London, 1902). Emphasis is on garden design making much use of ramblers and early climbers. Fine photographs in black and white.

Keays, F.L. *Old Roses* (Macmillan, London, 1935). Strong on noisettes, hybrid perpetuals and early tea roses.

Kordes, W. *Roses* (Studio Vista, London 1964). Translation of an account of rose history and cultivation by a famous German breeder and nurseryman.

Krüssmann, G. *Roses* (Timber Press, Portland, Oregon, 1981 and Batsford, London, 1982). An updating and translation of the German classic work *Rosen, Rosen, Rosen* of 1974. Extremely comprehensive but idiosyncratic in its choice of subject and emphasis. Strong on illustration from all periods.

Lawrance, M. *A Collection of Roses from Nature* (1799). Contains 90 plates from coloured etchings by the author, giving a unique contemporary record.

Le Grice, E. *Rose Growing Complete* (Faber & Faber, London, 1965). A very fine guide by a great authority.

Lindley, J. *Rosarum Monographia* (Ridgeway, London 1820). Written and illustrated by the man who was to become such a distinguished botanist.

McFarland, J.H. *Roses of the World in Colour* (Houghton Mifflin, Boston, Mass. 1937). Hundreds of colour photographs, variable in quality but just the same giving a unique picture of the roses in commerce in the 1930s.

—— *Modern Roses 8* (The McFarland Company, Harrisburg, Pa. 1980). The latest edition of this international check list of roses since the death of J.H. McFarland compiled by the International Registration Authority. The additions this time leave a lot to be desired as far as accuracy is concerned, tragic in a work long considered the last word.

Mansfield, T.C. *Roses in Colour and Cultivation* (Collins, London, 1943). 80 full-page colour plates, descriptions and cultural information.

Moore, R.S. *All About Miniature Roses* (Diversity Books, Kansas City, Mo. 1966). A practical book by the master-breeder of miniature roses.

Park, B. *Collins Guide to Roses* (Collins, London, 1956). Valuable for its comtemporary descriptions and colour photographs of varieties.

—— *The World of Roses* (Harrap, London, 1963). 230 roses, both old and at that time new, photographed and described by Park, a noted authority.

Parsons, S.G. *Parsons on the Rose* (Orange-Judd, New York, 1969). Previously published as *The Rose, Its History, Poetry and Cultivation*, 1947. This latter title fully describes the contents.

Paterson, A. *The History of the Rose* (Collins, London, 1983). Rose history beautifully presented and illustrated by many contemporary plates in colour and black and white.

Paul, W. *The Rose Garden* (Kent, London, 1848). A milestone in rose literature by a leading nurseryman of his day. The first edition had colour plates; these were later dropped for cost reasons.

Pemberton, Rev. J.H. *Roses, Their History, Development and Cultivation* (Longmans Green, London, 1908). Authoritative if a little solid, but very attractive illustrations. Do not get the early editions if you want to read about the hybrid musks.

Pyle, R. *How to Grow Roses* (Conard & Jones, Westgrave, Pa., and later Macmillan, New York). By an American nurseryman who introduced many fine European roses to the USA. Through its many editions, covers a long period of rose growing and hence change.

Redouté, P.J. *Les Roses* (Paris, 1817–1842). The original folios contain 170 of the roses painted almost without exception in the Empress Josephine's Garden at Malmaison.

Bibliography

Ridge, A. *For Love of a Rose* (Faber & Faber, London, 1965). The story of the Meilland family and of their rose 'Peace'.

—— *The Man Who Painted Roses* (Faber & Faber, London, 1974). The author's coy style makes this difficult to read, but there is much information on the life of Redouté that is not available elsewhere.

Rivers, T. *The Rose Amateur's Guide* (Longmans Green, London, 1837). This was a leading British nurseryman's contribution to the rose literature of his day and is a most interesting and authoritative one.

Shepherd, Roy. E. *History of the Rose* (Macmillan, New York, 1954). A standard American work, very comprehensive on species.

Sitwell, S. and Russell, J. *Old Garden Roses Part 1* (Rainbird/ Hutchinson, London, 1957). *Part 2* by Wilfred Blunt and Russell (Rainbird/Hutchinson, 1957). These were the only volumes produced of what should have been a six-volume work. Part 1 covers mainly rose history, Part 2 covers rose literature and the gallicas.

Steen, N. *The Charm of Old Roses* (Jenkins, London, 1967). A book of great charm and authority on the old roses in New Zealand.

Stevens, G.A. *Climbing Roses* (Macmillan, New York, 1933). One of the few books devoted to this group of roses.

Thomas, Capt. G.C. *Roses for All American Climates* (Macmillan, New York, 1924). A book by a great breeder of climbing roses.

Thomas, G. *The Old Shrub Roses* (Phoenix House, London, 1955). This book established Graham Thomas as the leading authority on the subject.

—— *Shrub Roses of Today* (Phoenix House, London, 1963). Completes the coverage by bringing in the species and modern shrubs.

—— *Climbing Roses Old and New* (Phoenix House, London, 1965). The last of a remarkable trio of books, all of which have gone through many editions.

Thompson, R. *Old Roses for Modern Gardens* (Van Nostrand, New York, 1959). A lot of information on the early hybrid teas.

Willmott, E. *The Genus Rosa* (Murray, London, in two parts, 1910 and 1914). A beautifully illustrated treatise on wild roses of the world.

Young, N. *The Complete Rosarian* (Hodder and Stoughton, Sevenoaks, 1971). No cultural details so not 'Complete', but fascinating and very controversial on rose history and many other aspects of the subject.

Glossary

Anther The male sex organ on the tip of the stamen.

Axil The angle between a leaf stalk and the shoot on which it grows. The point from which an axillary or leaf-axil bud grows.

Balling This occurs when wet petals of a rose bloom stick together.

Bareroot rose A rose sold with bare roots and not in a container.

Bicolour or bicolor One side of a rose's petals a different colour from that of the other.

Blind shoot A shoot, usually occurring early in the season, that does not produce a flower.

Blueing Deep-red roses often 'blue' – turn a purplish-blue – with age.

Bract A modified leaf immediately under the flower.

Bud (a) A bud that will develop into a flower, to be found at the end of a main or side shoot. (b) A bud that will become a shoot, to be found in a leaf-axil.

Budding Propagating a rose by inserting a leaf-axil bud into the neck of a rootstock.

Budding union The point on the rootstock into which the bud was inserted and from where the shoots of the new rose will grow.

Calyx The collective term for the five sepals.

Cane A rose shoot.

Carpel The stigma, style and ovary, making up the female parts of the flower. See **pistil**.

Chlorosis Lack of soil nutrients causing a change in the natural green colouring of leaves. Often they turn yellow.

Crown The point from which the shoots grow on the rootstock.

Cultivar A cultivated variety.

Cut-back A rose bush in its second season after budding, i.e., after its first pruning.

Dead-heading The removal of dead or damaged blooms.

223

Glossary

Die-back Fungus entering a shoot after frost or other damage causing it to turn brown, usually from the tip downwards.

Disbudding The removal of side flower buds at the tip of a shoot, or the main bud in a cluster-flowered rose truss. The former gives a bigger main flower; the latter brings all the other flowers out simultaneously.

Dormancy The cessation of growth during short days of low temperature during the winter months.

Earthing-up Also known as hilling or mounding. The drawing up of earth round the crown of a rose to protect if from cold.

Eye The same as a leaf-axil bud.

Flush A peak period of blooming. Many roses have two or more during the summer.

Foliar feeding Feeding through the leaves with a spray of liquid fertiliser.

Footstalk The flower stalk or pedicel.

Genus A group of plants consisting of one or more species, which have common structural characteristics.

Habit The way in which a rose grows.

Half-standard A standard rose on a 2-ft (60-cm) stem.

Heading back The cutting back of the growth of a rootstock when the variety budded on to it has grown away.

Heeling in A temporary planting of roses in a shallow trench until they can be planted properly.

Hep Another word for hip.

Hip The seed pod of a rose.

Humus Used for improving the soil texture. Dark brown or black residue of decayed vegetable matter usually formed in a compost heap.

Hybrid A rose variety resulting from a cross between two different species or varieties.

Hybridising The transfer of the pollen of one variety or species to another to create a new rose.

Inorganic A chemical compound such as a fertiliser that does not contain carbon and is not derived from plants or animals.

Lateral A side shoot growing from a main shoot.

Loam Difficult to define precisely, but basically a soil of medium weight and texture made up of clay, sand and humus.

Maiden A rose in its first season after budding.

Moss On a moss rose, resin-coated bristles or glands.

Mulching Covering soil with a layer of material, preferably humus-forming, to hold in moisture and smother weeds.

Mutation An alteration in the characteristics of a plant due to a genetic change.

Neck   The short straight part of the rootstock just above the roots into which a bud is inserted in budding.

Organic   A substance such as a fertiliser derived from once-living material.

Ovary   The female part of the flower containing the seeds.

Own-root rose   A rose from seed or from a cutting that is growing on its own roots.

Peat   Fibrous organic material used to improve soil condition and to increase water retention and acidity. It can also form a mulch.

Pedicel   The same as a footstalk.

Pegging down   Tying down the tips of long and flexible shoots to short wooden pegs driven into the ground to encourage flowering side shoots to form.

Petaloid   A partly formed petal sometimes found in the centre of a bloom.

pH scale   This measures soil acidity and alkalinity. Below 7.0 on the scale and the soil is progressively more acid; above it and it is progressively more alkaline. Round about 6.8 is ideal for roses, but they are amazingly tolerant.

Pillar rose   A moderately vigorous climbing rose suitable for training on a pillar.

Pinnate   A rose has a pinnate or compound leaf, having five or more leaflets.

Pistil   The stigma, style and ovary, making up the female part of a flower. Several carpels collectively in one flower.

Pointel   A small green growth at the centre of a few old garden roses, e.g., 'Mme Hardy'.

Pollen   Fine yellow grains produced by the anthers and which carry the male cells to fertilise the ovules.

Pollen parent   A hybridising term for the rose that provides the pollen in a cross. Always given second when quoting parentage.

Pompon   A rounded bloom with regular short petals.

Pruning   The cutting back of the shoots of a rose to encourage strong new growth and remove dead and diseased growth.

Quartered bloom   One in which the petals arrange themselves into four distinct parts.

Replant disease   See **rose sick**.

Reverse   The outer surface of a petal.

Reversion   When a hybrid reverts to the characteristics of one or more parents or the rootstock takes over from the budding variety.

Rootstock   A rose species or variety on to which another rose is budded to give extra vigour and other qualities.

Rose sick Used of soil which has grown roses for some years and in which new roses will not thrive. Thought to be of bacterial origin.

Rosette A rather flat and very regular bloom formation with many short petals.

Rugose Botanical term for a leaf with a wrinkled surface as found in rugosa roses.

Scion A bud used for grafting on to a rootstock.

Seed parent In hybridising, the rose that receives the pollen that fertilises its seeds. Given first when stating a rose's parentage.

Semi-double A bloom with two or three rows of petals.

Sepals The five triangular divisions of the calyx which protect the flower before it opens.

Shield The piece of bark cut from a shoot when budding and containing the bud or eye.

Single bloom One having five petals, but sometimes incorrectly used for flowers with up to seven or eight.

Species In botanical classification, for plant individuals that have distinct, unique characteristics and breed true in the wild. A division of a genus.

Split centre Irregular formation of petals in the centre of a flower, generally used to indicate a departure from the normal high centre of a particular variety.

Sport A mutation in which a shoot bears flowers or has a habit of growth different from the other shoots on a plant.

Stamen The male organ of a flower made up of the filament bearing the anther. It produces the pollen.

Standard Also known as a tree rose. One in which the variety is budded on to a 3 ft 6 in (107 cm) stem.

Stigma The end of the pistil or female flower organ.

Stipule Leafy growth along both sides of a leaf stalk.

Stratification The breaking of dormancy of rose seeds after gathering by careful tempertaure control.

Style The stem of the pistil which joins the stigma to the ovary.

Sub-lateral A side shoot from a side shoot.

Sucker A shoot growing from the rootstock instead of the variety which is budded on to it.

Synstylae A group of ramblers in which the styles of the flowers are in one column above the ovaries. The scent comes from this and is freely released into the air.

Systemic Used of an insecticide or fungicide that enters the plant system, making it toxic to pests and disease spores.

226

Trace elements   Soil-borne chemicals needed by plants in very small quantities.

Tree rose   See **standard**.

Truss   Flower cluster, generally used for that of cluster-flowered roses.

Understock   The same as rootstock.

Variety   A naturally occurring variation of a species, whether a sport or a hybrid, but popularly used for any distinct form, including a cultivar, which is actually only produced in cultivation.

Viable   Seeds that will germinate.

Weeping standard   A rose, generally a rambler, budded on to a stem 5 ft (1.5 m) or more high so that the shoots hang down or 'weep'.

Winterkill   A rose killed by extreme cold in winter.

Index of Roses

'Adam' 72
'Adolph Horstmann' 75
'Aimée Vibert' 145
'Albéric Barbier' 19, 144-5
'Albertine' 20, 144-5
'Alec's Red' 76, 174
'Alexander' 76
'Alfred de Dalmas' *see* 'Mousseline' 51
'Allain' 69
'Allgold' 162, 174
'Aloha' 14, 135
'Alpine Sunset' 76
'Altissimo' 135
'Amanda' 103
'Anabell' *see* 'Korbell' 111
'Angela Rippon' 10, 151
'Angelina' 122
'Anna Ford' 103
'Anna Olivier' 72
'Annchen Muller' 101
'Anne Cocker' 103
'Anne Harkness' 104
'Antoine Ducher' 74
Apothecary's Rose, The 34
'Apricot Nectar' 104
'Archiduc Joseph' 72
'Arthur Bell' 104
'Austrian Copper' *see* R. *foetida bicolor* 74-5
'Austrian Yellow' *see* R. *foetida* 74-5
'Autumn Damask' 24, 26, 40, 56
'Autumn Sunlight' 21, 136

'Baby Crimson' *see* 'Perla de Alcanada' 153
'Baby Darling' 17
'Baby Gold Star' 151
'Baby Masquerade' 151
'Ballerina' 10, 98, 121
'Bambino' 151
'Banksian Yellow' 136
'Bantry Bay' 137
'Baron Girod de l'Ain' 64
'Baronne Edmond de Rothschild' 77

'Baronne Prévost' 64
'Beauty Secret' 17
'Belle de Crécy' 35
'Betty Prior' 101
'Betty Uprichard' 73
'Blairii No 2' 57
'Blanc Double de Coubert' 120, 122
'Blessings' 77
'Bloomfield Abundance' 53
'Blush Damask' 41
'Bobby Charlton' 77
'Bonfire' *see* 'Bonfire Night' 105
'Bonfire Night' 105
'Bonn' 121
'Bonnie Prince Charlie's Rose' 44
'Bonsoir' 78
'Boule de Neige' 58
'Bright Smile' 105
'Buff Beauty' 123
'Bullata' 48

'Cameo' 98
'Camphill Glory' 78
'Canary Bird' 13, 29
'Capitaine John Ingram' 50
'Cardinal de Richelieu' 36
'Cathedral' *see* 'Coventry Cathedral' 106
'Catherine Mermet' 69
'Cécile Brunner' 53, 97
'Cécile Brunner, Climbing' 19, 137
'Celeste' 45
'Celestial' *see* 'Celeste' 45
'Celsiana' 41
'Centifolia' 48
'Cerise Bouquet' 123
'Châpeau de Napoleon' 49
'Charles de Mills' 36
'Cheshire Life' 78
'Chicago Peace' 79
'Chinatown' 10, 120, 123
'Cinderella' 152
'City of Belfast' 105
'City of Leeds' 105
'Coeur d'Amour' *see* 'Red Devil' 91

'Commandant Beaurepaire' 57-8
'Common Monthly Rose' see 'Old
    Blush' 54
'Common Moss' 50
'Communis' 50
'Compassion' 14, 137
'Complicata' 35-6
'Comte de Chambord' 57, 60
'Comtesse du Cayla' 54
'Congratulations' 79
'Constance Spry' 120, 124
'Coralin' 152
'Cornelia' 12, 124
'Coventry Cathedral' 106
'Crested Moss' 49

'Dainty Bess' 74
'Dainty Maid' 102
'Dame of Sark' 106
'Danaë' 121
'Dance du Feu' 136
'Darling Flame' 10, 152
'Dearest' 106
'De Meaux' 49
'Devoniensis' 70
Dog Rose 24
'Donald Prior' 101, 107
'Doris Tysterman' 79
'Dorothy Perkins' 145
'Dorothy Wheatcroft' 120, 125
'Dortmund' 14, 138
'Double Delight' 80
'Dr Grill' 72
'Dr W. Van Fleet' 145
'Dublin Bay' 138
'Duchesse de Brabant' 70
'Duchesse de Verneuil' 50
'Duchess d'Istrie' see 'William Lobb'
    51
'Duchess of Portland' 56
'Duftwolke' see 'Fragrant Cloud' 83
'Du Mâitre d'Ecole' 36
'Dutch Gold' 80

'Easter Morning' 10, 152
'Echo' 101
'Electron' see 'Mullard Jubilee' 87
'Elizabeth Harkness' 80
'Elizabeth of Glamis' 107
'Else Poulsen' 101
'Empereur du Maroc' 64
'Empress Josephine' 35, 37
'Ernest H. Morse' 81, 174
'Escapade' 107
'Estrellita de Oro' see 'Baby Gold
    Star' 151
'Europeana' 11, 108
'Evelyn Fison' 108
'Evening Star' 81
'Excelsa' 145

'Eye Paint' 108

'Fairyland' 16
'Fairy Prince' 16
'Fantan Latour' 49
'Fashion' 102
'Fashion Flame' 17
'Felicia' 121
'Félicité et Perpétue' 146
'Félicité Parmentier' 44-5
'Ferdinand Pichard' 59
Field Rose 43
'Fire Princess' 10, 152
'Fountain' 125
'Fragrant Cloud' 82, 174
'Fragrant Delight' 109
'Francofurtana' see 'Empress
    Josephine' 37
'Frau Dagmar Hartopp' 12
'Frau Karl Druschki' 65
'Fred Loads' 10, 120, 125
'Freiherr von Marschall' 72
'Fritz Nobis' 121, 126
'Fru Dagmar Hastrup' 12, 120
'Frühlingsgold' 13, 29, 120-1, 126
'Frühlingsmorgen' 13, 29, 120, 127

'Galway Bay' 21
'Général Jacqueminot' 65
'Général Kléber' 50
'Général Schablikine' 70
'Georg Arends' 65
'Gioia' see 'Peace' 89
'Glenfiddich' 109
'Gloire de Dijon' 72, 138
'Gloire de France' 37
'Gloire de Mousseux' 50
'Gloria Dei' see 'Peace'
'Golden Showers' 14, 139
'Golden Sunblaze' 154
'Golden Times' 83
'Golden Wings', 13, 120, 127
'Goldfinch' 147
'Grace Abounding' 109
'Grandpa Dickson' 83, 174
'Great Double White' 28, 44
'Great Maiden's Blush' 45
'Green Rose, The' see R. chinensis
    viridiflora 54
'Gruss an Aachen' 101
'Guinée' 139
'Gypsy Jewel' 152

'Hamburg' 121
'Handel' 21, 139
'Harison's Yellow' 31
'Henri Martin' 50
'Homère' 72
'Honey Favorite' 83
'Hume's Blush Tea-scented China' 69

Index of Roses

'Iceberg' 110
'Irish Beauty' *see* 'Elizabeth of
  Glamis' 107
'Irish Fireflame' 74
'Irish Gold' *see* 'Grandpa Dickson' 83
'Ispahan' 41

'Jacobite Rose' 44
'Jacques Cartier' 61
'Jeanne de Montfort' 50
'John Waterer' 84
'Judy Fischer' 153
'Jules Margottin' 73
'Just Joey' 84

'Kathleen Ferrier' 127
'Kerryman' 110
'Kiftsgate' 147
'Kobold' *see* 'Sue Lawley' 118
'Königin von Danemarck' 44, 46
'Korbell' 111
'Korp' 111, 174
'Korresia' 111, 174

'Lady Hillingdon' 70
'Lady Mary Fitzwilliam' 73
'Lady Plymouth' 72
'Lady Sylvia' 87
'La France' 25, 62, 84
'Lakeland' 85
'Landora' *see* 'Sunblest' 94
'La Reine Victoria' 59
'Lavender Jewel' 153
'Lavender Lassie' 128
'Leverkussen' 21, 140
'Lilli Marlene' 112
'Little Flirt' 153
'Little White Pet' 98
'Living Fire' 112
'Louise Odier' 59
'Lovers' Meeting' 112

'Macrantha' 15
'Mme A. Meilland' *see* 'Peace'
'Mme Berkley 72
'Mme Bravy' 72-3
'Mme Butterfly' 86
'Mme Delaroche-Lambert' 50
'Mme de Tartas' 72
'Mme de Watteville' 72
'Mme Edouard Herriott' 73
'Mme Ernst Calvat' 60
'Mme Gregoire Staechelin' 141
'Mme Hardy' 41
'Mme Isaac Pereire' 14, 59
'Mme Jules Gravereaux' 72
'Mme Pierre Oger' 59, 60
'Mme Sancy de Parabére' 134
'Mme Scipion Cochet' 72
'Mme Victor Verdier' 73

'Mlle Bertha Ludi' 101
'Magic Carrousel' 153
'Maiden's Blush' 45
'Maigold' 21, 140
'Maman Cochet' 71
'Ma Paquerette' 97
'Margaret Merril' 113
'Marguerite Hilling' 13, 128
'Marie van Houtte' 72
'Marjorie Fair' 10, 99
'Marlena' 113
'Masquerade' 102
'Matangi' 113
'Max Graf' 15
'Memento' 114
'Mermaid' 28, 140
'Message' 88
'Midas' 85
'Minuetto' 152
'Mischief' 86
'Mister Lincoln' 86
'Monsieur Tillier' 72
'Moonlight' 12, 121, 128
'Mountbatten' 114
'Mousseline' 50, 51
'Mozart' 121
'Mrs John Laing' 66
'Mrs Oakley Fisher' 74
'Mullard Jubilee' 87, 174
Musk Rose 24
'Mutabilis' 54

'Natalie Nypels' 99
'National Trust' 88, 174
'Nevada' 13, 29, 129
'New Dawn' 141
'New Penny' 153
'News' 114
'Niphetos' 71
'Nozomi' 16

'Ocarina' *see* 'Angela Rippon' 151
'Ocaru' *see* 'Angela Rippon' 151
'Old Blush' 40, 54
'Old Master' 115
'Old Pink Moss' 50
'Opa Potschke' *see* 'Precious
  Platinum' 91
'Ophelia' 87
'Orleans Rose' 97

'Papa Gontier' 72
'Parade' 141
'Parkdirektor Riggers' 142
'Parks' Yellow Tea-scented China' 69
'Parsons' Pink China' 54, 56
'Pascali' 88
'Paul Crampel' 99
'Paul Neyron' 66
'Peace' 3, 89

'Pearl Drift' 129
'Peer Gynt' 89
'Penelope' 12, 129
'Perla de Alcanada' 153
'Perle de Panachées' 35
'Perle des Jardins' 72
'Persian Yellow' *see R. foetida persiana* 74
'Picasso' 102
'Piccadilly' 89
'Pink Favorite' 90
'Pink Grootendorst' 120, 122, 129
'Pink Nevada' *see* 'Marguerite Hilling' 128
'Pink Parfait' 115
'Pink Perpetue' 142
'Playboy' 115
'Portland Rose, The' 56
'Pot o' Gold' 90
'Precious Platinum' 91
'Président de Sèze' 37
'Prince Camille de Rohan' 66
'Pristine' 91
'Prominent' *see* 'Korp' 111
'Prosperity' 12, 129

'Quatre Saisons' 40
'Queen Elizabeth' 8, 10, 102, 116

'Raubritter' 15, 130
'Rayon d'Or' 74
'Red Ballerina *see* 'Marjorie Fair' 99
'Red Devil' 91
'Red Dorothy Perkins' *see* 'Excelsa'
'Red Riding Hood' 101
Red Rose of Lancaster 34
'Red Star' *see* 'Precious Platinum' 91
'Reine des Violettes' 66
'Rise 'n' Shine' 154
'Rob Roy' 116
'Robusta' 131
'Rochester' 101
'Roger Lambelin' 64
'Rosa Mundi' 34-5, 37, 38
Rosa × alba incarnata 45; × *alba maxima* 28, 44; × *alba semi-plena* 34, 40, 44; *arvensis* 43-4, 144; *banksiae lutea see* 'Banksian Yellow' 136; × *borboniana* 56-7; *bracteata* 28; *canina* 24, 26, 43; × *centifolia* 28; × *centifolia cristata* 49; × *centifolia muscosa* 28, 47, 50; *chinensis minima* 150; *chinensis viridiflora* 55; *corymbifera* 26, 28, 43; × *damascena bifera* 40; × *damascena semperflorens* 40; × *damascena versicolor* 40; × *dupontii* 30; *ecae* 29; *fedtschenkoana* 31; *filipes* 'Kiftsgate' *see* 'Kiftsgate' 147;

foetida 31, 74; *foetida bicolor* 74; *foetida persiana* 74; × *franco-furtana* 37; *gallica* 24; *gallica* 'Officinalis' 34; *gallica* 'Versicolor' 37; *gigantea* 134; *glauca* 32; × *harisonii see* 'Harison's Yellow' 31; *holodonta* 32; *indica* 52; *indica sulphura* 69; *kordesii* 138; *lucens see R. longicuspis* 148; *luciae* 144; *longicuspis* 148; *moschata* 24; *moyesii* 13, 31; *moyesii* 'Fred Streeter' 32; *moyesii* 'Geranium' 31; *moyesii rosea* 32; *moyesii* 'Sealing Wax' 32; *multiflora* 25, 97, 144, 196; *odorata* 69; × *paulii* 15, 32; × *paulii rosea* 15, 32; *phoenicia* 24; *pimpinellifolia* 27, 29, 31, 126; *pimpinellifolia altaica* 32; *polyantha* 25, 97; *rouletii* 150; *rubrifolia* 32, 156; *rugosa* 120; *rugosa alba* 11; *rugosa* 'Scabrosa' *see* 'Scabrosa' 132; *sempervirens* 144; *soulieana* 29; *spinosissima* 27; *virginiana* 32; *wichuraiana* 15, 144, 196; *xanthina spontanea* 29
'Rose d'Amour' 32
'Rose des Peintres' 48
'Rose Gaujard' 92
'Roseraie de l'Hay' 11, 120, 131
'Rosette Delizy' 72
'Rosy Cushion' 16
'Royal Dane' *see* 'Troika' 95

'Safrano' 69, 71, 73
'St Mark's Rose' 32
'St Nicholas' 42
'Sally Holmes' 132
'Sanders's White Rambler' 19, 148
'Sarah Van Fleet' 132
'Scabrosa' 11, 132
'Scarlet Fire' 35, 120, 132
'Scented Air' 117
'Schoolgirl' 136
'Seagull' 19, 148
'Sheri Anne' 154
'Silver Jubilee' 92
'Silver Lining' 93
'Skyrocket' *see* 'Wilhelm'
'Slater's Crimson China' 52, 56
'Snow Carpet' 16-17, 154
'Soleil d'Or' 74
'Sombreuil' 71
'Southampton' 117
'Souvenir d'Elise Vardon' 72
'Souvenir du Docteur Jamain' 67
'Spanish Beauty' *see* 'Mme Gregoire Staechelin' 141
'Spartan' 102
'Stargazer' 117
'Starina' 154

Index of Roses

'Stephen Langdon' 118
'Sue Lawley' 118
'Summer Holiday' 93
'Sunblest' 94
'Sunsilk' 118
'Susan Ann' *see* 'Southampton'
'Sutter's Gold' 94
'Swan Lake' 142
'Swany' 16
'Sweet Fairy' 154
'Sweetheart Rose' 53

'Temple Bells' 148
'Tenerife' 94
'The Bishop' 48
'The Fairy' 99
'Tipo Ideale' *see* 'Mutabilis' 54
'Topsi' 119
'Toy Clown' 17
'Tricolore de Flandre' 35
'Triomphe du Luxembourg' 72
'Troika' 95
'Trumpeter' 119
'Tuscany' 35, 38

'Vanity' 133
'Variegata di Bologna' 57, 60

'Veilchenblau' 149
'Victor Verdier' 73
'Ville de Chine' *see* 'Chinatown' 123
'Virgo' 88

'Warrior' 119
'Wedding Day' 16
'Wendy Cussons' 3, 95
'Whisky' *see* 'Whisky Mac' 95
'Whisky Mac' 95
'White American Beauty' *see* 'Frau
    Karl Druschki' 65
'White Knight' *see* 'Message' 88
White Rose of York 34
'Wilhelm' 121, 133
'William Francis Bennett' 73
'William Lobb' 50-1
'William R. Smith' 72
'Williams' Double Yellow' 31
'Will Scarlet' 121

'Yesterday' 100
'York and Lancaster' 40
'Yvonne Rabier' 100

'Zambra' 8
'Zéphirine Drouhin' 57, 143

General Index

A Book About Roses 6
Alba roses 26; classification 27
All-American Rose Selection 158
Anaphalis 23
Aphid *see* Greenfly 187
Artemisia 'Lambrook Silver' 23
Ayrshire roses 144

Banksian roses 134
Barbier ramblers 145
Bengal roses 52, 75
Bennett, Henry 73
Bibliography 219
Black spot 189
Boerner, Eugene 102
Bourbon roses, 24, 40
Boursault roses 134
Bréon 40, 56
British Association of Rose Breeders 158
British Rose Growers Association 114
Budding 204; standard roses 206

Cabbage roses 28
Calcutta Botanical Gardens 52
Canker 189
Canterbury Bells 23
Castle Howard 156
Catenary 19; at Queen Mary's Rose Garden 20; at Wisley Gardens 20
Caterpillars 181
Centifolia roses 26; classification 27
Chafers 187
China rose hybrids 25
China roses 24
Classification of roses 26
Climbing roses as shrubs 22; for hedges 12; other uses of 19
Cultivated Roses 63
Cuttings 196; miniature roses from 151
Cyrene, Rose of 2

Damask roses 27; classification 191
Dead-heading 191

de Vink, Jan 150
Disbudding 192
D'Ombrain, H.H. 6
Dot, Pedro 150
Dupont, André 30

Exhibiting 207; cluster-flowered varieties for 208; large-flowered varieties for 207; judging standards 210; miniatures 208; miniature varieties for 211; RNRS rose classification for 209; show schedules 212; timing 211

Fair Rosamund 38
Fantin-Latour, Jean Théodore 43
Far Tee nurseries 52
Fertilisers 176; ingredients 176
Floribundas 25
Foliar feeding 177
Foster-Melliar, A. 6
Foxgloves 23
Froghoppers 187

Glossary 223
Grandifloras 26
Greenfly 187
Greenhouse, roses in 174; varieties for 174
Guillot, Henri 73, 97

Hardiness zones 216
Harkness, Jack 114
Henry IV Part I 40
Hole, Dean Reynolds 6-7
Holland roses 47
Hume, Sir Abraham 69
Hybrid musks for hedges 12
Hybrid perpetual roses 25
Hybrid polyanthas 97
Hybrid tea roses 25
Hybridising 201

Ile du Bourbon 40

General Index

Jekyll, Gertrude 6
Josephine, Empress 5, 30

Kiftsgate Court 38
Kordesii climbers 26
Kordes, Wilhelm 29, 135

Laffay, H. 50
Lambert, Peter 121
Lancaster, first Earl of 34
Lavender with roses 23
Lavendula 'Loddon Pink' 23
Leaf-cutting bee 187
Leafhopper 187
Leaf-rolling sawfly 188
Le Grice, Edward 101
Les Roses 5, 52, 69
Lilium regale 23; *rubellum* 23;
    speciosum 23
Luxembourg Gardens 30

Malmaison, Villa 5
McGredy, Sam 102, 135
Mildew, powdery 189
Miniature roses 17; indoors 17; uses
    of 18
Moore, Ralph 150
Moss roses 47; classification 27
Mulches 177

Natural History (Pliny) 39
Noisette roses 134

Paestum 39
Parkinson, John 1
Parks, John Dampier 69
Paul, William 32
Pegging down 63, 173
Pemberton, Joseph 6, 27, 98, 121
Pernet-Ducher, Joseph 74
Pernetiana roses 74, 134
Pest and disease chart 187-9; spray
    techniques 186
Planting bush roses 165; climbers 167;
    container-grown roses 168;
    standard roses 168
Pliny the Elder 2, 39
Polyantha pompon roses 25
Polyanthas, hybrid 26
Portland, Duchess of 56
Portland roses 24
Potentilla 'Beesii' 23; *mandschurica*
    23; 'Vilmoriana' 23
Poulsen, Svend 101
Prince Otto 75
Provence roses 47
Provins roses 34
Pruning climbing roses 184; cluster-
    flowered roses 184; large-flowered
    roses 183; miniature roses 185; old

garden and shrub roses 185;
    ramblers 184; reasons for 179;
    standard roses 184; technique 181;
    timing 181
Prunus 'Kanzan' 23

Queen Mary's Rose Garden 156

Ramblers, uses of 19
Redouté, Pierre Joseph 5, 37, 52
Red spider mite 188
Robinson, William 6
Rootstocks 204
Rose Directory 114
Rose leaf miner 188
Rose nurseries, America and Canada
    217; Europe 217-18; slug-worm
    188; trials 157
Roses: buying container-grown 160;
    colour blending 9; colours of
    early 2; cultivated by Romans
    39; cultivation, soil 164, site
    164
Roses for Amateurs 6; for bedding
    8; for ground-cover 14; for
    lining paths and drives 10;
    importing: UK 161, USA 161;
    in the green-house 174; other
    plants with 22-3; standards for
    plants 159
*Roses, Their History, Development
    and Cultivation* 6; use of standards
    in bedding 9
Rosmarinus officinalis 23
Royal Horticultural Society, The
    69
Royal National Rose Society, The 6,
    26; awards 158; gardens 156
Rugosa roses 26
Rust, rose 189

Salvia officinalis 23
Seed, sowing 203
Senecio greyii 23; 'Sunshine' 23
Soil acidity 165
Spraying techniques 186
Stachys byzantina 23; *lanata* 23
Stevenson, Robert Louis 75
Stratification 203
Suckers 193

Tea roses 25; early history of 2
The Book of the Rose 6
Theophrastus 2
Thrips 188
Tortrix moth 188
Training: climbers 169; ramblers 169;
    weeping standards 171
*Trees and Shrubs Hardy in the British
    Isles* 126

Tudor rose 34

Walsh ramblers 145
Wars of the Roses 34
Winter care 195

Wisley Gardens 32, 156
World Federation of Rose Societies
  26

Yellow Rose of Texas 31